The Business of Champagne

The world of champagne offers a fascinating insight into the complexity of modern business management and marketing. Champagne is at the same time a wine, a luxury product and a regional brand – it is tied to the place from which it comes, and can be made nowhere else. It therefore highlights a range of characteristics which make it interesting to the modern business world.

This is the first book to offer a complete overview of the way in which champagne as a product is organized, managed and marketed, and what its future prospects are. The book covers the entire range of issues surrounding the management of the champagne industry by reviewing the current context of champagne (structural, economic and legal), the role of 'place' (identity, terroir and tourism), marketing the 'myth' of champagne (image and competitive advantage) and the management of the industry (account-ability, people and the territorial brand). The book brings together leading academics and examines the Champagne region from multidisciplinary perspectives.

Examining the Champagne region provides insight into a range of management, production-management, branding and consumer-related issues and will be of interest to students, researchers and academics inter-ested in Gastronomy, Wine Studies, Tourism, Hospitality, Marketing and Business.

Steve Charters is Chair of Champagne Management and Director of the Reims Research Centre for Wine-Place-Value, France, as well as being a Master of Wine.

Routledge Studies of Gastronomy, Food and Drink
Series editor: Michael Hall
University of Canterbury, New Zealand

This groundbreaking series focuses on cutting edge research on key topics and contemporary issues in the area of gastronomy, food and drink to reflect the growing interest in this as academic disciplines as well as food movements as part of economic and social development. The books in the series are interdisciplinary and international in scope, considering not only culture and history but also contemporary issues facing the food industry, such as security of supply chains. By doing so the series will appeal to researchers, academics and practitioners in the fields of Gastronomy and Food Studies, as well as related disciplines such as Tourism, Hospitality, Leisure, Hotel Management, Cultural Studies, Anthropology, Geography and Marketing.

Published:

The Business of Champagne
A delicate balance
Edited by Steve Charters

Forthcoming:

Alternative Food Networks
David Goodman, Michael Goodman and Melanie DuPuis

The Business of Champagne

A delicate balance

Edited by Steve Charters

Routledge
Taylor & Francis Group

LONDON AND NEW YORK

First published 2012
by Routledge
2 Park Square, Milton Park, Abingdon, Oxon OX14 4RN

Simultaneously published in the USA and Canada
by Routledge
711 Third Avenue, New York, NY 10017

Routledge is an imprint of the Taylor & Francis Group, an informa business

British Library Cataloguing in Publication Data
A catalogue record for this book is available from the British Library

Library of Congress Cataloging in Publication Data
The business of champagne / edited by Steve Charters.
    p. cm.
    Includes bibliographical references and index.
    1. Wine industry—France—Champagne-Ardenne. 2. Champagne (Wine)—Economic aspects. 3. Wine and wine making. 4. Wine industry. I. Charters, Stephen.
    HD9385.F82C433 2011
    338.4'7663224—dc22   2011001377

ISBN: 978-0-415-59440-0 (hbk)
ISBN: 978-0-203-80876-4 (ebk)

Typeset in Times New Roman by
Book Now Ltd, London

Contents

Illustrations

Figures

Tables

Contributors

Steve Charters is Chair of Champagne Management and Director of the Reims Research Centre for Wine-Place-Value, France, as well as being a Master of Wine. Before moving to France in 2007 he taught and researched the business of wine in Australia. He has authored many academic and popular articles about wine.

Tim Dodd is at Texas Tech University, USA and his fields include consumer economics, restaurant and hotel management, marketing and tourism. He is head of the Texas Wine Marketing Institute and Associate Dean (Operations and Finance) in the College of Human Sciences.

Olivier Dusautoir is a consultant to various businesses in the wine and spirits sector, and a lecturer at a number of business schools in France in commerce and export. He formerly worked for both small and large producers in Champagne in the field of export management as well as other wine and spirits companies

Theo Georgopoulos is a Senior Lecturer at Reims Law School, France and Director of the Wine and Law Programme, in charge of legal research into wine business at the University of Reims Champagne-Ardenne, France. An Attorney-at-Law, he has published 8 books and over 50 articles on European law, wine law and constitutional law.

Philippe Jeandet is Professor in Applied Biochemistry at the University of Reims Champagne-Ardenne, France, Director of its Laboratory of Enology and Applied Chemistry, and Adjunct Director of the Research Unit 'Vine and Wine of Champagne, Stress and Environment'. He has published 210 articles in refereed publications and presented 180 communications to numerous conferences.

Martin Kunc has worked in business schools in Latin America and the UK. His research interests are: regional innovation systems and managerial capabilities. He has carried out consultancy with private firms and governments in Latin America, Europe and Africa within industries such as wine and tourism.

Nick Lewis works at the University of Auckland, New Zealand where he is a Senior Lecturer in Geography, concentrating on the relationship of business to space and governance – with a particular interest in wine and the wine industry, and how it changes and is represented; much of his work has focused on the New Zealand wine industry.

Larry Lockshin is Professor of Wine Marketing at the University of South Australia. He spent more than 20 years working with the wine industry and has published over 100 academic articles on wine marketing. His research interests are consumer choice behaviour for wine and wine industry strategy.

David Menival has a PhD in economics and is a specialist in the champagne industry lecturing at Reims Management School, France. He is an active member of the Reims Research Centre for Wine-Place-Value. His research is mainly focused on the reputation of wines and wine regions.

Richard Mitchell is a Senior Lecturer in Tourism at the University of Otago, Dunedin, New Zealand, former visiting professor at the Reims Management School, France and has previously worked in Australia. He has wide ranging research interests in regional development and tourism, rural tourism and the relationship of tourism and place to food and wine.

Al Seaman is Professor of Accounting Studies at the Business School, Humber Institute of Learning and Design, Toronto, Canada. He has many years of professional experience providing accounting and consulting services, and his interests include the relationship of accounting to corporate governance and accountability.

Liz Thach is a Wine Business Professor at Sonoma State University, California, USA. In addition, she has 15 years of executive and management level experience in major companies and has done consulting projects for more than 30 different wineries. Liz lives on Sonoma Mountain where she tends a small hobby vineyard, makes homemade wine and is a Master of Wine.

Acknowledgements

I want to express my thanks to all the contributors, who made the academic study tour of Champagne such a success with their insights, and who have distilled their ideas into these chapters. I specifically need to acknowledge the contribution of my colleague David Menival, who has engaged me in vigorous and stimulating debate about champagne and how it functions over the past four years, and who had to suffer over much of Christmas 2010 with my demands for information and assistance to help finalize the book. Daniel Lorson of the Interprofessional Committee for the Wines of Champagne also commented helpfully on Chapter 1. Additionally, I must acknowledge those who helped to make the academic tour such a success, gave of their time and knowledge, and created the opportunity for this book to be produced. Particularly I would like to thank the Interprofessional Committee for the Wines of Champagne, Champagne Nicholas Feuillatte, the Syndicat Général des Vignerons (and especially Sandra Cizeron), Champagne Laurent Perrier (particularly the former President of the Directory, Yves Dumont), Champagne Taittinger and Pierre-Emmanuel Taittinger, Pierre Cheval of Champagne Gatinois, Piper and Charles Heidsieck and in particular Ludovic Panciera, the Crédit Agricole including Bernard Mary, the Union des Maisons de Champagne and Ghislain de Montgolfier and Vranken Pommery – notably Paul Bamberger and Nicolas Lombard. Finally, Elisabeth Patin of Reims Management School was invaluable in the planning and organization of the tour which gave rise to this work.

I also wish to acknowledge the permission of the Interprofessional Committee for the Wines of Champagne for use of the map in Chapter 1, and of the Kemerer Group Inc. for the use of the figure in Chapter 11.

Abbreviations

AOC	Appellation d'Origine Contrôlée
BOB	Buyer's own brand: a wine made to the specification of a distributor (usually a retailer) with their own label on it
BOGOF	'Buy one and get one free': a form of price discounting used by some large retailers
CIVC	Interprofessional Committee for the Wines of Champagne
CO_2	Carbon dioxide
DO	Designation of origin
EEC	European Economic Community: forerunner to the European Union
EU	European Union
g/l	Grams per litre
GI	Geographical indication
ha	Hectare (an area 100 metres by 100 metres)
hl/ha	Hectolitres per hectare
INAO	Institut National des Appellations d'Origine: French national body overseeing the AOC system.
kg	Kilogram
kg/ha	Kilograms per hectare
LVMH	Moët-Hennessy Louis Vuitton: a luxury goods group which owns a number of the largest champagne producing houses.
NM	*Négociant-manipulant*, or merchant of champagne. This includes almost all the large producers
NV	Non-vintage
R&D	Research and development
RC	*Récoltant-cooperateur*: a grower who is a member of a cooperative and sells a wine that has been made for him/her by the cooperative
RM	*Récoltant-manipulant*: a grower who also makes his/her own wine for sale to the public
SAFER	Société d'Aménagement Foncier et d'Etablissement Rural: French state body empowered to support rural development
SGV	Syndicat Général des Vignerons: the union of growers

SO$_2$ Sulphur dioxide – added to wine as a preservative
UMC Union des Maisons de Champagne: the coordinating body for the houses négociants

Introduction

Steve Charters

Champagne[1] forms a fascinating wine region to examine from the business perspective. Despite occasional downturns it has shown a sustained growth since 1945. It is both part of the wine industry and yet also perceived to be a product apart; in that context it is both a product that is very strongly branded yet reflective of the place from which it originates. It has dimensions that are both agricultural and from the world of luxury.

This book came out of a tour of the region by a group of academics in 2008, organized with the specific aim of gaining an external perspective on the way the region is organized and managed and the means by which it engages with its consumers. The members of the tour were specifically selected to represent a range of disciplinary perspectives (management, marketing, human resource management, accounting, tourism, hospitality and economic geography) as well as a variety of origins. All except one were Anglophone. The contributors are therefore effectively witnesses to champagne – to its current state, to its own analysis of why it has been successful and to the future that it faces; witnesses, albeit ones trained to understand how a business works, specifically a wine business, and one based in a specific place.

The tour took place at the time of peak prosperity for the world economy and therefore for champagne so that the initial exposure to the region featured success and the concomitant concerns it created; however, the chapters were written as the worst crisis for decades struck and the book is published as champagne appears to be emerging reasonably well from the crisis. The context for this work thus covers a range of experiences and expectations.

Yet this is not designed to be a short-term analysis of champagne, nor of how it has dealt with an economic crisis that may last for a few years at most. Indeed, it is one of the premises of this work that the success of champagne – and many of the challenges it faces – goes well beyond the short-term limits of economic cycles. Further, this is not a textbook in how to manage a sparkling wine or its place of origin. Rather it is an engagement with one specific product in its totality, an exploration of its myths, history, paradoxes, contradictions and future – and based very much as champagne is now, at the start of the second decade of this century. To this extent the book is meant to have a relevance far beyond its specific region in France, or the category of wine. It is designed to contribute to debate in the fields of the management of agricultural goods, place-based products, tourism, regional management, branding and the distribution of luxury products. Part of the purpose of this text is to analyse why the Champagne region and champagne has worked so well. However, the world of wine is now changing very rapidly, and champagne faces challenges and problems for the future – so a second aspect of the book is to examine what those problems might be and how champagne is adapting to a new, more globalized world of wine.

The book is broadly structured in four parts plus a conclusion. Part I (Chapters 1–4) is contextual, and is provided by academics who are local to the region, and have a detailed understanding of how it is structured. These chapters offer background information about the history and geography of the region and how the management of champagne is organized internally (1), how the wine is made (2), the legal constraints within which wine producers and the regional organizations work (3) and the economic development of champagne (4). A section on producing champagne may seem superfluous in a book about the business of the wine, but the constraints of the processes involved are such that making it has a major impact on how it is managed and marketed; nevertheless, those readers who are already familiar with the production methods utilized for champagne could omit Chapter 2. Additionally, readers who have previously studied the organization of the region may find Chapter 1 unnecessary.

Parts II–IV (Chapters 5–12) are the result of the study tour, and represent the external analysis. They are organized thematically: Part II examines the place and the land; Part III then considers the mythology and marketing of the wine and Part IV explores the management of the industry and the businesses of champagne. One of the members of that team (Richard Mitchell) also spent a further period in Reims, and so Chapter 5 – which considers how champagne and Champagne are represented to outsiders – is the product of an extended research project in the region. Chapter 9 is written not from the external perspective but by local authors; it was felt that the subject of distribution was so important to understanding the business of champagne that it needed writing, and that specific local knowledge and engagement was necessary for this to be done comprehensively. Other chapters cover the construction and representation of the idea of terroir in the region (6), the positioning of champagne and its image (7), the management of the champagne brand (8), creating and sharing value (10), accountability (11) and the role of people (12).

The chapters vary substantially in style, something which was explicitly encouraged. Thus some chapters are very factual – how the champagne industry works (1–4), others are more theoretical, engaging with substantial literature context (5 and 6), reflective (7 and 11) or managerially focused (8–10 and 12). The perspectives are consequently personal and individual.

They do not always agree, and contradictory positions can be found. No attempt has been made to smooth them out, because each view has some validity, and to see the different points of view is important both for the champagne industry and for those who are interested in wine, place and territorial brands. Some are more positive about the region than others; some more likely to accept the received wisdom of the quality of champagne and others more ready to challenge a perceived mythology. Likewise, each contribution comes with a personal style which I have not tried to reduce to a single 'authorized' style; it is important that the individual voice comes through, however 'academic' the aim of the study. Each chapter is intended to be self-contained; the result is that there is occasional repetition – but I felt that this was preferable to the situation where a reader of a single chapter loses the thread because key elements have been covered elsewhere.

One caveat about a book such as this relating to figures and statistics must be mentioned. Despite – or perhaps because of – the careful record keeping maintained in the region, figures available for some core activities (e.g. number of hectares planted) often vary even for the same year, and there are regular changes from year to year. We have attempted to use figures that are as consistent as possible in this work but – especially given that it has been prepared over three vintages – there may be some slight variation from author to author.

Note

1   The word Champagne is used throughout this book for the region in north-east France, and champagne is used for its eponymous wine. Note that this latter term only applies to wine from this place and not, as in the USA, as a generic term for any sparkling wine, whatever its origin.

Part I

Context

1 The organization of champagne

A historical and structural introduction

Steve Charters

Introduction: champagne the wine

Champagne is a product which is rooted in its place and in history. The business of champagne cannot be understood without some knowledge of where it comes from and how the past has shaped the way the industry is structured, managed and perceived by those who run it – and these factors form the core of this chapter. As a preliminary, however, it is necessary to remember that champagne is a wine, and certain things are distinctive about wines. Most significant in this context is the fact that wine cuts across primary, secondary and – at times – tertiary industries (Carlsen & Charters, 2006). It is primary as it is based on an agricultural resource – the grapes. It is secondary because there is production involved (the process of manufacturing wine from grape juice). It is often tertiary when there is a service element attached to it, most clearly with wine tourism. This produces clear management challenges which do not apply to most other industries; the skills required to grow quality wine grapes, make good wine and provide a great experience for the public are not necessarily the same.

Wine is also self-evidently alcoholic, a fact which makes it attractive to many consumers and provides a level of marketing advantage but which also brings with it attendant management difficulties centred on issues of health and abuse concerns. Further, champagne is also by definition an effervescent wine. This is significant physiologically, as it is well-established that carbon dioxide accelerates the uptake of alcohol in the blood stream, thus speeding its euphoric effect. It is, thus, no coincidence that sparkling wines and specifically champagne have become the wine of celebration, as they make drinkers feel relaxed and cheerful more rapidly than other wines.

Finally, it should be noted that champagne is locally a very significant industry. The Champagne-Ardenne region of France is seeing a greater population decline than any other. In that context any industry which employs around 30,000 people and is worth 4.5 billion euros is important. In turn, as will be seen in Chapter 4, this has an impact on land values and it also acts as one of the major attractions for tourists, contributing yet more to the local economy as well as to social life and stability in a very rural area.

The geography and history of champagne

Champagne is produced in the north of France, in a region centred on Reims and Epernay, about 130 kilometres east-north-east of Paris (the geography of the region is shown in the map at Figure 1.1). This is a cool wine-producing region – as far north as grapes for high-quality wines are grown in France. The region divides into a number of sub-regions (between four and six, depending on which system one follows) and up to 20 sub-sub-regions (Anon., 2010b). The key sub-regions are: the *Montagne de Reims*, which curves around the south and west of its eponymous city (including sub-regions such as the Massif de St Thierry); the Marne valley, which stretches westward from Epernay to within 70 kilometres of Paris; the *Côte des Blancs*, southwards from Epernay, and including the region around the town of Sézanne; and the *Côte des Bar* (the Aube), separated from the previous three regions and about 100 kilometres south of Epernay.

Three hundred and nineteen villages currently possess the right to have vineyard land within their area. There are just over 34,000 hectares of land available to plant within the *appellation d'origine contrôlée* (AOC) area, and 34,051 are now planted – meaning that the entire demarcated area is effectively in use. Additionally there are almost 275,000 individual plots of viticultural land each averaging less than 1,250 square metres; land use and ownership is thus highly dispersed. Almost all of the wine-producing villages are in the Champagne-Ardenne region of France. Most of these villages (72 per cent of vineyard land) are in the *departement*[1] of the Marne, with a further 21 per cent of vineyard to the south in the Aube.

Wine has been produced in this region for over 1,500 years (Unwin, 1996),[2] but sparkling wine has only been made for around 350 years, and until the end of the nineteenth century most production was still wine (Guy, 2003). The mythology of the region claims that the effervescent wine was invented by the monk, Dom Pérignon (Kladstrup & Kladstrup, 2005), who was responsible for the provisions of the Abbey of Hautvillers, just outside Epernay. However, the truth is likely to be much more prosaic than that. Three random factors coincided to create the conditions for sparkling wine. The first was a 'mini ice age' which dominated Europe from the late medieval period until the nineteenth century, reducing average temperatures. In cold autumns this temperature change slowed down the fermentation of wine, often stopping yeast activity temporarily before it restarted in the late spring of the following year (Phillips, 2000). The other two factors were technological: the development of harder glass in England, making bottles a convenient and strong container for the first time, and the realization that cork could be an effective and airtight closure for those bottles (Phillips, 2000). Until the time these two developments occurred, if fermentation was arrested and then recommenced any carbon dioxide created by yeast activity dissipated into the air from the casks in which the fermenting grape juice (known as the must) was contained. Once the must, not fully

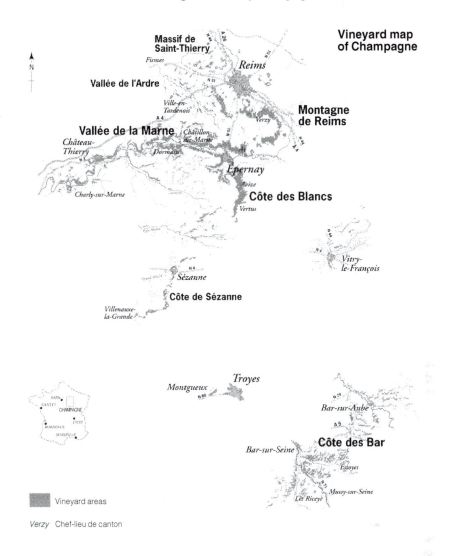

Figure 1.1 Map of Champagne. (Source: CIVC)

fermented, was placed in a corked bottle, when fermentation recommenced in the spring following a cold winter the gas was trapped in the bottle, making an effervescent wine.

The first evidence of sparkling wine being made from champagne in fact records its production in England, by adding sugar to still wine, and dates from at least 1662, some years before the period that Dom Pérignon was managing the cellars at Hautvillers (Stevenson, 1998). Nevertheless, it was evidently being produced in the region by the end of the seventeenth century, albeit in small quantities (Brennan, 1997). However, these styles of wine were not what we would recognize as champagne. Initially they were only mildly sparkling and were cloudy (because each bottle still contained many millions of yeast cells). The history of much of the following three centuries was one of refining the process by which the wine was made (something outside the scope of this introduction, but which is explained in detail by Kladstrup & Kladstrup, 2005). Additional information on the development of production and its human context can be found at the beginning of Chapter 12.

As in most of France, growing grapes in the Champagne region was part of local agriculture and thus carried out by many small agricultural producers, who often practised polyculture and might have a very small vineyard area. However, improving the production of sparkling wine was costly, as was the effort required to distribute the product in the markets of Paris and (later) London, St Petersburg, Berlin and New York. The capital and knowledge needed to do this meant that – for sparkling wine at least – production became the domain of merchants (*négociants*) who had the time and money to invest in it. These merchants, known also as the *maisons* (houses), owned little land, but purchased grapes from the small-scale growers (termed *vignerons* in French). From the mid-eighteenth century, when the maisons became more and more important, there was substantial hostility between them and the growers, much of which was focused on the issue of grape price; the vignerons naturally wishing to be paid as much as possible, the houses seeking to minimize that payment. Around this a host of other factors, such as the creation of the legally recognized identity of 'Champagne' as a wine-producing region, added other sources of conflict (for an excellent examination of this see Guy, 2003).

Even for the négociants, however, sparkling wine was initially less attractive than still wine. It was costly and time-consuming to make, whereas still wine could be sold more rapidly. However, in the eighteenth century, as transport systems began to improve throughout France, there was growing competition for the still wines of Champagne in the major market of Paris, particularly as increasing numbers of wines from Burgundy, often more full-bodied, were being sold there (Brennan, 1997). This competition threatened the viability of traditional still wines from the region, and so merchants began to increase the amount of sparkling wine they produced, by way of differentiation (Brennan, 1997). The fact that in the bottle a wine could last longer without spoiling allowed for greater potential in export markets also, for lengthy transport in casks was potentially damaging to the wine.

The sustained export efforts of the houses, especially during and after the Napoleonic period, meant that champagne became one of the few internationally recognized wines. National consumption was modest during the nineteenth century, rising from just over two million bottles a year in the 1840s to less than three million forty years later. Conversely, exports went from five million to 18 million between 1840 and 1880. As a result of this international reputation champagne (and the houses which made it) faced problems with fraud as others tried to trade in on its reputation. Consequently, in 1882 the houses formed a grouping which became the *Union des maisons de champagne* (UMC) in an attempt to face the problem jointly. Meanwhile, in the face of a series of agricultural depressions and the devastation of the Champagne vineyards by phylloxera[3] in the 1890s, the growers decided to pool their resources, forming several small unions. These in turn united in a federation in 1896 to develop more power in the face of the houses, becoming a single representative body, the *Syndicat général de vignerons* (SGV), in 1904.

The SGV opposed the UMC over a series of issues, including grape price, the delineated area of Champagne and issues relating to the 'fraudulent' production of champagne (Guy, 2003). Antagonism was such that there were riots in the region in 1911 (examined in more detail in Chapter 5). There was an irregular grape supply, causing difficulties for both sides of the champagne industry and a reduction in sales worldwide had caused a surplus of stock. However, the First World War showed both sides of the industry that they had more substantial enemies than each other, a perspective reinforced by the continuing agricultural depression in the 1920s and the more general economic decline of the 1930s, which resulted in a period of international protectionism. In order to counter this decline the two Unions created the *Commission de propagande et de défense des vins de Champagne* (committee for the promotion and defence of the wines of Champagne), designed to support their wine. Arguments about the price of grapes remained the key point of dispute between the groups, so out of this body the *Commission de Châlons* (named after the major local administrative city) was created in 1935, representing the two sides of the industry equally, and with the power to fix the grape price in a way that was fair to both growers and houses.[4]

As this process was cementing the relations between two opposing elements of champagne production, another was adding to their cohesion – the desire to delineate the boundaries of the area in which grapes could be grown and champagne produced. Again this was essentially to protect the houses against fraud from other wine producers and to protect the economic monopoly of the growers over grape production by excluding outsiders. Although this notion of a delimited area had been disputed in the nineteenth century (Guy, 2003), from 1911 onwards both sides came to realize the need for a coherent definition of the geography of production. As shown in more detail in Chapter 5, this development saw interregional disputes, even amongst the growers, as well as between growers and houses, but eventually this was finalized in 1927, and incorporated into the *Appellation Contrôlée* (AOC)[5] system in 1936, with the boundaries established being essentially those which exist today. The grant of AOC status did not just determine the borders of the region for producing champagne – it also introduced rules designed to improve the quality (and thus the reputation) of the wine for the benefit of all. Thus viticultural techniques were prescribed. These included determining the grape varieties which could be planted (excluding the less high-quality ones which had been introduced in the wake of phylloxera) as well as pruning methods. It also set compulsory production techniques (harvesting, pressing, storage, etc.), again in an attempt to guarantee the quality of what was in the bottle and thus enhance the region's fame.

Effectively, what had been an antagonistic production environment developed into one which was more cooperative. This was formalized in 1941 when the *Commission de Châlons* became a permanent organization called the *Comité interprofessionnel du vin de Champagne* (CIVC), thus giving legal validity to inter-professional cooperation. The organization's executive committee was constituted with exactly the same number of growers and négociants and it was (and remains) jointly chaired by the presidents of the SGV and of the UMC. In 1946, the CIVC was given a role to organize, control and direct the production, transformation, distribution and the exchange of wine produced in Champagne, and it has quasi-governmental powers over aspects of the viticulture and wine production in the region, with the ability to set legally binding decrees over these issues. Since the early 1990s the CIVC has lost its power to set or even recommend a grape price at harvest as a result of European Union (EU) action to stimulate free markets in goods, but the other responsibilities it subsequently developed have been retained (see below).

The contemporary organization of the champagne industry

The producers of champagne

The crucial issue in the organization of champagne remains the balance between growers and houses. The growers own 90 per cent of the land bearing champagne grapes, but are responsible for selling less than one quarter of all bottles of wine. The houses make over two thirds of the sales but own less than ten per cent of the vineyard land. The two groups are thus interdependent, and the situation is made more complex by the existence of a number of growers' cooperatives.

There are 20,000 *Champenois* (people who come from Champagne) who state that they own land on which champagne grapes can be grown. Of these, 15,200 are grape growers, meaning that almost 5,000 own land but have it managed by someone else. The average holding of vineyard land is 2.22 hectares – a small area but, with a potential gross income of €130,000 p.a., still financially viable. Of these growers around 4,800 sell champagne under their own label (they are known as *récoltant-manipulants* (RMs)) but they cannot effectively buy grapes or wine on the open market, so generally they are of a small size – and few of them are well-known outside the region; indeed most of their sales are made only in the region, at the cellar door.

The growers sell about 23 per cent of all bottles of champagne, but over 92 per cent of all the growers' sales are made in France (where they sell nearly four bottles in ten).

Many of the vignerons (around 13,000) are members of one of the 137 cooperatives in the region. These began to be founded during the agricultural depression of the first half of the twentieth century, and were created in French agriculture generally to provide small-scale producers with access to capital that they could not individually obtain, and to strengthen their bargaining power in the face of the superior economic power of merchants and middlemen. Cooperatives are mutual organizations where each member who sells grapes has an equal share (but not equity ownership) of, and vote in, the enterprise. The cooperative, meanwhile, is obliged to buy the grapes which the members have contracted to deliver to them.

There are more cooperatives in Champagne than any other French wine region and essentially they were set up to process grapes and sell juice or still wine to the houses. In practice they now have four basic ways of handling grapes: (1) they can just press and sell juice; (2) they can make a still wine which they sell to the houses; (3) they can put the still wine through second fermentation in bottle, which they then sell to a house for it to market as its own product; and (4) they can produce an effervescent wine which they sell under their own label, in competition with the houses and other growers, although only 67 of the cooperatives do this, selling their own brand. Additionally, cooperatives may also make finished champagne for their own members to sell under their own label. These vignerons are known as *récoltant-coopérateurs* (RCs). However, it is important to note that the cooperative does not in this case make a specialized *cuvée* just for the vigneron. Rather, they make a general wine for sale that all their members can buy and brand as their own. Thus it is possible in one village to have a number of vignerons who are all RCs and thus all sell their own brand, but the wine in the bottle is identical between each of them.

Many cooperatives are small, just serving some of the vignerons in a few villages, but increasingly federated groups of cooperatives are developing. This is most obviously the case with CVC (*Centre Vinicole de la Champagne*) Nicolas Feuillatte, which brings together 80 smaller, more localized cooperatives in one enterprise, thus indirectly uniting around 6,000 of the vignerons in the region. Nicolas Feuillatte sells wine to some of the houses, but also markets its eponymous brand, now the fourth or fifth largest in the world by volume.

The cooperatives have tax advantages, granted to them because in the 1920s and 30s they were perceived to be agents of local social and economic solidarity. As long as they only existed to provide the houses with juice or wine this was not contentious. Now that they produce and market their own brands this is giving rise to complaints that they are being given unfair fiscal privileges at the expense of their commercial competitors.

There are around 325 négociants and only they have the right to buy grapes or wine on the open market. It is these négociants who produce almost all the well-known international wine brands. In recent years many of the houses have been brought together in larger groups, concentrating ownership and management. Five groups now account for about 60 per cent of the value created by all the maisons. The largest of these is the luxury goods brand Moët-Hennessy Louis Vuitton (LVMH), and includes Moët et Chandon, Veuve Clicquot, Krug, Ruinart and Mercier. Other large groups include: the wine and champagne company Vranken Pommery; BCC, which owns Lanson, Boizel, and de Venoge; Laurent Perrier which also comprises the champagne labels Salon and Delamotte, and; the multinational drinks groups Pernod Ricard (owning Mumm and Perrier Jouët) and Remy Cointreau (Charles and Piper Heidsieck). A further 17 medium-sized enterprises account for about 33 per cent of value, including many of the best-known family companies, such as Taittinger, Louis Roederer, Bollinger and Pol Roger. These large and medium enterprises include about 50 brands in total – so a further 275 négociants are responsible for a mere 7 per cent of the value created by the houses, and these are often little more than large growers who happen to have the status of a négociant including the right to buy fruit from other growers.

The CIVC

In the years following 1941 the CIVC existed to organize and reinforce the interprofessional relationship. As noted above this focused initially on negotiating the price of grapes, but it also included intervening to guarantee a supply to the market when production was inadequate, or to support it when there was a surplus. The CIVC determines each year what the harvest size will be and what proportion of grapes harvested can be used immediately to produce wine for sale, and what proportion will be 'blocked' – i.e. reserved to be released onto the market to cover future demand. In this way the CIVC can moderate the flow of wine onto the market in response partly to the vagaries of weather (and thus harvest size) in a marginal wine production region and in part according to fluctuating demand for the product. Additionally the CIVC has intervened strongly in the relations between grape growers and négociants. This included helping in the creation of standard long-term interprofessional contracts, all of which must be approved by the organization.

As noted earlier, defending the Champagne region and name in the light of its reputation for high quality has been important in the history of the wine, and is now handled by the CIVC, which launches 800–1,000 court actions per year worldwide in its defence. These include some famous cases, such as that brought against Yves St Laurent in 1993 when the latter launched a perfume called 'Champagne'; a court decision forced a change of name.

The CIVC also pursues a research function. It has two experimental vineyards where it can test different ways of growing and treating vines and their environment, thus, for example, developing a body of knowledge about sustainable viticulture in the region over the last 15 years. It also has a well-equipped small-scale winery allowing it to test and develop new production methods and has sensory laboratories for carrying out wine evaluation activities.

The CIVC has a responsibility for the general promotion of champagne, a role which has grown substantially in recent years. It now operates *bureaux* in thirteen countries worldwide – the ten leading markets for champagne and China, Russia and India. These bureaux have wide remits which can include general promotion of champagne, defending it against passing off by other products (a continuing issue in the United States which refuses to recognize the integrity of the intellectual property of the name champagne), running trade tastings and organizing champagne events.

Finally, the CIVC has a role in attempting to maintain product quality. This includes things such as recommending pruning methods, determining the start date of the harvest and setting regulations for the production of the wine, including, for instance, minimum ageing times following the second fermentation. As part of this general function of promoting quality there is also a downstream quality-control function, with tasting of wines on the shelves in a number of outlets and the ability to request change if it appears that any product is of insufficient quality.

The CIVC remains, as it began, controlled equally by the SGV and the UMC and is jointly chaired by the head of each, although there is also a government commissioner who can intervene in the event of deadlock. It has a budget of around €20 million p.a. (raised by a levy per kilo of grape picked and per bottle sold) and it employs in the region of 120 people. For more information on its role see Chapter 10.

The future of the appellation

As has been previously noted, there is no more land to plant within the defined appellation area. Nevertheless, as will be shown in greater detail in Chapter 4, since the 1950s, sales of champagne have been rapidly increasing, and over the 15 years from 1992 to 2007 shipments increased by 55 per cent, although they have since declined a little. In response to this increased demand the area planted has also been increasing. In 1980 it was about 29,600 hectares and, as noted above, it is now 34,051 hectares, so that there is no further vineyard land to plant. The impact of this is a projection that – even with a decline in current sales due to the downturn in global economies, at some point between 2014 and 2019 demand is likely to exceed the maximum available supply of between 380 and 405 million bottles p.a. As a result the proposal was made early in the new millennium that the Champagne vineyard area could be reviewed and possibly expanded. The process is complex and time-consuming. In 2008, 40 additional villages were identified which could include new vineyard land; two were also proposed for deletion from the current area. This list is currently under review and, if approved, a commission then needs to establish precisely where the new vineyards might be appropriately situated. This process may (with further appeals) only be completed some time between 2016 and 2018. Once the grapes have been planted there is a minimum of three years before any crop can be picked and seven years before a substantial volume could be harvested. Thus this expansion, if it proceeds, would begin to have an impact from about 2024 onwards, and a substantial impact only from the end of that decade.

There has been criticism that any expansion of the appellation will reduce wine quality. However, before phylloxera the total vineyard area in Champagne was at least 60,000 hectares in total, and thus double its current size (Anon., 2010a). The proposal to expand the vineyard area is thus in part designed to restore previously used vineyard land to grape growing. Additionally, the quality of the wine produced from grapes in these areas will only be poor if the revision allows low-quality land to be brought into use. There is every indication that the bodies responsible for the process, including the CIVC, are intending to select land strictly for its high viticultural potential and to avoid an increased flow of poorer quality wine onto the market.

Conclusion

A number of key issues result from this contextual introduction to champagne – all of which are developed further in the chapters which follow. The first is that the growth and success of champagne has been emergent (Beverland, 2004), and certainly not planned – even though it is carefully managed now. Whilst the current organization of the region may imply that its success has been carefully orchestrated and the technology very precisely developed, key formative factors have been the result of chance. These include the combination of climatic change and technical innovation, the effect of effervescence on the body, the emergence of key actors over the generations, and even the impact of war as a stimulus for cohesion in the industry. What can be credited to the actors, however, is their willingness to seize these emergent opportunities and to work collectively to pursue them.

The second conclusion is to note the importance of two equally powerful groups – the négociants and the growers (and, as part of the second grouping, the cooperatives as well). This compares with a region such as Cognac where, again, négociants are responsible for the overwhelming volume of production, yet where the growers have never developed a united voice nor negotiated with the merchants from a position of equality. What makes this more interesting, moreover, is that although these groups work together to manage the industry, and although they are mutually dependent in terms of grape supply, they are also competitors when it comes to dealing with consumers. A vigneron may sell grapes to a cooperative and to a house, but also wine to a consumer in competition with both the cooperative's own brand and that of the house. This idiosyncratic system of mutually managed

cooperation and competition seems to operate, at least to this level of organization, nowhere else in the world of wine.

The result of this is, therefore, the key role of the CIVC. The production
system for champagne (and parts of its distribution) is very *dirigiste* – in
complete contrast to the typical *laissez-faire* New World approach to wine
production and distribution, where it is unlikely that a producer would
accept, for the overall good of the territorial product, controls on yields and
production methods or of the amount of wine to be released onto the
market. Indeed there can be few if any other industries which unite both
primary and production enterprises in a common body, as well as the
competing businesses within each half of that system. Companies which are
rivals in the American or Chinese markets also meet regularly under the
aegis of the UMC or the CIVC to discuss promotional or supply policy.

As noted, history has moulded the development of champagne, and as a
result the social context of production has become crucial. Champagne
cannot be separated from its soil, nor from the people who grow the grapes,
nor from the economies of the towns and villages in the area. While most
settlements have businesses on which they depend for their existence, the
converse is rarer; businesses which depend on the place for their existence.
Whereas most enterprises can transfer production to another country if the
economies of making the product are more attractive there, that cannot
happen with champagne. Consequently economic power is interrelated with
social relationships; the houses depend on who they know in which villages;
the cooperatives unite economically those who live, spend and socialize in
one or two villages – including the politicians, the community leaders and
the activists.

The consequence of this, and of the fact that the notion of 'champagne'
acts to strengthen the overall reputation of the individual brands, means
that the intellectual property of the place and its name is vigorously
protected. Clearly, significant energy is expended to limit the use of the
name to those involved in producing the product, but also effort is made to
promote the place, its mythology (as with the monk Dom Pérignon), its
history and its appeal. This promotion of place is primarily the responsibility
of the CIVC, but it is actively supported, and even undertaken, by the
houses and vignerons as well – so that the use of regional identity has both a
collective and individual significance. Whilst this notion of place has a clear
mythological function it is also, in the minds of its proponents, a very physical thing; one can note, for example, the distinction between the two types
of chalk sub-soil, one viewed positively and the other not. Ultimately place
is used as a means of inclusion and exclusion.

Notes

1   The equivalent of an English county.
2   The early history of Champagne is set out at the start of Chapter 12.

3   Phylloxera is a small insect of North American origin which eats the roots of vines and kills them. It devastated European vineyards in the seventy years following its arrival in the South of France in the early 1860s.

4   The two sides of Champagne often refer to themselves as 'the two families'; such a term, suggesting something gently domestic, is a good metaphor for the change in attitude of the growers and the houses. Families can be neighbours; they may occasionally argue but have common interest in protecting and improving their community.

5   *Appellation contrôlée* is the system of vineyard demarcation and production controls (including limits to the grape varieties which may be planted) introduced into France in 1935 and now, with some variations, ubiquitous throughout Europe. There is effectively a single AOC for Champagne, although a couple of minor AOCs for still wine exist.

2 Producing champagne

Philippe Jeandet and Steve Charters

As noted in Chapter 1, the start of champagne as a sparkling wine was essentially accidental, but this accident quickly became the subject of empirical research by wine-makers in order to refine the product. Thus, over 300 years, those involved in producing champagne focused very much on guaranteeing quality grapes, preserving the quality and finesse of the wine, ensuring that it was crystal clear and maintaining its balance. Modern processes are all focused on these aspects of champagne production. This chapter examines those processes, particularly within a management context, in order to give those interested in how the business of champagne functions an idea of the constraints placed on enterprises by the way the wine must be made. This is, however, only an outline, and those who seek further information should refer to Jeandet *et al.* (2010).

Champagne is undoubtedly the most prestigious effervescent wine throughout the world and around 300 million bottles of this wine are produced per year. It has become a symbol of lifestyle, and is used for all forms of celebration. Yet champagne is, above all, a blended wine. Most wines tend to be blended from a few sites and very often from a number of grape varieties. This is the case for champagne but in addition it is generally produced by blending wines from more than one year – something which is unusual in the world of quality still-wine production.

As with all wine, there are two key elements to the process. The first is growing grapes. The second is turning the grape juice into wine. However, with champagne this second element is split into two equally important stages: making a still base wine, and then creating the effervescent wine. These aspects of the process will each be addressed in turn, followed by a description of the various styles of champagne and a reflection on what provides the distinctiveness which is perceived to exist in the wine. It is important to note, however, that there are various methods of creating effervescence in a bottle. The *méthode champenoise* (champagne method) is the most complex, time consuming and expensive of all of these possible processes, and this has been adopted as the process of choice for all the highest quality sparkling wines around the world. A cheaper method is to mass-induce the carbon dioxide (CO_2) into the base wine in large tanks, and then filter, dose and bottle the wine under pressure to avoid the dissolved gas escaping. Cheaper still is to inject CO_2 into wine which is in motion; this produces a mousse of large bubbles, which dissipate rapidly and feel aggressive in the mouth, and is of a decidedly inferior quality.

Viticulture

In Chapter 1 we noted that Champagne naturally divides into a number of sub-regions. These regions have important historical and cultural contexts, but they also provide a viticultural context. Thus, for example, each is associated with one of the three major grape varieties used. The two best-known grapes are chardonnay and pinot noir. Both of these are found throughout the region, but the former is dominant particularly in the *Côte des Blancs* and the *Côte de Sézanne* and the latter in the eastern part of the *Montagne de Reims* and in the Aube. A third significant variety, pinot meunier, is dominant in the western end of the *Montagne de Reims* and the Marne Valley. This division is in part the outworking of the French notion of *terroir*, whereby grape varieties are each matched to the characteristics of a particular site – its soil, mesoclimate and topography.

At the same time each variety provides something distinctive to the blend. Pinot noir, a black grape variety, gives champagne its aromas of red fruits, as well as their strength and body; pinot meunier, another black cultivar, is characterized by its suppleness and spiciness, giving champagne roundness and fragrance. Finally, chardonnay, a white grape variety, provides champagne wines with their finesse, elegance, as well as floral and, in some instances, mineral notes. The two pinots are black-skinned grapes – thus are capable of giving red wine that is used for rosé wine-making – so that the production processes have to concentrate on extracting pale juice only. Other varieties have been authorized in the past, but they are now less than 0.3 per cent of all plantings, and of no more than very localized significance. The average price of grapes is currently €5.50 per kilo, making it the most expensive raw material of any wine region in the world.

Historically a process of site classification developed, grading the grape-growing villages according to their perceived quality, the *échelle des crus*. The villages were awarded a figure on a scale which now operates from 80 to 100 per cent. Any village awarded 100 per cent is considered to be a *grand cru* – which translates literally as 'great growth' but essentially means a great site. There are 17 of these, although a few are classed only for chardonnay or for pinot noir but not for both. Below that are the *premiers crus* (first growths) which score 90–99 per cent on the scale, of which there are 41. The other 261 villages are classed at 80–89 per cent. In the past the scale was linked directly to grape price; these days the price is less deterministically fixed, but there remains a general acceptance that some villages are better than others, and many producers will trade off the fact that their wines (or a prestige *cuvée*) is made only from *grands crus*. It is important to note, however, that the *cru* applies to the whole village and all the villages contained in it, in comparison to Burgundy, where it only applies to a single vineyard, or Bordeaux where it relates to a particular chateau or producer.

As noted in Chapter 1, Champagne is a very cool grape-growing region, with a mean annual temperature of 11°C (only just enough to ripen grapes) and rainfall of around 700 mm per year (CIVC, 2010). The climate is on the border between a maritime and continental climate, with year-round rainfall. The soils are very calcareous, with a preponderance of chalk in the most highly regarded vineyards, and chalky marl elsewhere, although a distinction is made in the region between sub-soils based on belemnite chalk (which is viewed positively) and micraster chalk (which is not acceptable for vineyards). Chalk is one of the best rocks on which to grow grapes, providing both excellent drainage but good water retention at lower levels which provide an excellent resource for the vines in dry years (Hancock & Price, 1990).

The vines are managed in a way that is traditional in temperate climates in Europe. They tend to be close spaced, with between 1 and 1.5 metres between rows and 0.9–1.5 metres apart along the rows, making around 6,750–10,000 vines per hectare (which compares with a norm of 1,000–4,000 in New World countries). Only four pruning systems are authorized by the AOC regulations. *Taille chablis* and *cordon royat* are the most important, and must be used in the *grands* and *premiers crus*. In other villages *guyot* and *vallée de la marne* can also be used.

There is a fixed yield of grapes at the time of harvest. The maximum that can be set in any year is 15,500 kilograms per hectare (kg/ha). However, as noted in Chapter 1, each year the CIVC sets an annual maximum which takes account of both the weather conditions for that year but also current market conditions and likely future demand. Thus in 2007, at a time of growth, the CIVC set a maximum yield of 13,000 kg/ha; in 2009, after the onset of the economic crisis had reduced demand this limit also reduced to 9,700 kg/ha and in 2010 it was 10,500. By French standards these are comparatively high yields: 15,500 translates as about 96 hectolitres per hectare (hl/ha), whereas typical yields for top red burgundy will be less than 30 hl/ha or Bordeaux, where the red wine may be around 35–40 hl/ha.

Wine production

Base wine

The first part of the process of turning the grapes into champagne is the production of base wine. The aim is that this wine should be as light and delicate as possible, and to avoid any coarseness. Champagne is also generally a white wine so it is crucial, given that two thirds of all the grapes harvested have red skins, to avoid any uptake of colour during the production process. Consequently harvesting is by hand only, to guarantee whole bunches of unbroken grapes which will not start to leach colour or tannin from the skins. High-quality musts (the extracted juice) are obtained by the use of proper picking and pressing conditions. For example, sorting to remove rot-attacked grape clusters is needed during picking, since it has been shown that grey mould caused by the phytopathogenic fungus, *Botrytis cinerea*, can have deleterious effects both on the foaming properties of champagne and on the taste of the wines. This was particularly a problem in 2010, for instance, with attacks of rot in some vineyards of between 20–24 per cent. In order to guarantee that grapes are ripe enough throughout the region the harvest date is specified by a *ban*, a regulation made each year by the CIVC that determines the earliest date on which picking can take place; varies slightly from village to village according to the season. Despite this, the grapes are picked with a comparatively low sugar content (usually around 9–10 per cent), resulting in juice with a high level of acidity and fruit flavours which tend towards the light or green, rather than rich and intense. Because there is a limited time for harvest (with the continual danger of wet weather, which favours the development of fungal disease including grey rot), and as it has to be done by hand, around 100,000 people have to be mobilized to take part, many of them coming in from outside the region.

Grapes must be transported as intact as possible to preserve freshness, and to avoid skin maceration in the juice and the effect of oxidation. Because many of the houses own or buy grapes from vineyards some distance from their production centres they often have 'press houses' in the vineyard areas where they can process grapes before transferring the juice to their headquarters. The entire grape clusters are pressed lightly (with pressures ranging from 1.5 to 2 bars) without crushing. Traditionally the pressing has been done in shallow basket presses which are powerful and fast – again minimizing colour and tannin uptake – but recently pneumatic presses which are gentle but can also be rapid have become popular. Rules govern the amount of juice which can be produced. A maximum of 2,550 litres can be pressed from every 4 tonnes of grapes; the *cuvée* is the first 2,050 litres, which is considered to be the finest, and the *taille* is the last 500 litres, generally a coarser juice and often not used by those producers most focused on high quality wine. As soon as the must is extracted, sulphur dioxide (SO_2) is added at doses varying from 3 to 8 g/hl, mainly depending on the pressing fraction (*cuvée* or *taille*) and the level of grey rot in the vineyard, to protect it from oxidation.

The wine is allowed to settle, the so-called *débourbage*, which allows much solid material to fall out of the must (18 to 24 hours at temperatures ranging from 6 to 15°C), before fermentation begins, generally in stainless steel tanks, and almost invariably using pre-prepared and inoculated yeast. Fermentation temperature tends to be around 15–18°C. Given the low natural sugar levels of the grapes the wine is generally, though not always, chaptalized (the addition of sugar to increase the alcohol level in the finished wine) so that at the end of fermentation there is a still, white wine of around 11 per cent alcohol by volume, termed the base wine. Controlled malolactic fermentation of base wines, that is, biological deacidification of wine by transforming green malic acid to softer lactic acid with the use of lactic acid bacteria, is now widely used in champagne production. This is done to avoid the unplanned occurrence of this fermentation subsequently in the bottle, which could lead to an increase in unpleasant volatile acidity and the appearance of unwanted lactic aromas in the taste of the wine.

The next crucial stage in the process is the blending (*assemblage*). This takes place some months after harvest and is the means whereby a consistent 'house style' is created. The practice of blending wines from different grape varieties, different origins (*crus*) and different years (reserve wines) is essential to maintain the quality of champagne and the house style unique to every champagne producer. Reserve wines are kept two or three or even up to ten years (sometimes on yeast lees) in tanks at 12–13° C and protected from oxygen. For many small producers blending may merely entail the selection of different wines from the current vintage to form the base for different types of wine (normal, rosé, off-dry, etc.). However, for most producers it involves blending wines from more than one year, in order to iron out variations in vintages resulting from the different weather conditions of the years; further, for the medium-sized and larger companies it will also involve blending the grapes of different villages (and therefore with different taste characteristics) from across the region, as well as wines made from the three different grape varieties. For the largest houses this can be a complex process, requiring the senior wine-makers to taste and re-taste hundreds of wine samples, and to use their knowledge of the wines, the vineyards and past blends to re-create the product in a way that is consistent with the brand in the past. This role requires both high levels of training and also a substantial experience with the past wines of the house and the way they have developed over the years.

Second fermentation

The base wine for champagne is light, still, acidic and low in ripe-fruit intensity; it is not particularly pleasant to drink. It is both given its character and made palatable by the second fermentation, which creates the dissolved CO_2, and is the basis of a sparkling wine. This process is outlined below, although readers seeking more information about the science of CO_2 are referred to recent research on the topic carried out by the University of Reims (Liger-Belair *et al.*, 2008, 2009).

The base wine is placed in a bottle to which is added the *tirage liqueur*. This is a mixture of wine, prepared yeast and (for a standard bottle) 16.5–18 g/l of dissolved sugar. The bottle, sealed usually with a crown cap, is then left in a cool cellar, and over a period of some weeks a second fermentation occurs. This increases the alcohol level of the wine by around 1.25 per cent but crucially also produces CO_2 – the other by-product of fermentation. Because the bottle is sealed the CO_2 cannot escape and remains dissolved in the wine, producing finally about 5–6 atmospheres of pressure (the equivalent of a truck tyre). The cooler the cellar, the longer the time taken for the second fermentation; the longer the time taken, the more completely the gas dissolves in the liquid, and thus – when the wine is drunk – the less aggressive and more 'creamy' the feel of the mousse in the mouth.

Although the second fermentation is over in around six to eight weeks the wine is not yet ready to drink. The rules of production require the wine to stay in the cellar for a minimum period: 15 months for a non-vintage wine and three years for a vintage. In practice the wines from producers most concerned about product quality will lie in the cellar for much longer – generally 30–42 months and four to eight years respectively. This process helps to integrate and age the wine, but critically it also adds another element to the final flavour. Following completion of the second fermentation yeast autolysis occurs, that is, the enzymatic self-degradation process of yeast cell constituents which follows the death of the cells at the end of fermentation. The wine is enriched by yeast components such as amino-acids, proteins and aroma compounds that influence the wine's ability to foam and its sensory properties – adding a subtle bready, briochy character, something considered to add to the quality, interest and appeal of the wine. Autolysis characters only occur during the production of Champagne wines that have at least 12 months in contact with yeast in the bottle.

The wine is now drinkable, but it is not clear, for during the second fermentation the yeast cells have multiplied rapidly, and create what is effectively a hazy wine. Over the last two centuries a method developed to extract the yeast without losing fizz or too much wine. The first problem is to get the yeast to agglomerate; to this end, the wine is matured on its side. However, the agglomerated yeast cells are not particularly fluid; getting them from the side to the neck of the bottle is something which takes days or weeks, with a regular twisting, raising and banging of the bottle, to obtain a gradual shift of the deposit. Over this period bottles start horizontally and finish at a substantial angle. Traditionally this was done by hand with the bottles stacked in riddling racks (*pupitres*), something still on display to tourists in the cellars of many of the major houses. A skilled riddler could riddle 40,000–60,000 bottles per day. However, labour costs and the unwillingness of workers to spend all day in semi-darkness turning bottles means that generally the wines are now riddled by machine in large crates of 504 bottles at once.

With riddling completed the bottles are stacked *sur pointes* – upside-down with the deposit of yeast in their neck, until the time comes for them to be finished and disgorgement takes place. During disgorging, the inverted bottle is partially immersed in a low-temperature brine (about minus 20°C), freezing the neck of the bottle and entrapping the yeast and other deposit. This produces a small plug of ice in the neck of the bottle which includes all the dead yeast cells. The bottle is then turned upright, the crown seal removed and, under the pressure of the gas, the plug pops out of the bottle. This is known as disgorgement (*dégorgement*). The advantage of freezing the bottle's neck is that it also chills down the rest of the wine inside. At a cooler temperature the CO_2 escapes less quickly, so although the ice plug is evacuated no wine and very little gas is lost; during this operation, there is a loss in the CO_2 pressure ranging from 0.5 to 0.8 bar. The bottle is then topped up with the *liqueur d'expedition*, a mixture of mature wine and a small amount of sugar and antioxidants (SO_2, citric acid or ascorbic acid). This liquid naturally replaces the volume of wine lost during disgorgement, but it also adds to the wine's style. The amount of sugar added (which gener-ally varies from 6–13 g/l but for some particularly dry wines may be as little as zero) helps shape the final style of the wine, and softens the aggressive nature of the wine's acidity a little. The wine is then corked with an agglom-erated cork that has two natural cork disks on its base, the bottom one of which is stamped 'champagne'.

For medium and large producers, disgorgement and the addition of the *liqueur d'expedition* is now highly mechanized, and from the time that a bottle leaves the icy brine bath to the insertion of the final cork may be no more than ten seconds in total.

What makes champagne distinctive?

Lovers of champagne maintain that it is the best sparkling wine in the world. Such a judgment inevitably has a subjective element, but it is undoubtedly true that certain factors combine to make champagne distinctive. Many of these can be replicated elsewhere, some of them, at least in the way that they interact in champagne, cannot.

As noted in the section on viticulture, certain key factors are crucial in the production of champagne. The quality of the soil for viticulture has been noted. Additionally, the grape varieties used are widely viewed as the best available for sparkling wine. Indeed, in those parts of the world which have most recently developed sparkling wine, such as North America or the Antipodes, wine-makers striving for the highest quality almost invariably choose chardonnay and pinot noir. Finally, the climate offers a delicate balance, between being cool enough to make light, elegant wines and too cool to produce good wine at all. The fact that in some years the weather veers towards the latter is one reason why most champagne is produced as a non-vintage blended wine.

The method of making the wine is fundamental. It is designed to be non-extractive, again to preserve the freshness, delicacy and elegance of the wine. Blending is crucial, offering the chance to produce a more balanced wine than would be the case if single sites or vintages were used, and of making a more complex-flavoured wine. The slow second fermentation provides an attractive mouthfeel and the long maturation on lees adds further complexity. Neither of these factors exist with more commercial sparkling wines, where the aim tends to be to get the product onto the market as speedily as possible.

Paradoxes of production

It is worth noting that there are aspects of the production of champagne that are unusual, particularly in the highly regulated system of wine production in Europe. As already stressed, this is a cool wine region; if it did not produce sparkling wine it would probably not produce wine at all now, yet what it does make is one of the most reputable wines in the world.

Uniquely amongst European wines, champagne is made with the addition of sugar to sweeten the wine. Otherwise sweet wines in Europe must be made using natural grape sugars. The blending of red and white wine to make pink wines has been explained – yet this is unique in European wine production, where the rules normally prohibit using white wine to make pink and only red grapes can be used.

Further, there is a single AOC for the whole of the region, a system which exists in no other major wine-producing region in France (there are 57 AOCs in Bordeaux and over 100 in Burgundy). Yet the label on the bottles does not mention the fact that this is an AOC wine – again the only exception to this rule in Europe where it is otherwise *de rigueur* to show that the product comes from a quality wine region. Finally, a whole village can be a *grand cru*. This compares with Burgundy or Alsace where *grand cru* sites are very specific, and a number may exist alongside each other in one village.

Drinking champagne

Styles of champagne

Champagne comes with a range of sugar levels. Historically it was a very sweet wine, but over the last 150 years the amount of sugar added in the dosage has been reduced; nevertheless, one of the strengths of the wine is that the range of sweetness allows different wines to be produced to appeal to different tastes. The most common wine is '*brut*', with a level of residual sugar of up to 15 grams per litre (g/l); however, this range is quite substantial, and a wine dosed at around 13 g/l will look noticeably softer and sweeter than one at 8 g/l. Ascending levels of sugar go with the designations of *sec* (dry), *demi-sec* ('half' dry) and *doux* (sweet); the most common of these, as a sweet champagne, is *demi-sec*. Another style is based on a minimal or non dosage, termed *extra-brut* which has less than 6 g/l residual sugar (also known as *brut-sauvage* or *non-dosée* when no dosage is added at all); this style is currently becoming more popular, in part because it is thought to be a more 'true' reflection of the *terroir* and the true nature of champagne, and in part in reaction against the use of sweetening to mask flavour in food. However, it has been open to criticism that the wines can be unbalanced (with an excess of apparent acidity) and that they do not age as well as wines with a little sugar added.

There are a number of styles of champagne. Thus one brand can be extended substantially to gain deeper market penetration. The varying styles depend on the grape varieties used, the provenance of the grapes, and the maturation methods.

The most widely drunk style of champagne (about 90 per cent of all sales) is termed non-vintage. This is the standard style, and most producers say that it is the wine by which they wish to be judged, even if it is not their most prestigious product. Different houses will typically focus more on one variety than another in moulding their style: thus Taittinger and Laurent Perrier tend to use more chardonnay, Veuve Clicquot and Bollinger more pinot noir. Many of the smaller producers in outlying areas will concentrate on pinot meunier.

Vintage wines are, as their name suggests, produced from a single year's crop. Whilst they may still be blended from different grapes and different villages they do not have wine from previous years added to smooth out the characteristics added by the weather of the year. Traditionally they have been made a few times a decade in the warmest years, when the acid in the wine is not too aggressive.

Blanc de blancs wines are made only from chardonnay grapes – the title means white from white (grapes). As a result they tend to be lighter, fresher and with more evident acidity, but consequently with high ageing potential.

Blanc de noirs, conversely, are made only from red grapes. They may be rounder, and fruitier, but less fresh and acidic than other wines. Their weight and character means that they are sometimes considered a less successful style than *blanc de blancs* wines (Faith, 1988).

Pink (*rosé*) wines have proved increasingly popular in the last ten years, in line with the rise in popularity of pink wines generally. Two methods may be used for their production. The first is to use red grapes and macerate the must with the skins for a period (12–36 hours) to extract some colour, before pressing the must and finishing the fermentation without the skins (*rosé de saignée*). This is considered by some to be a risky process; if the skins are not removed from the must at the right time the wine is too deeply pink, and will not fit into the house style. More common is the method of blending red wine with white, to produce pink.

Prestige cuvées are now produced by most major companies – following the lead of Cristal, made by Louis Roederer, Dom Pérignon from Moët et Chandon, and Krug. These are designed to reflect the best wine the company can possibly produce whilst remaining within the overall style of the house, and can sell at a very high premium.

Tasting champagne

Champagne is one of the most famous effervescent wines throughout the world. This is in part linked to the perceived elegance of its sparkling and foaming properties. Consumers appreciate both a regular and durable effervescence, leading to a foam ring composed of small bubbles on the liquid surface, the so-called *collerette*. Before smelling and tasting a champagne wine, consumers will pay attention to the appearance of foam. Professor Gérard Liger-Belair said the following in his remarkable book, *The Science of Champagne*:

> Bubbles form on several spots on the glass wall, detach and then rise toward the surface in elegant trains, like so many tiny hot-air balloons. Listen carefully also. When they burst at the surface, the bubbles make a crackling sound and produce a cloud of tiny droplets that pleasantly tickle the taster's nostrils.
>
> (Liger-Belair, 2004)

Whilst champagne has particular appeal for consumers, tasting it is not necessarily easy, and there is evidence that even experienced wine tasters find it more difficult than ordinary wines (Charters, 2005). As well as the appearance of the wine, the aromas are often more subtle than with other wines, and require particular attention. Further, just as champagne requires attention to the appearance of the foam, so when tasting it one must think about the mousse in the mouth. The ideal mouthfeel should be smooth, almost creamy. A wine with large bubbles which explode aggressively will be much less pleasant.

Champagne aromas can be divided into three types: those of young champagne, mature champagne and aged champagnes. The most characteristic aromas are the following:

- *Young champagnes (up to two to three years).* Fresh aromas (white flowers, white fruit, red fruit, citrus fruit), leaf aromas, fermentation aromas (yeast, doughy bread), mint, grapefruit, raspberry, strawberry, mineral notes.
- *Mature champagnes (from three to four years up to six to eight years).* Mature aromas, high aroma intensity and roundness: yellow fruit (cherry, plum, peach, pear), dry fruit, cooked fruit, pastry, sweet, spicy, cinnamon, caramel, brioche, blond tobacco, cherry.
- *Aged champagnes (more than six to eight years).* Complexity, aromas of mature fruit sometimes with animal notes, candied fruit, honey, undergrowth, grilled roasting coffee, fungi, dried grape berries, candied fruit, toast, morel mushrooms, gingerbread.

3   The legal context of champagne

Theo Georgopoulos

Introduction

The Champagne region is in all ways one of the most highly regulated wine production areas in the world. International, European, national and local rules cross each other in this rather small part of the wine world and fix a particularly complex legal status for the wine of Champagne. The prestige and the reputation of champagne and the globalization of the wine markets partly explain this complexity. The most important element, however, in the making of champagne's legal status is its rich and even turbulent history. Legal settlements, especially related to the decision-making process, express compromises or lessons from the past. In fact, these settlements are the expression of an original system of checks and balances which remind us in many ways of the control mechanisms of political science and constitutional theory. Instead of giving full power to one single institution or organization, decision-making stems from the cross-fertilization of points of view and the clash of different, not always converging, interests.

The role of law in this sense is two-fold. On the one hand, it fixes the procedural rules and the institutional framework for the decision-making process. On the other hand, it gives form and legal authority to the content of the compromises reached by the action of different players in the wine business.

Thus, it appears that the balance of the champagne business is based on a multi-level governance system. Whereas at the local level, a particularly original system is established, both the national and the European authorities also intervene, asserting the checks and balances of the model.

Local governance: the CIVC model

The regulation of the champagne business is above all a matter of balance between the growers and the wine-makers/distributors. The institutional settlements around the sharing of power and the decision-making process are designed in an attempt to ensure this balance.

The key features of an institutional balance

The structure of the CIVC is a unique system of checks and balances that reminds us of the balance of powers among political institutions. In order to better understand the institutional originality of the regulatory system of champagne, one should take into account both the historic and the economic system of the region. Land owners and wine-makers have been obliged to coexist, sometimes under difficult circumstances, in order to ensure the stability and further development of champagne. Especially since the eighteenth century, the establishment of well-known champagne houses progressively gave champagne its reputation and ensured international sales. However, in contrast to other wine-making areas like Bordeaux, there was no concentration of the production of grapes in the hands of brand-name owners. The geography of land ownership remained scattered and with few exceptions grapes still belonged to small or medium land owners, who lacked the infrastructure, know-how and above all the brand name and the distribution network that would allow them to challenge the champagne houses. This situation inevitably created the conditions of a delicate balance of power in terms of price policy: grape producers could not freely impose prices on the négociants without taking the risk of having their product going rotten on the vines and, inversely, champagne houses were obliged to make an effort towards the holders of the 'source' of the precious wine.

At the beginning of the twentieth century, a long-standing tension in the champagne world that eventually led to riots in the very beginning of 1911 – known as *les émeutes* (Kladstrup & Kladstrup, 2005) – was decisive for the future development of the institutional and legal framework of the champagne industry. Local vignerons reacted violently to the 'importation' of wine coming from other parts of France to be turned into champagne. Growers were complaining that they were being driven out of business in this way, whereas champagne houses were worried about stability and the further development of the wine production in a difficult period because of phylloxera and unfortunate climatic conditions. The social and political crisis that followed the action of mobs sacking champagne houses soon made clear that a long-standing institutional solution needed to be found. This settlement should not only take into account the need for a balance between the two major actors of the champagne business but also had to assert the specific characteristics of champagne. In other words, any long-standing and efficient solution should come from a rational regulation of the champagne business rather than through the interference of external factors, such as the importation of wines or decisions coming directly from central government.

The creation of the CIVC stands as the achievement of these objectives. As noted in Chapter 1, its structure is based on a federated system ensuring equal representation of the interests of winegrowers and champagne houses, and it forms the institutional meeting point of the two major players of the champagne business. The CIVC is not, however, a simple forum for discussion of questions related to the wine sector. It has a regulatory power delegated by the State. Even though it is an organization of private law, from a functional point of view it acts as an administrative authority within the limits that have been fixed by law. The *Conseil d'Etat*, the French Supreme Administrative Court recognized that public mission entrusted to the CIVC and confirmed that the decisions taken by its organs are administrative acts whenever they are related to the exercise of public authority (Conseil d'Etat, 13 January 1968). Besides, as we will see further, these prerogatives justify the presence of State representatives in the decision-making process of the CIVC.

Thus, major questions of the champagne wine sector including price-fixing, productivity (volumetric efficiency) and the commercialization of vintage wines are settled through the decision-making process of the CIVC. The consensus ensured by this common action of the two major actors of the champagne industry guarantees legitimacy in the governance of one of the most regulated wine areas of the world. The regulatory action of the CIVC together with customary practices in the champagne business which are repeated over time stand as a unique example of local law which enjoys its autonomy from general rules established at the national level.

The decision-making process lies upon the balance of powers between the two major actors. The decisions on production volume or prices take the shape of an inter-professional agreement. All members of each professional organization are bound by the agreement. The consensus that is necessary for the regulation of such important questions each year obliges both vine growers and wine-makers to compromise. This process not only absorbs conflicts between the two professional branches but also integrates divergent opinions among vine growers or distributors. The SGV especially is one of the most highly representative professional organizations in France given that 99 per cent of the champagne vine growers are members. Its organization is based on a system of local sections, each one of them corresponding to a wine-producing village. Local sections can debate over different questions of the wine business and, through a bottom-up process, they can bring their ideas or worries before the central organs of the Syndicat. Besides, they can express their point of view on projects for regulatory measures. The Syndicat's central organ, the Executive Committee – whose members are supposed to take into account these views while negotiating – acts on the basis of this legitimacy. The UMC, which counts some one hundred champagne houses as members, including the major brand names, is also a representative organization, even though it does not cover all champagne négociants. Only those that fully control the wine-making process as well as distribution can have access to membership of the UMC. However, as the champagne produced by the members of the UMC equates to two-thirds of the whole of the wine production, this gives the UMC the legitimacy to negotiate with the SGV.

We should underline the fact that the presence of these two professional organizations in the decision-making process is based on both legal provisions and developing professional practice. The 1941 decree enumerating the organizations that are legally authorized to participate in the decision-making mechanism of the CIVC (Decree of 8 September 1941), refers explicitly to three organizations for grape producers, including the SGV, and five organizations representing the champagne houses of which none have survived nowadays (Diart-Boucher, 2006). Therefore, the organization of the decision-making process and the representation of the most important professional organization of the champagne business are based upon evolving empirical practice. The institutional settlements of the CIVC reflect a real balance of existing powers at the local level rather than any prior choices or visions of the central legislative power.

An imperfect balance

This balance is not, however, without exceptions at the legal level. The SGV and the UMC do not decide together on all questions related to the champagne business. The professional organization of vine growers has prerogatives in certain fields where the intervention of the UMC is excluded. This is mainly the case with the general requirements which give access to the prestigious appellation of origin (AOC) Champagne. Historically, the *Institut national des Appellations d'origine* (INAO), the national authority in charge of the AOC system has worked in close relationship to wine syndicats. Since the 1884 Law on the freedom of syndicalism, trade unions within the wine sector have been fully recognized. With the emergence of the AOC system (with the legislative decree of 30 June 1935) these professional organizations were officially associated with the registration and the protection of the appellations of origin (Bahans & Menjuncq, 2010). At the European level, under the new common organization of the wine market (Art. 64 of Regulation 479/2008), it is stated that 'producer organizations' can be recognized by the Member States. This is the case of the existing French organizations – already recognized under the previous Regulation (1493/1999) – including the SGV. We should underline, however, that EU Law clearly distinguishes between producer organizations and interprofessional organizations which intervene under specific circumstances and in order to pursue relevant objectives (Art. 65 of Regulation 479/2008). From the combined application of Articles 37 and 49 of Regulation 479/2008, it appears that only producer organizations and not interprofessional bodies may apply for any registration or amendments to a registered appellation of origin or geographical indication (GI) protected at the European level. Thus, the CIVC could not replace the SGV in such a procedure.

Given that 'Champagne' as an appellation of origin is already registered and legally protected, any amendment related to the AOC Champagne may concern either the delimitation of the wine-producing area that benefits

from the prestigious appellation of origin designation or the product specifications for wine-making that justifies the use of the AOC Champagne. In
these situations, according to French law the recognized organization for
the protection of the AOC (*'syndicat de defense'*) should be consulted
before any decision is taken by the Ministry of Agriculture. According to
French case-law (Council of State, Judgement of 29 June 1998), there is a
legal obligation for national authorities to consult these organizations
before taking any relevant decision. In fact, this association is usually the
group of producers of the wine sold under the relevant AOC. This is reasonable given that vine growers and wine producers know best the methods of
wine-making and the specificities of the 'terroir', so can propose amendments that are likely to correspond to real needs of the sector. Thus, it is not
surprising that the SGV participates in the decision-making process, given
that it is recognized as an organization for the protection of the AOC champagne. Recently, it has been consulted for the new product specifications
for the wine-making of champagne which were adopted by a decree on 22
November 2010 (Decree No. 2010-1441 of 25 November 2010, Official
Journal of the French Republic, No. 0273, p. 21013).

On the other hand, the UMC is excluded from this decision-making
process. Of course, the expectations of the professional branch are supposed
to be taken into account at least unofficially. But, from a legal standpoint,
there is no obligation on the national authorities to involve other organizations in this decision-making process. In other words, the balance of powers
is not complete and it depends on the level of governance of the champagne
business. At the level of designing the requirements for the AOC Champagne, the SGV, as a 'producer organization', is far more involved in the
decision-making process, whereas regarding the year-to-year management
the two representative organizations are equally present.

The balance between employers and workers

Furthermore, each one of the two professional organizations is responsible
for the collective bargaining between employers and trade unions. This is
also an important question for the champagne business. In the past, social
conflicts have impeded the development as well as the peaceful function of
the wine sector in the region. The SGV and the UMC organize voluntary
negotiations between employers and employees (between 3,000 and 4,000
working for the wine-makers, some 6,000 workers in the vine-growing
sector, plus tens of thousands of interim workers for the grape harvest). For
the SGV, the first collective bargaining agreement was signed on 2 July 1969
regarding workers in the Marne *departement*. Later, the same agreement
was extended to workers of the rest of the wine production area. This agreement concerns employees in businesses with a preponderant agricultural
activity.

The case of wine-makers is even more interesting, for collective bargaining between champagne houses and their employees was already organized by the late 1920s and the first collective agreement was signed in 1936, following an important period of social struggle in France. This agreement is regularly revised through collective bargaining organized under the responsibility of the UMC, settling questions like wages and bonuses, family allowances, leave, working conditions, medical care, pensions, etc. The negotiations take place within the so-called *Commission Tripartite* (Three-Parties Commission) where the UMC is represented as well as two *syndicats* (trade union conglomerates). According to French law, the agreement is binding not only for the members of the UMC but for all wine-making businesses of the Champagne region, including those that have not participated in the negotiations (Decree of 6 June 1986).

The fact that collective bargaining is organized under the responsibility of the two major professional branches appears to be a rather good idea. Although some may argue that in this way the powers of the SGV and UMC are further enhanced and that the regulatory system in the field of labour law becomes too centralized one must recognize the advantages of this choice. First, the legitimacy of both professional organizations is likely to ensure negotiations open with a large participation by interested parties. Second, as representative organs of the professional branches they are aware of the problems and the perspectives of the champagne industry. Therefore, the arrangements crystallized through these agreements will probably take into account the specific context of the champagne industry at the moment of their signature. Both these elements contribute to the easing of the relationships between employers and workers in the sector. The difficulties and the struggles of the past which had shaken the champagne industry have once again dictated institutional and legal settlements which work towards the resolution of conflicts.

From local governance to national regulation

The regulation of the wine sector at the local level through CIVC action does not mean that nationwide authorities are excluded from the decision-making process. This would have been against French legal tradition which is generally based on a centralized administrative system. Besides, conflicts in the champagne industry through history explain the concern on behalf of the State to keep an eye on what is happening around the Champagne vineyards. Finally, the economic challenges related to the commercialization of what is arguably the most famous wine worldwide further justifies the intervention or, at least, the discreet presence of State representatives in the decision-making process. Thus, the autonomy of the champagne regulatory system is limited.

This is already affirmed at the level of the CIVC's function. Champagne's inter-professional organization is under the control of the Ministry of Agriculture. This justifies the presence of a governmental official

(*Commissaire du gouvernement*), a qualified public servant of the central government in the structure of the organization. This function is entrusted to the Prefect of the Region who has the power to sign all decisions taken by the common agreement of the representatives of the two structures at the basis of the CIVC system (SGV and UMC). This signature gives to the decisions of the CIVC the authority of binding administrative decisions. The presence of the representative of the State administration is not however purely formal. It allows surveillance and control on behalf of the State. These prerogatives may simply be expressed by form of mediation in case of conflict between the two professional organizations. The impartial and independent role of the State representative with regard to the corporatist vision of the SGV and the UMC can facilitate its role in the search of compromise. Nevertheless, it cannot be ignored that the State representative goes far beyond this discreet role and has and uses a real power to veto the agreements reached by the professional organizations (Diart-Boucher, 2006). Of course, as is common in most systems of checks and balances, this confrontation never takes the form of an open conflict. The point of view of the State is taken into account at the moment of the negotiations in order to reach an agreement that will best satisfy all the decision-makers within the CIVC.

Nonetheless, the presence of the State in the wine business, including champagne, is above all ensured by the role of the INAO. This public administrative establishment was created as a reaction to the failure of governmental authorities as well as courts to register and efficiently protect the system of AOCs. Thus, the law-decree of 30 July 1935 by which the modern AOC system was introduced also created a national committee of appellations of origin for wines that would later become the INAO. Nowadays, the INAO has enlarged its competence to other foodstuff as well as different types of labelling. Its main mission remains to propose the recognition of appellations of origin and GIs. In this sense, the INAO offers the necessary expertise for deciding upon new or existing appellations of origin (and GIs). It also recognizes professional organizations that, like the SGV, have the legal capacity to act for the defence of existing appellations of origin. Moreover, and it is one of its most important missions, it has the power of control over the wine industry to check whether the product specifications required by law have been respected, allowing the product to enjoy access to the appellation of origin (Visse-Causse, 2007).

In order to fulfil its mission, the INAO is based on a decentralized model. Apart from its central organs (which include representatives of the State, professionals and even consumers), it intervenes at the regional level through its regional committees. The regional representatives of the INAO, including those for the Champagne region, are in permanent contact with the professionals of the wine business. Thus, these committees stand as an interface between the local and the central administration of the wine sector, whereas at the same time the control of the respect of product specifications is entrusted to an authority that is distinct from the producers and wine-makers. The checks and balances system, once again, is affirmed.

The INAO itself is subject to the same philosophy. Despite its over-arching role at the levels of expertise and control it has no decision-making power. Decisions on the registration of appellations of origin or on the amendment of the product specifications or the wine-making geographical area belong to the State authorities and mainly the Ministry of Agriculture. The recent change of product specifications for champagne is a good example in this sense. The national wine and spirits committee of the INAO was consulted before the adoption of the decree on the new product specifi-cations for champagne, but the opinion of the INAO was not binding on the political authority, even though in practice its positions are generally followed without hesitation.

Under the new common organization of the wine market (Regulation 479/2008), the important role of the INAO is confirmed. As a control authority designated by France (Article 47) it has the power to check whether the requirements imposed by EU Law, including for the cham-pagne wines, are respected (see Bahans & Menjuncq, 2010, p. 132).

The European factor: new balance or new disorder?

The development of European wine regulations have nevertheless progres-sively questioned the delicate balance of legal powers fixed for champagne and finally transformed the game between actors of the champagne industry. Starting with the general provisions of the Common Agricultural Policy, the European Economic Community expressed from the very begin-ning its intention to regulate the agricultural sector. Wine could not escape this regulatory change. Regulations 816/70 and 817/70 introduced the common organization of the wine market which completely changed the methods of regulatory governance of the wine sector in Europe. Of course the Champagne region seemed to a certain point protected against this legal revolution for it was already a highly regulated system and European Community Law was rather deferential towards established regulatory systems in the wine industry. For instance, Regulation 817/70 made the distinction between table wines and quality wines which had an important impact on the wine sector throughout Europe. However, for champagne such a distinction did not have any serious impact on the established regula-tory system for local and national rules were far more rigorous. Nonetheless, different questions of major importance had to be answered in relation to European Community demands. The management of plantation rights of vines and above all the control of subsidies granted to wine-makers have confirmed the presence of the European Community (now the European Union) as a new factor in the governance of the champagne industry.

Indeed, all wine-producing areas throughout the European Union need to comply with the demands of EU Law, which stands as an important factor in the governance of the wine industry. Plantation rights for instance, fixed by the previous common organization of the wine market have had a decisive impact on global wine production among the Member States. The control of vine plantation tends to ensure a decent revenue for wine producers by limiting the supply of wine to the market while allowing the progressive renewal of the European vineyards. The plantation of vines in Champagne – either in the light of an extension of the producing AOC area or even with regard to plantation within the existing zone – has to observe rules imposed by these European constraints.

Besides, one should not neglect the fact that the establishment of the internal market as a primary objective of the European Economic Community, and subsequently of the European Union, has enhanced the legal protection of champagne's image and treatment abroad, in Europe as well as in third countries. The prohibition of tax discrimination of wine between Member States, further confirmed by the harmonization of excise duties and more generally the establishment of the free movement of goods, granted free trade of champagne throughout Europe (Georgopoulos, 2011). Moreover, the common organization of the wine market and the negotiation of international agreements with third states (like the agreement on wine trade with Australia) have limited cases of the improper use of the name of champagne for sparkling wines produced in other parts of the world. Thus, EU Law has also contributed to a better visibility of champagne, at least from a legal standpoint. This 'external balance' provided to champagne should not be underestimated: by protecting its name and its reputation in a continuously opening world wine market, champagne defends its position among other wines – or otherwise it would simply get imprisoned in it! In any case, EU Law stands as an important guarantee in the establishment of the status of champagne in the international markets.

A brand new perspective in the position of the European Union in the balance of powers in Champagne has been introduced through the new Common Organization of the wine market. Regulation 479/2008 has profoundly changed the balance of powers between the Member States and the European Union in the regulation of the wine sector. Questions like registration of appellations of origin and GIs and labelling are now mainly regulated at the European level (Bahans, 2009), whereas national authorities, including local organizations have only enforcement powers in this field.

The previous Common Organization of the wine market, established by Regulation 1493/1999, left to the Member States the exclusive power to decide on GIs and especially on quality wines produced in a specific region of their territory. This recognition was based on national criteria. Member States were simply obliged to forward to the Commission the list of quality wines produced in a specific region that they had recognized stating for each one of them the details of the national provisions governing their production and manufacturing (Regulation 1493/1999 Art. 54 para. 4). The

European Commission was simply in charge of publishing the list of wines without having any power to scrutinize the registration. Of course, the 1999 Regulation fixed a certain number of EU requirements, mainly that the name of a quality wine produced in a specific region should not be used to designate wine not produced in that region (Art. 52 para. 1). However, these elements were not accompanied by any enforcement powers given to the Commission apart from the general possibility to engage an infringement procedure against Member States that breach EU Law requirements.

On the contrary, the registration system of the new Common Organization for the wine market is based on the allocation of autonomous European power to grant European protection (positive and negative) on wine designations of origin (DOs) and GIs (Regulation 479/2008 Art. 45) and to decide on the criteria on the basis of which such a protection should be guaranteed (including major amendments of the product specifications). Especially for designations of origin, requirements posed by article 34 of Regulation 479/2008 are equivalent to the ones fixed by Art. 115-1 L of the French Consumption Code, the provision which is the basis for the defence of 'terroir wines' in France. Designation of origin is defined by Article 34 para. 1 (a) as follows:

> The name of a region, a specific place or, in exceptional cases, a country used to describe a [wine] that complies with the following requirements: (i) its quality and characteristics are essentially or exclusively due to a particular geographical environment with its inherent natural and human factors . . .

Therefore, the registration procedure is now based on European criteria which do not necessarily coincide with those applied by national authorities.

Of course, one may argue that this change will not have any major impact on the governance of the European wine sector through the AOC system for two major reasons. On the one hand, national authorities are always present in the administrative procedure given that they intervene in the registration procedure as a first step of control and they have a decisive role in the implementation of EU settlements at the national level. On the other hand, the Commission is unlikely to use the powers allocated by Regulation 479/2008, especially the ones granted by Articles 49 and 50, on the basis of which it can scrutinize and cancel existing wine names. Up to the present under Regulation 510/2006 related to the registration and the protection of appellations of origin for foodstuffs other than wine – which has served as a model for the new common organization of the wine market – the Commission has not totally exercised its scrutiny powers.

Therefore, it seems hard to imagine the European Commission putting into question the legitimacy of the champagne. Nevertheless, its role should not be underestimated as it may intervene with regard either to major changes to product specifications or, by contrast, to new appellations of origin that are likely to compete with champagne in the future. For the time being, this last perspective remains highly hypothetical. It is beyond any doubt, however, that from a legal standpoint the status of champagne depends also on the position (or the tolerance) of the Commission which stands nowadays as a public policy-maker in the wine business.

Concluding remarks

There is no doubt that the delicate balance of the champagne business is subject to continuous change. The triangle of growers–champagne houses–national authorities has created through historic evolution, and even serious conflicts, a system of governance that is surely original and probably stable. And yet, the emergence of the European Union as a new factor in the governance of the champagne industry is likely to influence in the future the balance of powers, as delicate, elegant and complex as the product itself.

4 The economic perspective on champagne

David Menival

Introduction

To define the economic context of champagne is hard to do. First of all, an economic context includes a wide set of elements. If we consider one definition of the economy, we have at least to focus on how the products are made, how they are exchanged and by whom (Samuelson & Nordhaus, 2005). That unites several disciplines such as history, sociology and politics. Such a context also presupposes an explanation for the creation and evolution of supply and demand and the relationships between them.

Faced with this challenge, the present chapter can only deal with the essentials: a focus on the current market and its likely evolution. Obviously, it is about the champagne market, but there is a further constraint. What kind of champagne are we dealing with? We have seen (Chapter 1), the supply is managed by several producers: cooperatives, négocants and some growers. If we want to speak about markets, we should focus on these actors. Additionally, we need to repeat this analysis for each market and each supplier. Achieving this would require at least one book which would be overtaken by changing data before it was ever completed! Therefore, our aim is simpler. This chapter will focus on the global evolution of the champagne industry and mainly the different aspects of supply. Consumer behaviour and distribution will be dealt with in subsequent chapters.

From this starting point, what are our next concerns? First of all, we will focus on the main characteristics of the global supply of champagne. Thus, we will analyse it through both its sources and destinations. That will lead to an obvious consideration of the success of champagne. Second, we will explain how this present success operates within a nine-year classic economic cycle. Third, we will consider the likely consequences of this economic development.

The economic success of champagne

The present strength of champagne cannot be surpassed when you think about its image. What other wines are always used to signify happiness, success and friendship? For general consumers, champagne signifies high value and is perceived as definitely the best sparkling wine. Several economic factors appear to confirm this point of view and to give us the idea of the 'king of wines'.

The supply of champagne has long been controlled by the négociants in champagne (see Chapter 1). However, this control has changed fundamentally during the course of the last century.

The first champagne merchants appeared in the seventeenth century with the creation of some houses which still exist, such as Ruinart (1729) or Moët et Chandon (1743) and most major international brands were formed during the first Industrial Revolution. They developed a strong promotional activity with the biggest names active outside France, leading them to specialize in export (Garcia, 1986). They became the only source of champagne until the end of the nineteenth century. Then, during the early twentieth century, new négociants appeared with a lesser reputation and mainly focused on the French market. This led to a change in the distribution of global shipments[1] of champagne, with the French market becoming increasingly important, receiving 30 per cent of bottles shipped on the eve of the First World War. This change continued between the World Wars, with the domestic market overtaking exports for the first time in 1922. The trend was amplified by the crash of 1929 and prohibition in America. Eventually, exports accounted for only 17 per cent of all shipments, only to return to 40 per cent just before the Second World War.

Despite this proliferation of négociants and the gradual expansion of the domestic market, the supply of champagne remained erratic until the 1950s (see Figure 4.1). Global shipments did not exceed 39 million bottles. This limitation was due to many phenomena. The first was simply the result of the troubled times that the world experienced until the end of the Second World War, leading to a sharp drop in exports. The second one was the technical limit of production. Whilst after 1850 the growth of champagne and the quasi-industrial technology of its preparation became such that négociants could, without too much difficulty, effectively re-ferment, mature and finish the wine, the production of champagne was restricted by harsh climatic conditions, causing regular crop failures (Clause, 1988). This was dramatically aggravated by the troubles linked to the phylloxera crisis. Paradoxically, the drop in grape production led to a reduction in the price of a kilo of grapes due to the use of grapes from other regions (Anjou, Midi) by négociants. This led to several riots by growers and a real instability of production until the eve of the Second World War (Clause, 1988). These social disturbances were partially resolved between the two World Wars and finally resulted in the creation of the CIVC in 1941, as noted in Chapter 1.

Thus it was only in the late 1950s that champagne began to have unprecedented successes. The volume shipped grew continually despite cyclical irregularities (see Figure 4.1).

Figure 4.1 Total shipments of champagne between 1900 and 2009. (Source: CIVC)

The first factor which began to stimulate the growth of sales began with the formation of cooperatives. Although the idea of cooperation started prior to the Second World War, the movement really developed in the 1950s, the number of cooperatives going from 50 to 110 in ten years. Their main functions were to improve the technical, economic and social aspects of production by giving growers access to capital, equipment and expertise (Draperi, 2001).

Today, the 137 cooperatives which are spread over the entire Champagne appellation press nearly half of the harvest. Of these 137 units, we can distinguish between (1) cooperatives which only press juice and make base wine and (2) others which provide finished champagne for their members to sell and also develop their own brands for sale (Garcia, 1986).

The first form of cooperative was the initial type developed from 1929 onwards. Indeed, pressing and wine-making services developed both in periods of fine harvests with a good financial return and during significant declines in shipments which resulted in a decline in prices. This included a decline in grape prices. To avoid a drop in income, some growers tried to combine their means of production to retain surpluses of grapes, make champagne and sell their own bottles – using the cooperative as the processing organization. This phenomenon developed during the interwar period, following the severe economic crisis that erupted at the end of the 1920s. Thus the cooperatives included 1300 growers in 1939 who were responsible for the shipment of about two million bottles, or 5 per cent of total sales of champagne. From 1960, they have become increasingly numerous and gradually formed a significant business sector (CIVC, 2010). These growers, the RCs, increased in number up to the beginning of the twenty-first century and have stabilized, since 2005, at around 55 per cent of the total growers who sell champagne under their own brand.

The second form of cooperative results from the experience acquired by growers in selling their own brands. By offering the service of wine-making for their members, cooperatives developed more and more expertise in the techniques of production and maturation. As a result, some of them decided to sell champagne directly under their own label. In 1950, nine cooperatives were direct suppliers of wines to consumers. This number has expanded to reach 45 today. Their share of the market steadily increased until 2003 and currently accounts for around 9 per cent of total shipments. This result comes from a high concentration of supply in three cooperative unions (Champagne Jacquart, CVC Nicolas Feuillatte and De Saint Gall) which combined were responsible for more than 72 per cent of shipments by cooperatives and 82 per cent of the cooperatives' exports in 2005.

The second development which explains the proliferation of suppliers of champagne results from the evolution of négociants. The number of négociants has increased since 1971, despite a decrease in the early 1950s. From 1956 to 1964, more than 45 disappeared due to difficulties in selling wine (Banque de France, 1969), but then, from 1971 to 2006, this number grew from 153 to 290. This development comes from the multiplication of *récoltants-négociants* – growers who wish to increase their supply by buying grapes, wine or finished champagne from other professionals, and who cannot do it merely as *récoltants-manipulants*. Therefore, they registered a change of status with the CIVC, becoming négociants. We can distinguish them from traditional négociants, especially those who are members of the UMC, which only considers a small number of the largest négociants as real 'houses' of champagne.

Finally, with the development of new suppliers, the pattern of global shipments changed with a new balance between the domestic and foreign markets. From a concentration on exports at the beginning of the nineteenth century, then a focus on the French market, champagne has become both a domestic and an international product (see Figure 4.2).

This part of the offer – exports – remains dominated by négociants (see Table 4.1). They are present both on the French market and on foreign

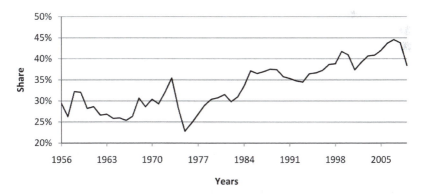

Figure 4.2 Share of exports in the global shipments of champagne. (Source: CIVC)

Table 4.1 Price and volume of champagne supplies, 2009

		Growers	Cooperatives	Négociants
France	Average prices without taxes	10.84	12.07	12.29
	Volume	69,402,647	14,744,603	96,616,352
	Share of their own shipments	92%	59%	50%
	Share of the domestic shipments	40%	9%	51%
Exports	Average prices without taxes	12.48	11.85	14.92
	Volume	5,418,487	10,210,058	96,931,909
	Share of their own shipments	8%	41%	50%
	Share of the export shipments	5%	9%	86%

Source: CIVC

markets and their bottles remain more expensive than those supplied by other categories of supplier. They are followed by the growers, who ship the second largest volume of bottles but are less common in international markets and whose product is valued lower than that of the other suppliers. The cooperatives are in third position in volume but they tend to focus on the international arena and they are in second position in terms of prices.

Despite the multitude of suppliers, it seems that the demand is still growing. Thus, the evolution of shipments to key markets is in sharp contrast to the trends of other wines (see Table 4.2). Moreover, this trend has been maintained in spite of an increase of the average price (see Figure 4.3). It shows a real development in champagne turnover. Whilst it is one of the smaller viticultural regions in France (4.2 per cent of national production area), it represents nearly 30 per cent of French wine exports by value and 10 per cent of the total value generated on the international wine market (FranceAgriMer, 2010).

However, this success is not without consequences on the economic context of champagne which has suffered from a nine-year cycle of crises since the 1970s.

Economic crises and champagne: a cyclical and repetitive mechanism

The flux of the economy by cycles is not something specific only to champagne. Schumpeter (1939) noted the main economic approaches which rely on the definition of repetitive periods of recession and expansion. He defined three kinds of cycles from the name of the initial economists who developed them. Among these, one is particularly significant in the

Table 4.2 Evolution of consumption of wines and champagne in the major markets in 2007 (percentage change)

Country	All wines	Champagne
France	–49%	89%
Italy	–57%	143%
Portugal	–51%	2,380%
Spain	–58%	1,461%
Denmark	183%	226%
Netherlands	100%	303%
Belgium	71%	67%
UK	280%	1,097%

Source: VINIFLHOR using figures from the OIV; CIVC for Champagne

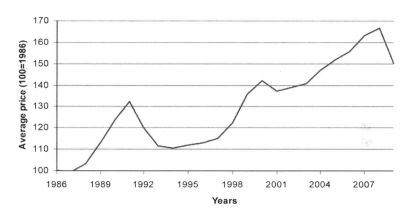

Figure 4.3 The evolution of the average price of champagne. All figures include tax. (Source: CIVC)

economic evolution of champagne. Called Juglar's cycles or Classic cycles, they were initially detected through some monetary and financial indicators and produce recurring waves of crises around every eight years.

Since 1970, the global shipments of champagne seem to have followed this cycle of eight to nine years, as seen in Figure 4.4. Far from having a simple deterministic origin, this trend results each time from very different international causes. The two first cyclical depressions for champagne arrived with the oil crises (1973 and 1979). The next coincided with the First Gulf War (1990), then the American financial dot.com crisis (2000), and most recently the subprime crisis (2007). However, the ways in which crises unfold in champagne are quite similar.

The first suppliers affected by crises are consistently the négociants. Due to their markets and prices, the drop in consumption resulting from

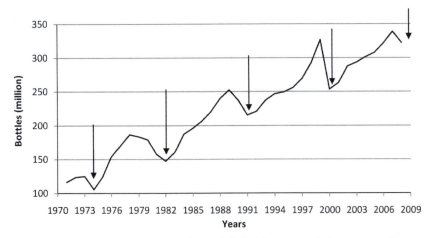

Figure 4.4 The nine-year cycles of the global shipments of champagne. (Source: CIVC)

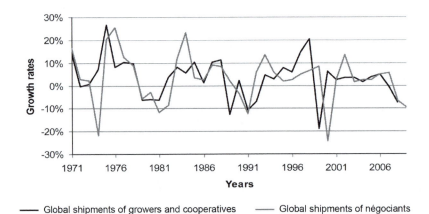

—— Global shipments of growers and cooperatives   ⋯⋯ Global shipments of négociants

Figure 4.5 The impact of shipment fluctuations by type of producer. (Source: CIVC)

international recession strikes them harder (see Figure 4.5). That is true for both domestic and international markets due to the high concentrations of shipments. Indeed, even though négociants specialize in exports, they are dependent overall on the economic health of the European Union, as can be seen during the last period of prosperity since 2001. Figure 4.6 shows the concentration of their shipments within the European Union, which remains substantial. Therefore, the stronger the impact of international crises on the European Union, the worse the situation of champagne négociants. That explains the short-term effect of the crisis in 2000, compared to the others, for the economy in the European Union was comparatively strong at that time.

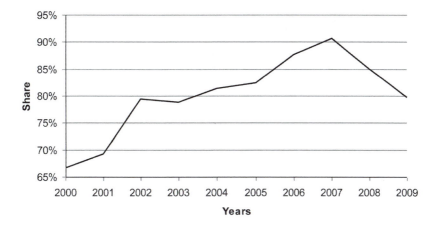

Figure 4.6 The concentration of shipments made by négociants in the European Union (percentage share). (Source: CIVC)

The decrease of sales leads to a worsening of the financial situation of négociants due to their dependency on the supply of grapes from growers. As noted in Chapter 1, the négociants own only 10 per cent of the total vineyard area but sell at least 66 per cent of all champagne, so they have to buy grapes from growers. However, several elements push grape prices up. First, the development of cooperatives and growers as suppliers of wine over the last half-century has reduced the availability of raw material. Second, the time for producing grapes from new vineyard plantings cannot legally be less than four years. Third, the ability to access new plantations has been limited since the 1970s due to the steady reduction in the availability of new vineyard land and a consequent sharp increase in the price of vineyard land (see Figure 4.7). This increase in land price is further complicated by the role of SAFER (*Société d'Aménagement Foncier et d'Etablissement Rural*), a state body which has the power to intervene in land sales in order to support the maintenance and development of dynamic and sustainable agriculture as well as support rural development and environmental protection. SAFER has the power to confirm land sales and can in some circumstances overturn agreed transactions and substitute a new purchaser if it considers it better for the local community.

In addition, the need for grapes can increase faster than the annual supply. To obtain one bottle of champagne, around 1.3 kg of grapes is required and it is necessary to wait at least 18 months between the harvest and the sale of the bottle (and generally longer in practice) (CIVC, 2010). That is why the demand for grapes will be higher than the sales of the year N to fit the potential rise of demand of $N+2$ during periods of prosperity. All these elements feed speculative activity by growers and explain the increasingly expensive price of grapes (see Figure 4.8).

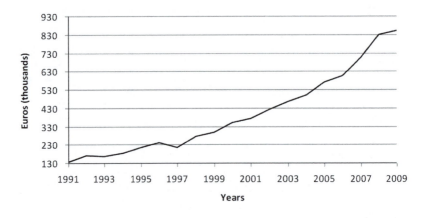

Figure 4.7 The average price of one hectare of vineyard planted in Champagne. (Source: SAFER)

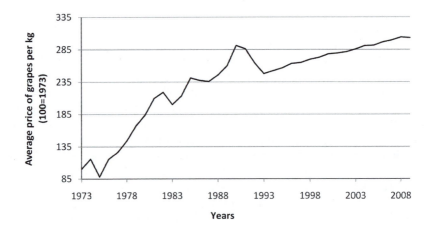

Figure 4.8 The evolution of grape prices in Champagne. (Source: CIVC)

This speculative activity is augmented by the trade in *sur lattes* wines. These are wines which have been put through the second fermentation by one producer (usually a large grower or a cooperative), and rest in bottle awaiting disgorgement,[2] but are instead sold on to another company, usually a house, before finishing. The purchaser will disgorge and finish the wines and sell them with the house's own label on, thus claiming them as their own. The use of this market is seen as overcoming temporary fluctuations in demand, and allows companies the opportunity to find extra stocks quickly without having to make and store wine which they may not ultimately need.

    Finally, stock costs are very expensive. The payment for grapes is traditionally made during the year following harvest but that expense is only

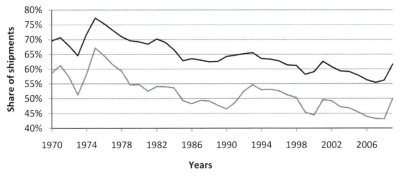

—— Share of domestic market in the global shipments

—— Share of domestic market in the négociants' shipments

Figure 4.9 The impact of the négociants' shipment strategy on the domestic shipments. (Source: CIVC)

recovered two years later, when the wine is finally sold. This delay makes négociants financially vulnerable, especially when they have to account to financial markets for their profits.

In this context, many négociants have to sell these stocks quickly to find cash in order to cover debts during the first signs of financial trouble. As exports are usually the sales most adversely affected during international crises, the négociants use the domestic market as a fallback position (see Figure 4.9), relying on their already strong positioning based on high reputation (see Table 4.1). However, this market is also affected by international uncertainty and growers and cooperatives, who sell mainly on the domestic market at lower prices, have a substantial market share. Therefore, négociants adopt a policy of price reductions on the domestic market in order to move stock (see Figure 4.10).

Inevitably, this policy affects the behaviour of other suppliers. The cooperatives, who encounter the same troubles abroad, try to reinforce their position in the domestic market but have a lower reputation than most négociants. Therefore, they finally adopt the same policy of price decreases (Figure 4.10). This approach, especially in supermarkets, significantly alters the perception of French consumers. Even if their purchase of champagne is not always made in supermarkets, they tend to refocus their idea of the perceived worth of a bottle of champagne. Consequently, growers (who tend to use other distribution channels than supermarkets) are the last to suffer from a loss of sales, in the wake of price reductions by the négociants and cooperatives. The growers' offer, based on good quality for a good price becomes obsolete due to more renowned labels having cheaper prices. Conversely to négociants and cooperatives, however, growers tend to modify sales only by a stabilization of the average price; a decrease would

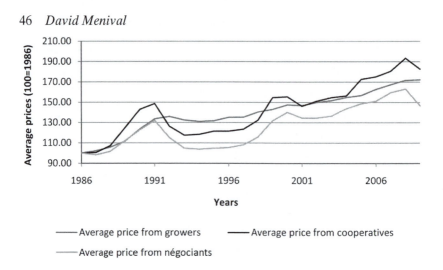

Figure 4.10 Evolution of prices by type of producer of champagne. (Source: CIVC)

be too risky due to their low margin linked to the fact that they offer the cheapest prices already.

Similarly, with the onset of any economic crisis, négociants need to buy fewer grapes and prefer to use their existing stocks of wine (see Figure 4.11). This results in a reduction in the quantity of grapes on the market, which, even if the price remains stable, affects the sellers because of the reduced volume sold.

These difficulties continue until the resurgence of the international economy, which allows négociants and cooperatives to revert to international markets and thus reduce the pressure on the growers, both as sellers of champagne and as sellers of grapes.

Conclusion

Champagne has had great economic success over the last decade compared to almost all the other wine-producing regions, French and foreign. It benefits from a highly reputed image throughout the world, its shipments have rocketed since the end of the 1950s and its price shows a steady rise. In this almost idyllic situation, all the suppliers have found success and generally enjoy a profitable financial existence. Thanks to the CIVC, this balance continues and is guaranteed in the medium term, especially because of the inter-professional contracts for grape supply. Obviously, this near-perfect world has its recurrent troubles. The success of the wine internationally locks champagne into a series of classic crisis cycles which challenge the mechanism of supply, prices and demand. However these dysfunctions have – so far – passed after the end of each crisis allowing champagne to recreate its success story.

Figure 4.11 Evolution of official yields in Champagne. (Source: CIVC)

Nevertheless, several issues can be underlined as relevant to the next steps in the classic cycle in champagne. First of all, champagne is not the only sparkling wine in the world and faces increasing French and foreign competitors. Until the last crisis of 2000, these competitors were only followers. For example, *crémant d'Alsace*, the sparkling wine of Alsace, was established in 1976 in a way which was designed to imitate champagne, with conditions of production as restrictive as champagne to try to guarantee the same intrinsic quality (CIVA, 2003). Now, however, it may be that such wines seek to supplant, rather than to imitate. In France, between 2008 and 2009, the average price of a bottle of champagne bought decreased by 5.3 per cent, whilst there was an increase of 4.9 per cent for all other sparkling wines (French and foreign) (FranceAgriMer, 2010).

Another issue relates to consumers' behaviour. Champagne still benefits from an image of happiness and celebration. Consequently, shipments are traditionally concentrated on the periods of special celebrations such as weddings, first communions, and Christmas and New Year parties. However, this trend has steadily changed over the last 40 years, with sales being less festively oriented in France and abroad, especially for the summer periods (see Figures 4.12 and 4.13).

Another issue relates to the perceived reputation of champagne through the evolution of prices. Usually, prices are used as signals of quality by consumers. In a perfect market, prices are the reflection of the set of characteristics which define the intrinsic quality of products. However, wine exists in an environment of strong asymmetric information between suppliers and purchasers – so that consumers have much less knowledge about what they are buying than those who make and market it. In this context, reputation is the sum of all expected quality criteria, symbolizing both objective and the subjective consumer expectations (Shapiro, 1982). Therefore, in turn, price reflects those objective and subjective characteristics which establish the product's reputation (Gerstner, 1985; Tadelis, 1999). The role of reputation in determining price has been confirmed already for food products, because

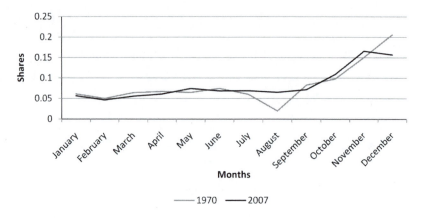

Figure 4.12 Evolution of domestic shipments, 1970–2007. (Source: CIVC)

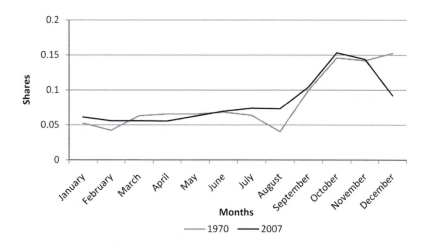

Figure 4.13 Evolution of exports, 1970–2007. (Source: CIVC)

they are generally considered as experience goods, with their quality only able to be determined at consumption (Quagrainie *et al.*, 2003). This has further been shown to be particularly important for the wine industry (Gergaud, 1998; Landon & Smith, 1997; Oczkowski, 2001). Consequently, with the cyclical movement of prices, the champagne industry could confuse consumers due to the incoherence of signals which support its reputation and finally challenge its current position as the 'king of wines'.

Until now, the high price of champagne has been accepted due to the wine's high reputation. That means that consumers associate a set of objective and subjective characteristics with champagne. However, since the 1970s, these characteristics – especially the more cultural and symbolic ones

– have been subject to change, such as, for instance, the shift of seasonal distribution of shipments.

Whilst we cannot be certain about the precise nature of this change in consumption patterns, it has been accommodated by cyclical decreases in prices – which themselves are supposed to be the signal of quality of champagne. Consequently, in a context where champagne may be consumed more and more as a normal wine rather than as an exceptional product, consumers may change their perceptions and less and less accept renewed price increases after a period of economic crisis. This change in consumer perspective will thus change the overall perceived reputation of champagne. Crucially, therefore, the combination of price instability and the changes in consumers' behaviour could threaten the wine's image.

Finally, it is worth noting the impact of the increase in the price of vineyard land on the future economy of champagne. Even with a substantial return per hectare of around €65,000, an average price of €830,000 per hectare for land planted with vines is not financially viable – let alone the figure of €1.5 million that was reached for some sales in 2007, before the start of the current crisis. The vignerons have begun accusing the négociants of making unreasonably high bids for land, in order to force the smallest producers out of the market; the négociants have been claiming that it is not worth buying vineyard land as the return to them (between 4.3 and 7.6 per cent gross) is not viable. All of this may be substantially unbalanced by the change in land values that an expansion of the AOC area will produce in the period after 2020, but for the time being any vignerons who are currently proprietors of reasonably sized land holdings are clearly very well-off, yet the barriers to entry to new potential vignerons are almost insurmountable – for the very little land left without vines planted on it the price is still around €300–350,000 per hectare. The impact of the high levels of French inheritance taxes on the value of these holdings is also likely to be a destabilizing factor over the mid-term.

Notes

1 It is common usage in Champagne to talk of shipments (both to France and other countries) rather than sales.
2 In the past they were stored on laths (*lattes* in French) in the cellars – hence their name.

Part II
The place and the land

5   A place of paradox

Champagne as it is presented to the outsider

Richard Mitchell

Introduction

Visitors to Champagne are presented with many paradoxical images of the place, the product and its brands. These images are presented to the visitor formally through tours, promotional material, advertising and public relations material and less formally, but equally as powerfully, through interactions with insiders of the profession. Myths are employed that reduce the tensions caused by paradoxes surrounding the production of champagne, imparting it with often mystical qualities.

Myths have long been connected with paradoxes and contradictions in the lives of people (Freilich, 1975, p. 210; Levi-Strauss, 1963) and in the way places (Tuan, 1977, 1991) and brands (Alexander, 1996) – especially wine (Charters, 2006) – are imbued with meaning. Champagne (product and place) is no exception to this, with the legend of Dom Pérignon – the Benedictine monk who is reputed to have 'discovered' champagne – being core to the mythology of the region (Beverland, 2005; Guy, 1999, 2003). Like other places (Wortham-Galvin, 2008) and brands (Alexander, 1996) these myths add considerable value for consumers of Champagne/champagne and they are at least part of the reason why champagne has become so iconic (Beverland, 2005; Holt, 2004). Indeed, Beverland asserts that brand owners (including champagne brands) use myths to craft and reinforce the authenticity of the brand.

This chapter discusses the role of paradox and myth in brand and place-brands and introduces the complex web of myths surrounding paradoxes in the production of champagne.

Paradox and myth

While the structural analysis of myths is not without controversy (Freilich, 1975), some of the outcomes of structural analyses are significant for the argument presented here. Most importantly, it has been established that 'myths resolve dilemmas, contradictions, paradoxes, and puzzles by identifying mediators' (ibid.) (see also Alexander, 1996; Levi-Strauss, 1963).

According to Freilich (p. 10), such mediators 'both separate and join conflicting ideas, since a mediator contains elements found in neither of the conflicting ideas and elements found in both of them'.

For champagne, myth is a critical mediator for the many contradictions that are present in the product, its production and consumption and the place-brand that it has developed and cultivated. Indeed, myths are central to the value that is inherent in the name champagne (Guy, 2003) and which the profession so vigorously protects around the globe (Mitchell, 2008). Like other place mythologies (Tuan, 1977, 1991; Wortham-Galvin, 2008), the myths surrounding Champagne (and champagne) blur the line between what is 'true' and what is 'imagined' in a way that reinforces the identity of the place and the people that live in it (Wortham-Galvin, 2008).

The role of place-brand

All places are grounded in both reality and myth and indeed, as Tuan (1977, p. 98) points out:

> Countries have their factual and their mythical geographies. It is not always easy to tell them apart, nor even to say which is more important, because the way people act depends on their comprehension of reality, and that comprehension, since it can never be complete, is necessarily imbued with myths.

The process of myth-making and the places in which they are made are 'intertwined with identity' (Wortham-Galvin, 2008, p. 32). Place-based myths are therefore a reflection of the people of that place, their culture, heritage and traditions. As such, 'mythologies of place' provide us with powerful ways to understand the dynamics of people and place in a way that traditional data cannot, as 'place has actions, characters, a setting, and points of view' (ibid., p. 38). This is certainly true of the business of champagne and the Champagne region, which are bound up in the people that work in the 'profession', their practices and behaviours. Indeed, the very fact that the Champenois talk of the champagne 'profession' when most other wine regions around the world talk of wine 'industry' highlights their singular view of champagne production.

Well-known myths can help people to bond with a place (Hopkins, 1998; Tuan, 1991) or a brand (Alexander, 1996; Beverland, 2005; Holt, 2004). According to Holt (2004, p. 8) myths that reside in brands allow individuals to

> stitch back together otherwise damaging tears in the cultural fabric of the nation. In their everyday lives, people experience these tears as personal anxieties. Myths smooth over these tensions, helping people create purpose in their lives and cement their desired identity in place when it is under stress.

Brand myths (including place-brands), then, have the ability to create meaning where none had existed before. This meaning is powerful as it allows people to negotiate paradoxes found in what they know and believe about a brand. Indeed, Alexander (1996, p. 3) suggests that 'the power of the brand myth seems to stand in direct proportion to the dynamism of the contradiction it resolves'. So, while high-involvement wine consumers might *know* that champagne is the product of what might otherwise be considered wine-making idiosyncrasies (e.g. under-ripe grapes grown in a marginal climate, yeast remaining in the bottle and the addition of sugar that increases alcohol levels), they are able to *believe* that it is a unique luxury product only able to be made in this small part of the world. This paradox requires mythologies that transmute 'odd' wine into a luxury and, because the place-brand (the very name Champagne) is so essential to the success of the myth, these myths are bound up in the place itself.

To this end, by the time of the *Belle Époque* at the end of the nineteenth century, Champagne (the place-brand) 'had become a "resilient totem", able to support . . . "varied mythologies" about [the French nation] without having to account for contradictions' (Guy, 1999 after Barthes, 1972). Champagne had become part of the mythology of France and Frenchness, as well as supporting its own set of mythologies about the region and profession that have grown to those present today (Guy, 1999, 2003). Over time these mythologies have developed into a series of interrelated beliefs that are cultivated, celebrated and communicated to consumers of champagne and visitors to Champagne. As Wortham-Galvin (2008, p. 38) points out, thoughts and feelings of a place, its people and institutions take on more importance than facts 'in part because the places described become detached from their original context and a new context is substituted'.

This chapter describes a number of the more overt paradoxical mythologies surrounding the champagne industry. In particular, it explores:

- *Harmonious conflict*: how the champagne profession projects an air of harmony that contrasts with (but is not necessarily incongruous with) historical conflicts and on-going tensions within the profession.
- *Micro- versus mega-scale production*: how thousands of smallholdings producing small amounts of grapes are reconciled with some of the world's largest wine production facilities.
- *Industrialized nature*: how a heavily industrialized process (sometimes on a massive scale) is presented as being a product of nature.
- *Innovative conservatism*: how innovation and conservatism are presented as two sides of the same coin.
- *Blended terroir (a specific and general place)*: how the region reconciles the concept of terroir (which is so intimately connected with specific qualities of the landscape) with wines that are blended from grapes from different landscapes (even though the soil is the same) and from different years.

The study

Data for this chapter were gathered over multiple visits to Champagne between 2005 and 2008. Visits ranged from three days (2005 and 2006) to five months (2007/8) and the final visit was for five days in 2008 as part of the study tour that was the genesis of this book. Data were gathered in many situations, including: tours and tastings at several champagne houses, growers and cooperatives; everyday life in the region as an expatriate; observations of and interviews with visitors to the region; unstructured interviews with champagne professionals, visitors and locals, and; formal presentations by champagne professionals. Many forms of data resulted from this field work, both documentary (publications from industry bodies such as CIVC, UMC and SGV, brochures from visits, etc.), aural (e.g. inter-view recordings and transcripts and notes of conversations and presenta-tions) and visual (e.g. video recordings, photographs and field observations).

This research suffered from the classic conundrum where 'qualitative analysis is often reported as an intuitive, personal journey for the researcher. Meanings "emerge" from the data in the form of themes and categories whose origins often remain unclear' (Clarke, 1999, p. 363). The breadth (across many forms) and depth of data (weeks of observations, dozens of hours of audio and video recordings and dozens of pages of field notes) meant that many forms of analysis took place over several months that iden-tified emergent themes within the data. To privilege one type of analysis over another in this chapter would be to underplay the role of being fully immersed in the data while living in the region (literally living in the data) as well as interacting with it upon my return home. As such, this reflects Schatzberg's (2008, p. 2) assertion that such 'ethnographic immersion' 'is a process that often begins while doing ethnographic field research, but then continues as one interacts with data, theory, and method in various other locales'.

Indeed, it has been observed that when analysing myths it is essential that the researcher has an intimate knowledge of the culture in which the myth is embedded (Freilich, 1975) (in this case the champagne profession). To this end, while living in Champagne and having constant contact with the profes-sion was an important factor, the rigour of the analysis was improved with the inclusion of analytical triangulation provided by two researchers resi-dent in Champagne: one French and a life-time resident of Champagne; the other, an Anglo-Australian resident in the region for around three years and having researched the profession for more than a decade. As themes emerged they were discussed with the researchers and refined using evidence from this study and that unearthed by the other researchers in their own studies of the region.

The paradoxical myths presented below (in no particular order) are those that have been distilled from the data through multiple levels of analysis.

While these do not necessarily represent all of the mythology surrounding champagne/Champagne, they are most certainly those that are the most prevalent in the formal and informal presentations made to the visitor.

Harmonious conflict

Champagne has long been a place of conflict (Guy, 1999; Kladstrup & Kladstrup, 2005). In fact, Kladstrup and Kladstrup point out that, as a major crossroads for trade routes between east and west, and north and south, it has been the location for some of the fiercest conflicts in European history. The First and Second World Wars also saw much bloodshed, with the Champenois united against the German invaders and the champagne profession providing many wartime heroes (ibid.). This historical backdrop of the struggle of the Champenois against invaders from abroad is a theme that is projected to visitors to several of the champagne houses, but which is absent from many others.

For example, at Laurent Perrier an integral part of the story told about the foundation of the modern incarnation of the company are the wartime heroics of Bernard de Nonancourt and his elder brother Maurice who was tragically killed during the Second World War. During our visit, we were told how Marie-Louise Lanson de Nonancourt, Maurice and Bernard's mother, herself a 'war widow', purchased Laurent Perrier in 1939 to secure her sons' future. Maurice, the eldest, was set to take over the company when he was 'tragically killed' while undertaking his 'Resistance work'. Bernard was the next in line for succession, but only after the war where he became an 'amazing historical figure for his involvement in the French Resistance at a very, very high level'. The story then seamlessly moves to his post-war induction into the champagne profession as he was 'trained into the art of champagne making'. This is starkly contrasted by the visitor interpretation at Champagne Pommery, which, according to Kladstrup and Kladstrup (2005), was heavily involved in frontline battles during both World Wars, yet almost no reference is made to the war by guides.

This, then, is the first and most obvious layer of interpretation of how conflict is an integral part of the culture and history of Champagne (the region) and champagne (the product and profession). It seems that how, and indeed if, this is presented to the visiting public is largely a choice that the individual companies make. If asked about this part of the history of the region, however, all will discuss with pride the role that those in the champagne profession played in both World Wars. For example, Pierre-Emmanuel Taittinger (of Champagne Taittinger) so poetically said in a meeting 'on this land where we drink the happiness, we lost so many families'.

Other aspects of conflict in the region are not so freely discussed by the profession, especially those that relate to internal conflicts in the region (such as the riots at the time of delineation of the AOC region or even minor disagreements over grape prices). Instead they constantly return to the rhetoric of collective action against invaders to propagate a myth of harmony within the region. This is not to suggest that there is overt conflict within the region; rather that mythology comes into play to help explain how the region has reached a harmonious outcome from a conflicted past.

The birth of the formally delineated Champagne wine region was the source of considerable internal conflict between different parts of the profession (growers and houses) and different parts of the region (the Aube and the rest of the region) (Guy, 2003; Kladstrup & Kladstrup, 2005). While the following is at risk of oversimplifying an important period of Champagne's history, it is used here to highlight the role that internal conflict has played in the mythology of the region and profession.

As noted in previous chapters, in January 1911, Champenois grape growers took to the streets in a violent uprising against the houses and the government (Guy, 2003; Kladstrup & Kladstrup, 2005). This followed years of disastrous crops (because of the invasion of phylloxera which decimated almost the entire vineyard), poor prices for growers and the discovery of grapes being brought in from other regions of France by champagne houses (another invasion by unwanted outsiders) (Kladstrup & Kladstrup, 2005). Imported grapes were thrown into the Marne river, buildings belonging to champagne houses were ransacked and burned, grapes were uprooted and wine was poured into the streets and rivers. Meanwhile, debate raged over the inclusion of the Aube within the boundaries of the region as it is some distance from the main part of the region and, according to many in the region at the time, produced inferior-quality grapes and wine (Guy, 2003). After dozens of heated public meetings and debates, and public rallies and riots involving tens of thousands of people, the Aube was first included in the region, then removed and then in 1927 finally reinstated as part of the formally defined AOC region.

This very public spat between grower and champagne house and the Aube and the rest of the region highlights a very real tension between the different elements of the region. Today the relationship is described as one of mutual respect and need for each other: growers need the capital provided by the merchants; merchants need the grapes produced on the land owned by the growers; the producers outside the Aube need grapes from the Aube to supplement supply; the Aube needs the rest of the region to take much of its crop. Indeed, Daniel Lorson from the CIVC described the situation as 'a type of socialist system' where growers and houses agreed on the parameters of the business. Each harvest growers and houses jointly set rules like yields per hectare, harvest dates, pressing limits, minimum potential alcohol (sugar levels) and, until the advent of EU laws forbidding it, a fixed price for grapes. The SGV describe this situation as a kind of 'alternative economy' where growers and houses actively manipulate demand and supply.

So, out of conflict has come a harmonious profession. This harmony relies both on the underlying conflict between the growers and houses and the potential for invasion from a common enemy. While both sides agree that there is greater advantage to be had projecting a united front and agreeing on matters that affect the whole industry, tensions at harvest time are obvious and both sides freely admit (although generally not in public) that negotiations do not always proceed without difficulties. In a sense these two parties are bound together by the institution and constitution that is provided by the CIVC and by the very conflict that pushed them apart in 1911; power over the supply of grapes. An important part of this is the continuation of the rhetoric surrounding the 'threat of invasion', this time from those who seek to misappropriate the name Champagne. According to Daniel Lorson, one of the core functions of the CIVC is the 'systematic surveillance' of products (of all types) that illegally use the name Champagne. This helps to unite the profession once again in the fight to protect the region from invasion.

Beyond the realms of the institutions provided by the CIVC, however, the fragile balance is starting to be compromised by a deterioration in the social fabric that holds the growers and the houses together. Many houses talk with great pride of the fact that many of their relationships with growers are long standing (often with several hundred of them) and that they are based on little more than a handshake and a gentleman's agreement. Growers too talk of the pride they have in the personal relationship that they have with the wine-maker or owner of a house. But recently these relationships have begun to breakdown for some, as the management of the houses becomes more corporate (with complex contracts) and/or distant (with head offices in Paris or elsewhere). As one representative of the SGV suggested, across the champagne profession 'one family' has started to become 'two families'.

In Champagne without conflict there is no harmony. This is a clear paradox evident in the rhetoric of the region and profession. Mythology surrounding conflict, and how the Champenois have dealt with it, maintains a fragile balance that allows the profession to function as it does and for the presentation of a very harmonious picture to the outside world. This theme of harmony is also evident in several of the other paradoxes presented in this chapter, not least of which is the harmony between the micro- and mega-scales of production.

Micro- and mega-production

A significant paradox in the production of champagne is the predominance of production scales at the micro- (grape production by the growers) and mega-scales (champagne production by the houses). The average land holding for grape growers is less than 2.3 hectares, with many of the holdings as small as 0.5 hectares or less. Contrast this with the champagne houses or corporate groups that control several houses. For example, the top three groups produce more than 100 million bottles per year (Mary, 2007).

This situation also has its historical antecedents. For example, the high number of land parcels and fragmented ownership has its roots in the French Revolution and the introduction of the Napoleonic legal code. The 1789 revolution saw the demise of feudal land ownership and new inheritance laws which saw the splitting of land amongst siblings, as well as ongoing crop rotation practices and a highly competitive land market that led to fragmentation of rural land holdings on a massive scale (Sargent, 1952). The present-day landscape of the Champagne vineyard (vineyard used almost exclusively as a term of the collective plantings of the region rather than an individual holding) is a patchwork of small holdings that at times are completely indistinguishable from one another, except for the odd block whose vines are planted at a slightly different angle to the rest. This belies the complexity of ownership hidden within the landscape; remembering that there are 275,000 different legal parcels managed by more than 15,000 different people and crammed into 34,000 hectares.

On the face of it this situation is not highly unusual with a very small number of large producers dominating sales and a large number of very small producers fighting over small percentages of the remaining sales in almost all wine regions around the world (Hall & Mitchell, 2008). The paradox in Champagne lies in the staunch determination of the growers to remain independent, when they are almost entirely dependent upon large corporate structures (the houses) of which they are, to all intents and purposes, a part. These structures have a strong influence over the past, present and future direction of the grape growers. The houses influence vineyard practices and other aspects of business management systems (record keeping, quality standards procedures, etc.), sometimes under the name of the CIVC. This paradox allows for a seamless story to be told that melds the micro and the mega together as a coherent unit, allowing the growers their 'independence' and the houses their 'control'.

Growers talk of the special relationship with the house that they supply and boast of the longevity of the 'gentleman's agreement', sometimes put in place by their father. These agreements are usually made with the 'cellar master' (head wine-maker) of the house who is likely to have been with the company for two or three decades. The personal nature of these relationships is important in allowing growers to justify, to themselves at least, their position of independence. For example, one grower indicated that the informal nature of the relationship was one that was extremely strong and heavily based on trust but that, should the trust be broken, he could easily move on and sell to another house such was the demand for grapes, especially in the *grand crus* vineyards.

The houses, too, tell a similar story of the pride they have for their personal relationships, one house describing how each of the more than 300 growers that supply grapes to them receives at least one personal visit from the cellar master every year. On the face of it this seems like a perfectly noble situation (and it is), but the nature of individual contracts between growers and houses is at least partially affected by strict standards set down in the AOC regulations and the collective negotiations between the growers (SGV) and the houses (UMC) under the auspices of the CIVC at harvest time each year.

Houses also talk of the 'artistry' of blending grapes from so many parcels of land to create the 'masterpiece' that is the house style of champagne. Indeed, Moët et Chandon directly use painting as the metaphor for the process of making their house-style champagne. A video presentation shown to visitors to the cellar explains how the cellar master works like an artist to bring together the different elements of the wine: the three grape varieties, the different styles from the different villages and different textures that create the final blend. A similar story, yet different metaphor, is told in the video of Champagne Pommery and is in the oral presentations of many of the other houses. The essence of this narrative is one of the house's careful selection of the raw materials that create their wine (they are in control) and of a highly skilled art (or craft) in bringing it together as a whole. By implication, this is a skill that does not rest with growers, but which resides in the hands of the houses.

So, a complicated dynamic of dependence, independence, control and interdependence exists that melds the micro and the mega together in one seamless story. The image of the region relies on the existence of both the micro (with its intimate connection between people, place and land – the essence of place-brand) *and* the mega (not just for the resources but for the collective and individual story of the houses and what they represent – their grandeur, their merchant-class heritage, wealth and access to the necessary social and economic capital for the development of a system of luxury production). The notion of a single profession that encapsulates both the growers (micro) and the houses (mega) is perhaps the most obvious way in which the story is conveyed and this is definitely also informed by the myth of harmonious conflict described above.

Industrialized nature

The paradox of industrialized nature is the mythology that has received the most attention from other researchers both in relation to wine in general (Beverland, 2005; Charters, 2006; Ulin, 1996) and champagne in particular (Beverland, 2005; Guy, 2003). For example, Beverland (2005, p. 1008, after Ulin, 1995) suggests that 'by defining wine as a natural product, as opposed to an industrial mass-produced product, social, cultural and historical claims of authenticity were naturalized'. Beverland also suggests that it is in Champagne, where this paradox is cultivated through the myth of Dom Pérignon, that this is most important in the creation and maintenance of brand authenticity. In particular, he states that the story of Dom Pérignon 'further entrenched the myth that Champagne was a natural product because Dom Pérignon was noted to have discovered Champagne by following ancient traditions' (ibid., p. 1007). Guy (1999, p. 229) too, is explicit in her analysis of the Pérignon myth: 'despite the almost industrial techniques used in sparkling wine production, the monk myth distanced sparkling wine from associations with assembly lines, technology, and back-breaking labor.'

However, the paradox of industrialized nature goes well beyond the myths surrounding Dom Pérignon and this is evident in much of the visitor interpretation of the houses, where large-scale industrial processes are the most common mode of production. In fact many of the houses now openly acknowledge and discuss the half-truths of the Dom Pérignon story, augmenting or substituting it with other 'de-industrialising' myths.

Even Moët et Chandon, the owners of the Dom Pérignon brand and the Abbey at Hautvillers where Dom Pérignon did his work use more than just the legend of Dom Pérignon to de-industrialize the image of their production. Dom Pérignon's statue stands at the entrance to the Moët et Chandon *cave* tours, so the association between the legend and the brand is still very overt. However, as described above, the metaphor of artistry and crafts-manship and, in particular, landscape art is used in the video presentation from the tour, distancing their production from the industrial and the mega. Beyond this the tour of the *cave* takes the visitor through the labyrinth of limestone cellars, deliberately avoiding sites of industrial production. Visitors see no stainless steel and no machinery, and even though they are told how large the cellars are (26 kilometres), visitors are never told how many bottles of champagne are stored in them. Only if asked do the guides reveal the total number of bottles produced at the facility every year and even then they do so reluctantly and under no circumstances will they reveal how many bottles of their *prestige cuvée* (Dom Pérignon) are made – this would destroy the image of craftsmanship, artistry and the natural.

A more common tool used by all of the houses and by the CIVC to rein-force the role of nature is images of vines, especially their different states across all four seasons. The very clear message is that, through the seasons, nature is in control, and video presentations developed by the CIVC and the houses and interpretation at *Le Musée de la Vigne* (Museum of the Vine) imply that 'we can but wait and hope'. The influence of the seasons is further reinforced by the institution of 'vintage' champagne, which is only made in the best years 'when nature allows'. Clearly this influences the rarity value of the *prestige cuvée* (top vintage wine) of the house, but it also reinforces the role of nature in the production of all of the wines produced by that house.

The use of vines and the seasons also reveals an oblique reference to what has been termed 'death-rebirth (or resurrection)' myth that has its roots both in the cosmic and the natural worlds (Henderson & Oakes, 1990). According to Henderson and Oakes, in nature autumn and winter represent death as leaves fall from plants (usually most directly associated with a 'sacred tree') and spring and summer represent rebirth as plants burst back into life. This is a very ancient myth (evident in most ancient civilisations) and it is at the core of modern Judeo-Christian belief (ibid.). Indeed, the myth of the Greek god of wine, Dionysos, is bound up in the death–rebirth myth and there is a very clear reference to this in the visual displays of the Champagne Mercier *cave* tour. As the elevator descends into the *caves* the doors close, a sound track begins and a scene is revealed through the glass wall at the back of the elevator. There is no commentary, instead enchanting music is over-laid with the sound of chirping birds and crickets and then, as a diorama of the vineyard is revealed there is the barking of a dog and the sound of seca-teurs pruning vines. The descent continues and the visitor is plunged into the 'underworld' with sculptures in the limestone of the dog, people tending vines and most importantly nymphs flying amongst the grapes. This is at the confluence of the natural (the vines themselves) and cosmic (the nymphs) myths of death and rebirth, where the nymphs in the vines are a direct refer-ence to Dionysos' crossing over to the underworld (ibid.).

The mystical and cosmological connections to nature were also evident at the now defunct Piper Heidsieck tour. Here nature was portrayed, not only as being significant in the vineyard, but she was also portrayed as 'doing her thing' inside the bottle in the creation of champagne. The narra-tive is definitely one of 'creation' over manufacture, where 'yeast [a living organism] begins the magical transformation' of still wine into champagne. Here 'the wine has become a living thing' that matures under the protection of mother earth in the 'tranquil' *caves* 'surrounded and protected by the Champagne limestone'. Nature is put forward as being totally in control as 'no human can hurry the wine, because now nature has taken over'. This too is a very ancient narrative, possibly dating back as far as the first accidental discovery of how crushed grapes were mysteriously transformed into a mind altering substance (Charters, 2006).

The paradox evident in 'industrialized nature', then, is one that is rein-forced and reconciled through myths and narratives that are deeply embedded in Western culture. They rely on the values we place on nature (including Judeo-Christian beliefs surrounding natural representations of death and resurrection) and the association between the mystical/cosmolog-ical and the natural. Nature is used to add value for consumers (Beverland, 2005) and to reconcile the paradoxes surrounding the mass production of a supposedly rare luxury good. It also intertwines with issues surrounding the scale of production discussed above, allowing both the houses (the mega) and the growers (the micro) to believe that they are connected by a greater power – nature and her influence over the grape production (the seasons) and the manufacture of champagne (the 'magic' of fermentation).

Innovative conservatism

As with the industrialized nature paradox, the paradoxical tension between innovation and conservatism relates to the production of luxury and this is highly evident in the material presented to visitors to the region. Indeed, it could be argued that the concept of innovative conservatism is so highly intertwined with that of industrialized nature that it perhaps forms part of a greater set of mythologies surrounding technology and its application to the champagne industry.

The concept of innovative conservatism is also evident in the academic literature and once again this forms part of Beverland's (2005) discussion of brand authenticity in luxury wines. In particular, Beverland singles out champagne houses as being at the forefront of using myths that attempt to strike a difficult balance between tradition (conservatism) and innovation, staying true to traditional craftsmanship while constantly adapting and developing new products and styles to stay ahead of their peers and adapting to consumer trends. According to Beverland (p. 1023) the use of modern production methods (that are 'publicly downplayed') ensures 'quality leadership' that 'enhances status and price premiums', while the public face of production favours 'images of traditional hand crafted methods and intuitive expertise [and] helps create a powerful image of commitment to past traditions, which helps convey a sense of authenticity'. He also suggests that the images of 'traditional' practices 'are often stylized versions of real events' (p. 1007) that result in 'the continuance of myths regarding production processes' (p. 1002).

As a result, all *cave* tours also tell visitors about production techniques that are now largely obsolete (such as hand-riddling) (see also Beverland, 2005). In fact, the tour at Champagne De Castellane opens with a self-guided tour of a museum full of antiquated champagne equipment and, on the main part of the *cave* tour, displays of historical champagne-making techniques are prominent and visitors can do their own hand riddling. As already discussed with previous paradoxes, tours also talk of the 'art' (or 'craft') of such skills as blending which also have high levels of technical and scientific input that are never revealed to the visiting public. The implication (and sometimes the overt story) here is that, as an art or craft, skills are passed down from generation to generation and learnt over decades rather than learnt through formal (scientific) education and, as such, are reliant on relatively unchanging traditional knowledge.

However, while technologically modern processes may be deliberately hidden from the consumer, many houses also cultivate the juxtaposition between tradition/heritage and innovation, with stories and images that have strong elements of both. So, for example, while de Castellane (and others such as Laurent Perrier) actively engage the visitor in the traditional/ historical methods of champagne-making, they also show the modern bottling line, *gyropalettes* (robotic riddling machines), stainless steel tanks and other elements of the modernized process. More broadly this is evidenced by the houses placing equal emphasis on both its lineage (e.g. the year it was established, the history of its ownership) to establish a strong sense of heritage and its role as an innovator by being the first (usually in the modern era) to develop a certain style of champagne or to open up a new international market. In fact, these are often discussed in direct connection with each other in the same part of the tour.

Interestingly, for several houses innovative conservatism is bound up in the stories of the matriarchal figures in the house's past. The most famous of these is Veuve Clicquot. Her story of courage in the face of adversity, when her husband died (*veuve* being the French for widow) is intertwined with stories of her ingenuity as she not only took on a male-dominated business, but also introduced technological innovations such as the riddling rack that were to be adopted by the entire industry. Meanwhile Pommery recounts the story of Madame Louise Pommery, herself also widowed and left to run the company in the nineteenth century, and how she was 'an avant garde spirit' (Vranken Pommery Champagne, 2008), developing and marketing brut (dry) champagne when all champagne of the time was sweet. She is also portrayed (quite rightly) as a pioneer of wine tourism, as she commissioned an artist to decorate several of the 120 *crayères* (Roman chalk pits) that she had purchased and converted into cellars and opened these for public viewing (ibid.). Today, Pommery continues this patronage of the arts by including regularly updated exhibitions of contemporary and often avant garde art within the cellars, and incorporates this within the *cave* tours. This very modern and ever-changing addition to the cellars is a very real expression of the tension between innovation and conservatism in champagne as it is juxtaposed against the backdrop of the neo-classical sculptures on the walls of the *crayères* of 130 years earlier.

Not all tours express such a tension, however, with the tour of the facilities of Champagne Nicolas Feuillatte being very firmly rooted in the realms of the modern, innovative and technologically advanced. Here there is no attempt to hide the modern or to overlay it with a sense of conservatism or heritage and this reflects a very deliberate strategy to do so. Champagne Nicolas Feuillatte is a cooperative union that was established in 1976 and as such it does not have the heritage or lineage of the other major producers and therefore has a unique selling proposition that sets it apart from the others. The tour of their production facility occurs on raised platforms that overlook some of the most advanced wine-making machinery in the world and visitors are told of the innovative use of technology and their above-ground 'state of the art' facilities. The champagne-making process is interpreted, as it would be in a New World winery, as being a modern, quite technical process that relies on technology and science (the art of blending is discussed, but remains in the background of the story).

The visitor to Champagne is surrounded by messages that meld conservatism (in the guise of heritage and tradition) with innovation. This can be done by either contrasting (especially past and present) production practices or intertwining the two concepts where visitors are told of a heritage of innovative behaviour within the champagne house and increasingly within some grower brands. Like other fashion (Kawamura, 2005) and luxury products (Vranken Pommery, 2008), being deeply rooted in the past of the place and the product is as important as being willing to extend beyond what exists to be the first to do something.

Blended terroir (a specific and general place)

Terroir is the source of much debate in the wine world (Charters, 2006; Vaudour, 2002). The French claim it as a term that defies translation into English (Charters, 2006) and many French wine-makers suggest that it can only exist in France. In general, the term terroir is considered to encapsulate the unique combination of natural and environmental (and, some would say, cultural) elements that is extant in a region which influences the character of a wine. This cannot be replicated as the way in which all these elements interact is so complex that it can only be expressed in the place where it naturally occurs. For the French it gives wine its soul and for many French it is something that is only expressed in French wines.

Terroir is the cornerstone of the French AOC system (Vaudour, 2002) and is core to the communication of what makes champagne unique. All communications from the champagne houses, growers, the CIVC and the other professional bodies of champagne are predicated on the very real belief that champagne has a singular and unique terroir from the Champagne region. Every visitor is introduced to the Champagne terroir, using maps, diagrams and photographs of the underlying geology. The key, the visitor is told, lies in the chalk that lies just below the surface and vineyards may only be planted where this chalk exists. Visitors are also told that Champagne's climate, on the northern-most limits of grape growing, also has a profound impact on the character of champagne. Aspect and micro-climate also play an important role in which grapes are planted where: pinot noir on the slopes of the *Montagne de Reims*, pinot meunier in the cooler *Vallée de la Marne* and chardonnay in the easterly slopes of the *Côte des Blancs* to the south (only rarely is the Aube ever mentioned in this discussion).

The facts of the story are undeniable, a unique terroir based on soil, aspect and climate does exist in Champagne and, on the face of it, there does not appear to be any paradox. However, as the story continues to unfold, the visitor is told of how the key to the unique style of each house (and some growers) is the careful blending of wines (*assemblage*) from across the region and even from different years (for non-vintage wines). Grapes for a single wine might come from vineyards that are more than 100 kilometres apart, some south facing, others easterly, some on hill slopes and others on the valley floor. Such blending would be anathema to wine-makers in many other regions of France, including Bordeaux where premium wines are made from different grape varieties, but where these grapes are grown in relatively small and tightly delineated sub-regions of Bordeaux.

As already discussed, the houses use the art and craftsmanship of the cellar master as a core component of the stories of champagne-making. At the core of this story of craftsmanship is the blending of dozens of different base wines to create the unique house style that is consistent from year to year. So houses are claiming that their house style is created both from the specificity of place and from blending together of different characteristics created by different conditions in different places. Houses also often produce their high-end wine (*prestige cuvée*) from grapes from single years (vintage champagne) or specific places (e.g. single vineyard like Krug's Clos de Mesnil blanc de blanc or wines from *grand crus* villages like Taittinger's Brut Prélude Grand Crus). Houses therefore claim to be both expressing place and creating a style that denies the specificity of place. It seems logical that this would be problematic for a place-brand that relies on the intimate relationship between place and product, but the story told seamlessly melds together place and manufacture in the same way that it deals with issues of scale and industrialized nature discussed above.

Conclusion and implications

The mythology of champagne (and therefore part of the value inherent in the place-brand) is reliant on the paradoxes and tensions that lie in the skill of knowing when to let nature take its course and when to control the process of the manufacture of champagne. The careful retelling of the myths that surround these paradoxes is a key element of the visitor experience in Champagne and is core to maintaining the place-brand identity of champagne.

The myths discussed in this chapter are by no means mutually exclusive and these elements are part of all interpretation for visitors to the region. Some experiences privilege some myths over others, but it is not possible to tell one part of the story without including the other elements. The near universal use of these myths in the visitor experiences of houses, growers and professional organisations highlights the strength of the belief and significance placed on these myths as the profession reconciles the paradoxes they are faced with.

The stories are retold with great accuracy by all involved in hosting visitors and there is a high degree of believability in the storytellers. This is vital to the continuing success of the mythology of champagne, but could also be undermining the value that is imparted by these myths. To this end, several of the visitors interviewed during this study commented that once they had undertaken one tour the repetitive nature of the story told at each subsequent visit began to bore them and somewhat cheapened the experience. Therefore, champagne houses and growers need to ensure that the stories they tell must be differentiated from the others in the region while still maintaining the mythology that the region and product is built on. This is particularly important for those visitors making more than one visit; the very visitors that are likely to be most involved in wine and the most likely to be heavier consumers of champagne.

6 Mobilizing brands and terroir in Champagne

Nick Lewis

Introduction

Terroir is a term used widely to highlight the territoriality of rural produce. A search on 'terroir' in Google Scholar yields more than 40,000 hits, which extends to 26 million on the web. Its popularity emphasizes the significance of geographical provenance in understanding and valuing rural produce, but also hints at the multiple interpretations of the term, an overwhelming number of which seek to define it (broadly or in finer detail). In this chapter, I am concerned more with how the term is used than debating an essential meaning. I ask how the discourse of terroir is deployed in Champagne and what this tells us about its work as a master discourse of political and cultural economy in wine. I argue that champagne demonstrates the contradictory ways in which terroir is used and exemplifies its malleability and its purchase.

As a geographer, I am trained to think about the interplay of human and biophysical dimensions, even though I work primarily in the cultural realms of economy and policy. In this work I adopt a post-structural political-economy approach that questions the categories of understanding by which we come to know the world (Le Heron & Lewis, 2010). Thus, for example, we should always ask what we mean by apparently self-evident categories such as firm, region, industry, or . . . terroir. A post-structural approach sets out to move beyond debates over the 'real' meaning of such categories to question the work that they perform, culturally, economically and politically. I begin with three observations on terroir: it is a master discourse in wine culture; it is used in reference to wine that is purported to be somehow genuine, traditional and crafted as opposed to industrial, generic and somehow flawed; and it is 'performative', or begins to make the world in its own image (the word thus becoming the object referred to). Whilst we should be more concerned with the work of terroir than with defining it, we should ask why others are determined to define it and to what effect, and how their different definitions perform in the world. In this chapter, I work through some of these questions in relation to the way I observed terroir being used (and not being used) in Champagne as part of an academic study tour in 2008.

The chapter begins by outlining what is meant by a post-structural political economy perspective. It then goes on to argue first for an interpretation of terroir as a master discourse of wine culture and then that the literature has so often missed the mark as a result of its obsession with definition and 'truth of concept' rather than proof of concept. The third section of the chapter examines what I saw of terroir in Champagne during a week in late summer 2008. It is necessarily a partial account of both champagne and terroir and one that draws primarily on the English language literature, but is one that demonstrates that terroir is deployed flexibly in Champagne in ways that help us to view the term more generally in more helpful light. This is not, as some have argued unhelpfully, because champagne is a brand and not a terroir. Rather, it is because terroir is asked to do different work in the region, work that articulates the different but not always contradictory organizational and marketing potentials of brand and appellation differently to other regions.

The concept of terroir

Complex territoriality of wine

The French concept of terroir is used as shorthand for the complex territoriality of production, appreciation, and regulation in wine. It posits determining relationships between the characteristics of a place and the wine produced there, and encompasses relationships between soils and climate and the physiology of the vine, place-rooted traditions of wine-making and viticulture, regional trajectories of wine industries, regulatory practices, and the strategic cultivation of associations between wine and place in imagery and text (Moran, 2006; Vaudour, 2002). Use of the term terroir, wittingly or otherwise, acknowledges both the central place held by French wine in wine culture and trade and the example of the AOC, which serves as the model to understand the application of terroir to regulating and narrating wine–place relations (Gade, 2004; Moran, 1993b). Terroir is deployed more or less explicitly, more or less forcefully, and more or less in line with understandings derived from French wine lore to suggest that wine is a product of its place. Its economic and social values are attributed to place and enhanced by multiple referents to geographical provenance at different scales. So too are its particular sensory qualities.

The terroir literature refers to cultural, political and environmental factors, but is generally dominated by an environmental determinism that draws a more or less direct causal relationship between soils and climate, the performance of vines, and distinctive sensory qualities in wine. This environmental determinism is commonly seen as defining the cultural and political economy of wine. In more reductionist interpretations (Van Leeuwen, 2009), place becomes soils and/or climate working through black-boxed (compartmentalized or bracketed-off) biophysical relationships, often with little reflection on the narrowness of this definition. Whilst biophysical scientists will occasionally refer to human determinants of terroir (see for example Jones, 2007), this is seen as 'the human contribution' (Bohmrich, 1996) via which humans respond and/or influence wine through their investments, viticulture, oenology, representation, and political organization. Such accounts still tend to place environmental endowments rather than human practice in geographical environments at the centre of geographical provenance. Although occasionally incorporated in sophisticated ways such as Bohmrich's (2006) 'intervention wheel' which identifies 'countless factors that humans bring to bear that could affect the expression of terroir', human involvement is externalized. It is commonly seen as designed to express the physical environment – an explanation that conveniently dovetails with the romance of terroir, the political invocation of which is an important dimension of what I term *terroiriste* or *terroirisme* to indicate some form of strategic deployment of the discourse of terroir to convince or to compel.

For human geographers (Barham, 2003; Gade, 2004; Lewis, 2008; Moran, 2006), humans are very much integral to terroir. They invest in land, generally in markets that are not parcelled by perceived wine qualities and almost always conditioned by access to both finance and land availability. They also alter land, with bulldozers and dynamite as well as fertilizer and water; and they breed and clone vines, write scientific texts, select varieties and clones, manage vines, make and judge wines, make meanings about places and wines, and so on. Humans blend across varieties and land parcels and draw boundaries around parcels of land and definitions of terroir at different scales (communal, regional, cadastral and so on). These moments and sites of human and biophysical co-constitutiveness diminish any claim that any particular wine derives its qualities from the physical environments of its production, and especially the claim that any place (vineyard, grouping of vineyards) generates wines of particular qualities.

Three questions might help make this point to doubting wine lovers: do different varieties respond in the same way to the same physical environment; does scale mean that terroir is always a blend; and if wine-makers make claims about different terroirs in the same bottle of wine, does this work the same way in *terroiriste* discourses about a single vineyard wine (and should it)? The answer to the first question lies in the biophysical black boxes, but either way erodes determinist claims about the terroir of blended wines. The second directs our attention to the inadequate consideration of the scaling of terroir as an imagined determinant of wine's sensory qualities. The geographical scale at which a wine is denominated and its environmental qualities imparted and from which grapes are drawn and made into wine is clearly pivotal to any claim about environmental effect and the capacity to identify such effects (Bohmrich, 1996, 2006). The answer to the third lies in the cogency of the claims about terroir, and the form and force of their making. That is, not only is terroir discursive and elastic but it is also highly political in the worlds of both culture and economics. As Wolikow and Jacquet (2010, p. 21) observe, 'terroir is a historic construct, an object forever redefined by a tumultuous history . . . [and] the fruit of the unavoidable construction of norms without which no market can function'.

All of this complexity enters into vineyard, winery, and market, which are treated as black boxes by environmental determinist accounts of terroir. The complexity of biophysical relationships at work in the black box of the vine as well as the problem of scale in terms of climatic and soil influence, all give further lie to environmental determinism. In each of these spheres, new research is opening up the black boxes. Seasonality, yeasts, varieties, clones, individual plants, growing phases, genetic triggers, and so on are all being opened up, not to mention their complex interrelationships.

Simple determinist accounts remain influential (see, for example White *et al.*, 2009). Interpreted as soil type and/or climate, terroir offers a simple, universalized language to law-makers fashioning and interpreting regulation, wine-makers narrating their wines (ironically, often when describing their own distinctive practices), wine enterprises marketing their wines, wine media looking for accounts that can be linked to visuals and tourism, and wine-tourism enterprises celebrating the physical environments of particular areas. It is also appealing to those whose science privileges either soil or climate, allowing them to claim and exercise advantage in the politics of knowledge production around wine. Human factors can be tacked on as external influences if and when needed. Politically determined territorial boundaries and territorialized regulatory structures often stand as proxy for the territoriality of environmental effect and the scale for identifying and representing it. Such regulatory frames, however, are political and once again place humans deep inside terroir's many black boxes in any real-world expression of them.

Terroir and regulation

Perhaps the most influential work of terroir is in framing and legitimating geographically denominated regulation. Terroir is heavily implicated in the AOC structure, and is invoked by different interests in more or less determinist accounts to explain, legitimate, or critique its political economy (Barham, 2003; Brouard & Ditter, 2008; Guibert, 2006; Moran, 1993b). It is also at work in the politics of international trade in wine, particularly in regard to access to European markets for non-European wines (Barker, 2004).

In the world of the AOC itself, the physical environment of origin is important, but neither exclusively so nor necessarily over-determining. Law-makers referred to the 'local, loyal and constant practices' that could be used to delimit an area associated with the protected geographical name. Designed to protect French wine producers against fraud, it built on established political boundaries (Moran, 1993a). Citing earlier work, de Sainte

Marie & Bérard (2010) argue that it was not until 1966 that a discourse of geographical environment was positioned as central in law – as 'a designation of origin . . . possessing a quality or characteristics which may be attributed to the geographical environment, including both natural and human factors' (2010, p. 181). Nonetheless, 'local, loyal and constant practices' remain central and 'geographical environment' is understood to encompass the knowledge of local actors and human interaction with nature. Such practices are argued to yield wines that are typical of their place.

As a regulatory expression of the discourse of terroir as well as a powerful and reinforcing frame for much of its work, the AOC therefore arises from an emphasis on human practices. Wines from a place are argued to display *typicité* and thus be expressive of place (physical and cultural) rather than be determined by an environment that will in the first (or final) instance necessarily produce 'placed' wines, hence the need to control production practices and to monitor what is produced. For Moran (1993a, 2006), as for de Sainte Marie and Bérard (2010), the link between qualities of wine and landscape can be discerned, understood, and seen to be defining through an examination of human practices from investment through viticulture and wine-making to marketing, appreciation, and commentary. The irony is that while this understanding is deeply embedded in the structure and performance of the AOC and well appreciated in practice in both France and in the New World, it is commonly distorted in popular and scholarly writing that proceeds from simple definition.

Finally, the AOC is a complex, multi-scalar and highly political governance framework (Barker, 2004). Whilst high-powered central and regional organizations set rules and arbitrate, the system rests on the work of multiple local organizations, principally, in Champagne, the SGV, which define and arbitrate over matters of *typicité*, collective values, and practices. This collective localism is entirely consistent with, if not a necessary precondition for, the idea of terroir. Indeed, it is in practice co-constitutive of the idea of terroir and with the vineyard as the origin of product, distinctiveness, and value.

Consuming terroir: a contemporary *terroiriste* wine consumption space

Normally read forward from the determinism of wine qualities by the biophysical (and then complicated to a lesser or greater extent by highlighting the significance of human factors), a more sophisticated account of terroir might work backwards from taste. Whilst wine professionals argue consistently for their ability to taste outside of external cues, this is known at best to be an inexact sensory science and does not extend to the wider public. At the same time, we also know that wine is a social product (Benjamin & Podolny, 1999). It carries social values, is consumed and valued in social settings, and is a positional good. Knowledge of a wine's provenance (where it was made, by whom, and from what grapes) is a significant dimension of the social aspect of wine consumption and will likely affect appreciation of the product. Certainly, the consumer behaviour literature confirms that region has an effect in consumption decisions (especially in 'statused' buying or consumption settings) (Perrouty *et al.*, 2006). This is even clearer if we allow for the ultimate desire to be social rather than biochemical, and thus some amalgam of taste, time, place, social relations and memory. Music psychologist Adrian North (2008) suggests that wine tastes differently when accompanied by different forms of music, involving sensory effects as well as cultural effects to do with the links between different types of music and cultural capital. If North is right, representations of terroir may interfere with our taste receptors, or at least our capacity to interpret them; and terroir will shape wine qualities through the social construction of taste itself as well as the cultural values of any particular wine.

Associations between wine and place connect with post-industrial aesthetics. Arguably, this connection, crafted by wine media, retailers and wine companies, together with its framing of social status has underpinned its successes of the last 25 years. Wine culture has exploded into global consciousness as part of a widespread reaction against sameness, anonymity, universality and functionality in foods as in other goods (Lash & Lury, 2007; Maye *et al.*, 2007). The local is seen to be traditional, artisanal, different, trusted, pure, healthy, safe, social, environmentally sustainable, different, and culturally referenced – all social values that have been translated into economic values in post-industrial production–consumption circuits. And if it is not our local then it should be someone else's local – which has the added values of the exotic. Wine, dripping in discourses of terroir, has been particularly well-placed to benefit from the demand for distinctiveness, the local and intimate, and the purportedly authentic (Paxson, 2010). As Gade (2004) suggests, terroir is deployed to generate a 'product salience' that mediates an 'interactive expectation between producer and consumer'.

In the world of wine, then, place and stories about place create as well as mediate and attribute distinctiveness value. Spatial imaginaries such as terroir have themselves become cultural economy products – subtly interwoven with the sensory qualities of wines in the narratives of wine enterprises, wine writers, wine retailers, waitresses, and hosts at dinner parties. They are produced and packaged for consumption in tourism and rural lifestyle programmes by travel writers, estate agents, film-makers, and those selling land for vineyards. Wines marked by place and price circulate through and become co-constitutive of this complex field of signs and status relationships. For marketers, retailers and producers of wine this is a field of opportunity to create products and segmented markets and market the values on which they rest. For image-makers and other mediators, it is an opportunity to create for themselves a more or less central role in production–consumption circuits.

Branding terroir

Brand managers leverage place to create and capture value from distinctiveness (Lury, 2004). Historically, Lury (2005, pp. 93–94) argues, a brand name 'was a mark of ownership intended to create trust in the consumer as a guarantor of the quality of particular products . . . an originary relationship between producer and products'. At the heart of branding practice lies building distinctiveness by accenting the point of origin – producer and place. That is, in socio-historical understandings of branding, terroir is branding. In contemporary branding, Lury argues, brands have become 'marks of transformation' in which 'value is attributed to transformation via the organization of a set of relations between products in time' (Lury, 2005, p. 94). Whilst not reflected upon by wine writers, this suggests that the meaning of origin in wine (or terroir) is constructed in the in-between relationships among taste, geographical imaginaries, construction and performance of status, social relations of purchase and consumption, and movement and communication of wine between producer and consumer. It should not surprise, then, that this meaning is elaborated and communicated by working on the relations in-between.

One consequence of this reflection on branding is that we should question any effort to construct a binary relationship or dichotomy between terroir and brand in wine, and examine its political rationality. Another is that we should not dismiss branding as crass or anti-terroir. Branding is remaking terroir, even if it not terroir *per se*. It is doing so because of the increasingly complex and often distanced relations between producers and consumers in a social world of much more extensive and faster mobility.

In wine, branding helps artisanal producers both to display and claim origin and all the meanings therein, and to extend their reach into post-industrial middle class demand for terroir. It also helps those organizing the production, distribution, and sale of high-volume products to extract marginal returns from references to place. Those involved in the production and organization of wine leverage terroir by attaching more or less authentic and more or less professionally adulterated indications of origin and wider meanings of quality and efficacy in the in-between. 'Difference' values are attached to volume products by romanticized reference to mythical places and relations of origin and by recognized indications of trusted organization (consistent qualities from price to taste across varietal brands, places of purchase and so on). More authentic 'difference' values are branded by origin, albeit often no less adulterated by image professionals. Terroir legitimates, authenticates and adds gloss to appellation. It provides objects and strategy for branding strategies who work place imaginaries hard in different market segments. The challenge is to distil and represent authenticity via reference to place.

This new potential of place to create and mediate value (and to brand organization as well as origin) is connected to an economy of distinctiveness and social status borne of processes in the reproduction of culture and the practices of multiple structuring agencies (Bourdieu, 1986). Place is a central organizing principle in the micro-practices of distributing, retailing, and advertising wine: retail shelving, media coverage of wines and wine-makers, distributor portfolios, the crafting of wine labels, websites, and other brand collateral, and the stories told by wine enterprises to distributors, media, and consumers. This turn to place is co-constitutive of the turn to quality and is fertile ground for *the mobilization of terroir in wine branding*.

Terroir, a master discourse of the cultural and political economies of wine

More sophisticated efforts to define terroir highlight multiple co-constitutive determinants of the relationship between place and wine and its political, economic and cultural construction. Wines are seen as products of interrelationships among: climate and soils at multiple and overlapping scales; the physiology of the vine; place-rooted traditions of wine-making; the passions and skills of wine-makers; the rent-seeking behaviour of capitalists; the development trajectories of regional industries; regulatory practices; the imagery that surrounds wine; the spatial imaginaries of particular places and the cultivation of images by marketers. Moran (2006), working with Vaudour's (2002) framework has proposed, for example, a model of at least six types of terroir: agro-terroir, vini-terroir, territorial terroir, identity terroir, promotional terroir, and legal terroir. Importantly, and in part to counter narrow environmentalist definitions and associated political deployments, he emphasizes the importance of focusing on both human factors and their interrelationship with the biophysical in this mix, especially their mutual dependence and co-constitution in the context of learning.

Accounts that seek to disentangle its multiple dimensions expose the complexity of wine's territoriality. They also reveal the cultural values and political potential associated with and exercised through this territoriality; and they allow commentators to escape the circularities of understanding imposed by their own knowledge bases. Nonetheless, they have yet to produce a fully relational account that captures the co-constitutiveness of the different dimensions of terroir that they identify – particularly in the co-constitution of consumption and production and biophysical and cultural knowledge. One direction in particular might prove promising in this regard. This is a focus on the ability of terroir to perform, the idea which I develop in this chapter. This approach focuses on how the term is deployed and the claims made in its name. In the accounts of terroir represented above, the political is seen as external to the definitional and the realm of truth, yet the politics of knowledge production are central. Geologists, for example, become engaged as scientific experts to testify to the distinctiveness of particular places in court cases about geographical provenance, often locking in their perspective as truth in the form of legal precedent centred on decisive findings. Similarly, biophysical scientists have begun to extract funding by hypothesizing the implications of climate change for wine production and wine industries, while business studies scholars have sought to build a distinctive sub-discipline named 'wine business'.

Interpreting terroir in wine marketing

Terroir has been an important term for the marketing and wider wine business literature – in setting research contexts and framing research questions, as well as providing relationships to be measured and explained. With notable exceptions (Charters, 2006), the literature has tended to treat terroir as a pre-defined and definitive term and to ignore its performative dimensions in a rush to delineate the components of price and value in wine, especially region and brand in consumer choice. In so doing, it distinguishes between place-based (region or terroir) versus branded wines as a basis for knowing and marketing wines, and tends to treat French wines as exemplars of the first and Australian or Californian as branded. Further binaries are used to differentiate between the New and Old Worlds of wine and account for presumed differences in regulation and business organization and practices (from production to marketing), as well as consumer behaviour. Croidieu and Monin (2006) talk of terroir versus brand logics and cite Thornton *et al.* (2005) to identify dimensions of the logics: organization or governance (family vs market), sources of identity (wine-making vs business), legitimacy (legacy vs market success), authority (tradition/appellation vs trademark/shareholder return), mission (terroir vs sales), focus in production (viticulture vs wine-making), strategy (legacy/lineage vs volume/growth), and investment logic (sustainability vs return). Table 6.1 seeks to capture many of the overlapping dimensions of these sorts of categorizations, which tend to frame accounts of the wine world in the literature and wider popular media. They are prioritized differently and read from different starting points, depending on the focus of study and interest (marketing strategy, value chain organization, historical geography, knowledge form, connections with place, or other).

Whilst potentially useful as a heuristic device, these binaries oversimplify the wine worlds that they purport to describe. Their reductionism and failures to represent the world accurately or intelligibly are recognized in the literature (Moran, 2006; Vaudour, 2002). The binaries are not as tight as they might appear to be, and do not establish simple brand versus terroir or New World versus Old World logics. Appellations perform as trademarks and vice versa, wine regions are often brands, family enterprises share features with corporate, and multinational firms have specialized terroir-based craft wines. Seeking to reduce the world into these categories has the effect of reproducing knowledge in these terms and thus in turn the world. The search for their ideal forms empirically is likely to be frustrated and frustrating. In real worlds, different wines from different places and at different times are created, narrated and marketed from different articulations of these features.

Nevertheless, the binary understandings presented in Table 6.1 are in circulation and have effects. Rand (2008), for example, points out that while terroir and appellation are 'related concepts' and derive their significance from their interrelationship, they have come to be understood as 'the same thing'. Wine writers and business scholars tend to ignore the complexity of their interrelationships. Less helpfully, however, she then goes on to draw a distinction between 'appellation' as marketing and terroir as genuine relationship with place. She uses two examples to make this argument – the Greater Australia 'appellation' and champagne. Although Greater Australia is a GI rather than an appellation in an AOC sense, her point is that appellations rely on a discourse of terroir for their justification. They are deployed as instruments of marketing. Not only do they represent what is produced as from a place, but they actively produce terroir through their prescription of vineyard and winery practices. Even GIs influence the practices of investors, wine-makers, marketers, regulators, and consumers. Both appellations and GIs condition production to ensure that wines from one place take on particular characteristics – to lock-in or even to produce place.

These points are well-illustrated in the case of champagne, Rand's second example. In the rest of this chapter, I will use this case to develop a third column for Table 6.1 that demonstrates the dialectical constitution and spatio-temporal contingency of the different dimensions of terroir.

Table 6.1 Binary *terroiriste* understandings of worlds of wine

Terroiriste *'starting point'*	*Other*
Terroir	Brand
Authentic	Commoditized/technologized
Traditional	Modern
Inherited craft: geography/tradition (alchemy)[a]	Codified science: technology/science (chemistry)[a]
Tacit/empirical knowledge	Codified/taught knowledge
Localized: 'typical'	Generic: 'standardized'
Artisanal	Industrial
Appellation (region)	Brand
Quality	High volume, low price
Place (origin)	Varietal
Single vineyard	Blend
Appellation	Trademark
Family	Corporation
Making wine	Making money
'Old World'	'New World'
Romantic	Modern

Note: [a]The italics are taken from Croidieu and Monin (2006)

Champagne terroir

The literature on champagne concurs that its success is based on a regional distinctiveness communicated by, if not residing in, its name. To the extent that terroir is about human practices in the context of geographical environments, champagne is a defining example. However, to the extent that it is understood and marketed as a micro-expression of distinctiveness (single vineyard and single variety), champagne is not like the Burgundian exemplar. Those arguing that champagne is industrial and brand-centric point to the centrality of *méthode champenoise* over vineyard expression, the practice of blending across villages and varieties, and the volume production of the houses and their emphasis on branding.

Champagne's success derives from generations of strategic stewardship and development of a reputation (regional brand) for a distinctive product (Charters & Menival, 2010; Guy, 2003). Product and brand are based on both a technological innovation and careful consolidation of the right of local producers to take exclusive advantage of product, reputation, and underlying technological innovation. The innovation, the *méthode champenoise*, is a particular human practice developed in association with the potential of geographical environments in a particular historical context of competition and industry organization. It involves practices in the vineyards (in relation to vine performance) and the winery (in relation to wine-making possibilities, technology, and yeasts), but centres famously on an in-bottle secondary fermentation and the production and management techniques necessary to make the approach work and produce high-quality wines.

Guy's (2003) analysis of the history of social relations in the wine industry in Champagne emphasizes the importance of representations and political deployments of terroir in the emergence of champagne's production, marketing, and regulatory practices. She writes of its implication in the formation of the AOC and the fight against fraud in production within Champagne and in wines coming from elsewhere which claimed to be champagne. In the early twentieth century, terroir was routinely invoked in shaping production, marketing and regulation, but intricately connected to 'industry' and to the hard political economy of grape pricing, land holding, and investment. Guy directs particular attention to the interplay of the politics of terroir, high yield viticulture, the *méthode champenoise* and investment opportunities which attracted capital to bigger-scale production. The technology facilitated large-scale production and a regional marketing of terroir, and in turn the growth of the champagne houses. However, this history remained subject to the wider politics of land and patrimony that inheres in terroir, such that the houses grew by purchasing grapes rather than land. Smaller producers developed behind domestic demand for cheaper, artisan produced *vin de deuxieme choix* (second-choice wine). Both benefited from the new regional appellation and a regional 'brand' built on discourses of terroir. The result was a history of complex social relations and messy relations between terroir and industry which were both facilitated and accommodated by the flexibility of terroir.

The point is that any suggestion that there is a simple binary between industry and terroir or brand and terroir obscures the complexity of which Guy and others write. Whilst its wine is generally multi-sourced, highly processed, and blended into a regional essence, champagne has an AOC and all of the symbolic capital, geographical imaginaries, regulatory capacities, and collective institutions that go with that. Its village structure differs from the finer grained vineyard-focused classifications of Burgundy and chateaux arrangements of Bordeaux. Rather, it supports the particular mix of place, marketing expertise, and brand that has become champagne. Terroir in Champagne refers to what Avellan (2009) terms 'the personality and versatility of regional characteristics'. The AOC provides a structure for organizing collective action, regulating prices, regional growth, and production practices in vineyard and winery, and mobilizing terroir in corporate and regional branding. As much as it derived initially from technology, this technology was intimately related to human practice in distinctive geographical environments. Its success as brand is built on terroir as understanding of place, distinctive practice and wine, the geographical trademark secured for it by geographical indications laws, the regulatory apparatus of the AOC that allows it to control the brand (thus again terroir as a concept), and clever marketing that links all this to exclusivity.

Reading complex terroirisme in the field

The different chapters in this book will point in different ways to the complex interweaving of production, consumption and regulation, much of this around notions of terroir. In this chapter, I use the experience of the academic study tour to make explicit some of the work performed by terroir in Champagne, focusing on the interplay between terroir, industry, and brand. In addition to background reading and the introductory remarks of the various informants to whom we were exposed across the week, four dimensions of our experience in the field opened windows onto this complexity: the tastings to which we were invited and treated; the accounts of the regulatory and political structure of champagne given us by leaders of regional wine organizations; the promotion of their wines by champagne houses and small enterprises; and proposed vineyard reclassification that dominated much discussion in Champagne at the time.

Tasting terroir

Across the five days of our visit we were invited to taste champagne at five champagne houses, four formal meals, and with four smaller producers. Possessing a non-trained palate, I was able to detect difference, but unable to interpret it. However, I was able to listen to the interpretations of others in multiple tastings. These interpretations related subtle differences in aroma profiles to different wine-making approaches, brand traditions, seasonality, and source of grapes. That is, participants (wine-makers and academics) conversed in a mixed language of terroir and brand in order to give meaning and values to the wines. They echoed the claims by wine-writers, such as Essi Avellan (2010), that it is possible to distinguish across communes, between for example the 'steely' chardonnays of Le-Mesnil-sur-Oger and the 'purist style' of Guy Charlemagne in 'the chardonnay heaven' of the *Côte des Blancs*, and between the 'subtle and feminine, sensuous wines' of Cramant and the 'stylish balance of power and charm' of Avize. Whilst the language invites some scepticism, the point is that terroir is at work in creating and communicating economic and cultural values. Champagne was being narrated and performed into its exclusive values, whilst terroir was being produced and reproduced at the same time. This was most apparent in the once in a lifetime tasting of Dom Pérignon with the wine-maker in the Abbey at Hautvillers. The wine-maker talked at length about his wines (including the 2000 vintage) and the origins of the grapes, weaving together the romance of the evening, the location, and the wine with stories of its history, its geography and its production. This was terroir, social status, and value in its creation.

When we met the SGV, we were treated to a tasting from three smaller producers, who introduced their wines and enterprises. Each emphasized the village(s) from which they drew their grapes, the environmental qualities of their vineyards, and the ways in which the micro-advantages of village and vineyard translated into and were expressed in their wines. Their accounts resonated with hundreds of others that I have heard in different regions and countries, including a later visit to a producer of grower champagne in his home village – land, enterprise and family-centred narratives of craft, industry and brand. For those speaking and listening, the event was yet another performance of the drama of terroir.

Accounting for terroir

Second, whilst terroir was always present in more formal communications about the history and organization of firms and region, it was deployed differently by different groups. Group discussions with regional organizations centred on trends in production and sales of champagne, the organization and regulation of production, and relations between growers and champagne houses. Leaders of both the SGV and the CIVC used notions of terroir to explain the geography and history of wine-making in the region and relations among growers, small producers, cooperatives, and houses. Leaders of both reverted to terroir to justify the current reclassification of vineyards (see below). The head of the UMC also used terroir to explain the collectivism, shared interests, and regional identity within Champagne. Indeed, after our meeting his next appointment was the crucial meeting to discuss the harvest for the year. The negotiation of collective action was high on his mind as he discussed the terroir that underpinned a regional brand.

For the CIVC and the SGV, terroir was more overtly about land. Maps were displayed and discussion developed about the particular qualities of sub-regions and villages. The region was narrated in a language of terroir. We were presented with the July issue of *La Champagne Viticole* (the SGV's trade newspaper), which in a series of stories effectively celebrated each of Moran's (2006) different dimensions of terroir. The publication performs roles in communication, but also scripts into being a Champenois identity centred on terroir, its organization, politics, and branding (see Table 6.1). The articles direct attention to the multiple organizations, sites and moments of local- and regional-scale governance, especially to the meetings and ceremonies that build identity. They not only reveal the building of regional identity in practice but participate actively in this construction. Specifically, they direct attention to the strength of 'brand champagne' and the challenges it faces, viticultural practices and information sources, trade shows for viticultural machinery, tastings, promotional events, stories about growers, patrimony, and images of vineyards and heritage. The magazine highlighted, legitimated, and reproduced a bottom-up construction of 'champagne' in an interplay of industry, brand and terroir.

Promoting champagne terroir

Third, the publicity material made available to the academic study group during our visits demonstrates the different ways that terroir is deployed. The champagne houses do not dwell on terroir. Indeed they make less reference to soil and climate than comparable material generated by the leading producers in New Zealand. In its A6 notebook-sized description of its seven brands, the closest that Laurent Perrier comes to making terroir-based statements about the qualities of its wines is to observe that the grapes for its *Grand Siècle* are 'supplied by twelve of the most prestigious crus or villages' and 'only the very best plots' from them. Rather, reference is routinely made to the production process, variety and style. The same is true of Taittinger's website, where even in the description of its own vineyards it refers to the prestige of crus and villages rather than the qualities of soils and climate directly. In its promotional material Pommery reserves mention of the source of grapes for its icon product *Cuvée Louise*. Although this mention claims that the grapes come from parcels 'chosen on the basis of their position in the terroir, their performance over the years, and the aromatic richness of their grapes', terroir is again used primarily to refer to the best grapes and best performing vines rather than to define the wine.

In interview, the heads of the champagne houses pointed proudly to their holdings in *grand cru villages*, but focused attention firmly on their brands, their history, and marketing and corporate organization. In tastings, the house wine-makers returned discussion to the origins of the grapes and to the qualities of the vineyards from which they were drawn and even to the arts of blending across vineyards with particular qualities so as to extract the best from each and add to them new sensory values. Nonetheless, 'champagne' was seen clearly as the value creator – both as brand more generally conceived and as designation of origin. The champagne house enjoys industrial scale production supported by blending and acceptance globally as a brand of luxury and quality, yet also benefits from control over a monopoly product given it by the AOC and access to the imagery and romance of terroir.

The smaller *récoltant-manipulants* to whom we talked each market their wines with more explicit reference to terroir. For example, the website of Champagne Tarlant, observes that

> our wines reveal the diversity of the sub-soil, the vineyards and the blends of our estate. Each parcel lays claim to its own identity and we listen to that complexity and do all we can to let it sing in the wine we make from it.

Champagne Pierre Gimonnet et Fils refer to 'terroir*s indispensables*' and emphasize that their vines are grown only in the Côte des Blancs. Both Tarlant and Pierre Gimonnet et Fils highlight the significance of family on their websites. Like the houses, however, reference is again centred less on distinctive qualities imparted by a particular site and more on the generic quality of the vineyards, particularly their contribution of particular elements of terroir across the blend. Thus, this is still a different application of terroir from that which you can see in Burgundy or even in New Zealand.

Reclassifying terroir

Finally, our visit coincided with widespread discussion of the review of vineyard classification launched by the SGV and the CIVC in 2003. The review examined delimited parcels of land within communes inside the *zone de production* and those outside which were pressing claims to be included. It was clearly designed to increase the supply of grapes to the houses, but had to negotiate the problem of drawing fixed boundaries on the basis of land use pattern at a point in time. Changing boundaries is not easy legally or politically in either the New or Old Worlds (Banks & Sharpe, 2006; Barham, 2003). Although the AOC is more flexible than normally portrayed in the Anglophone world (Kelly, 2007), change is always subject to complex multiscalar politics involving struggles at the local level and wider institutional politics (see Chapter 3). These politics must be contested in the language of terroir, even though they reveal the distinction between terroir and appellation.

In responding to questions from our study tour about the expansion of vineyard area planned as a result, respondents at champagne houses and officials of the CIVC, SGV and UMC, all referred to global growth in demand for champagne, the challenges of meeting this demand, and the rising prices of grapes and land. Prices of champagne had risen to a point where they were argued to be threatening the product's reputation, creating demand for substitutes, and putting pressure on stocks. Rising grape and land prices were putting pressures on the delicate balance of interests within the appellation and the capacity of the CIVC to control these tensions through the setting of prices and yields. The high grape prices and short supply were strengthening the hand of growers relative to houses, and allowing independent producers to benefit relative to the houses by resisting price rises and accepting lower income returns on their champagne, knowing that they were generating longer-term capital gains through the price of their land. Officials moved also to forestall any independent claims from owners of non-designated land stimulated by the lure of increasing champagne and land prices that might be fought through the courts.

We were told a consistent story that the original mapping of the vine-yards in 1927 occurred at a moment in time and included only vineyards in the ground at that time. The appellation included some land on which lesser-quality grapes were being grown and excluded land that had previously grown high-quality grapes for champagne, but had fallen out of production or been excluded as a result of the particular politics of the day. Daniel Lorson, communications director for the CIVC, argues that roughly the same number of hectares of vineyard land was excluded as included in the original mapping at a time when phylloxera had taken much land out of production. Lorson repeated to us the message he has passed elsewhere that 'in the mind of the people of Champagne, the terroir was always larger . . . For a person in a Champagne village, the terroir is everything that surrounds him, not just the land in the 1927 appellation' (cited in Rand, 2008).

This account was consistently relayed to our group by industry leaders, champagne houses, growers and small producers alike. It provides legitimacy for the review, and for its outcome, which classified new communes as part of Champagne, but removed two communes deemed inferior. The changes were justified in terms of terroir, and will, if Jefford (2008) is correct, rein-force a focus on terroir by encouraging more *récoltant-manipulants* at the same time as making more grapes available for the champagne houses and strengthening their capacity in negotiations with growers to drive further quality improvements.

The complexity of terroir in Champagne

In all these moves terroir is central – as a language and field of understand-ings within which to conduct the review and a legitimizing discourse for discussing its findings. Indeed, in each of these four sets of examples from the field, our study group was exposed to the breakdown of binary distinc-tions around terroir (Table 6.2). Rather than treating them as 'violations' of

Table 6.2 Fractures and co-constitutiveness in binary understandings of wine worlds

Binary	Champagne as example of co-constitutiveness
Terroir/brand	Selling wine on a distinctiveness generated by practices and environments of Champagne – regional brand supported by reference to vineyard qualities
Authentic /commoditized	Deep tradition of innovative technology 'in place' to produce unique commodity
Traditional/modern	On-going technical development around tradition based on defining technological innovation
Craft /science	Scientifically augmented traditional technology – technologically sophisticated craft
Empirical/codified knowledge	Wine-makers immersed in empirical and technical learning – and teaching others elsewhere
'Typical'/'standardized'	Particular product given distinctiveness by local technical expertise and regional name
Artisanal/industrial	Mix of artisans and volume production
Appellation (region)/brand	Regional brand – meaningful geographic indication
Quality/volume	High volume, high price
Place (origin)/varietal	Well-established, regionally specific blends
Single vineyard/blend	Regional meanings, sub-regional styles
Appellation/trademark	Region as brand protected by AOC and geographical trademark
Family /corporation	Family businesses, wine-making families, and corporate houses trading on family histories
Making wine/making money	Wine-making as passion in worlds of extraordinary wealth and highly lucrative business
'Old World'/'New World'	World of high class, luxury – drawing on 'Old World' elitism marketed to new elites
Romantic /modern	Clever articulation of high modernity and aristocratic imagery to create romance around elite luxury

competing codes and calling for even more fine-grained distinctions (Croidieu & Monin, 2006), our time in the field confirms them as co-constitutive. We were exposed to the inevitable articulations of terroir and brand, authenticity and industry and so on in practice and in place, albeit in a context where the binaries were indeed at work discursively in claims made by participants. Champagne is a product given distinctiveness by local technical expertise and its regional name, rather than the *typicité* of a particular land parcel. It is a regional brand, managed as a brand but narrated as place if not always as local as is understood in definitions of terroir.

In the field, our group observed the interplay of brand and place, high modernity and aristocratic traditions, family and global corporation, the romance of place and global chic, and terroir and technology. We witnessed exclusive boardrooms, an art gallery displaying avant garde art works in Pommery's historic cellars, and photographs of British royalty drinking champagne on winery walls at cooperative producer Nicolas Feuillatte. We interviewed the proprietor of a family wine enterprise in his family home, heads of large champagne houses and managers of global luxury goods companies. We listened to arguments about trends towards grower and single vineyard champagnes, where terroir is a more prominent concept. We were recounted the enterprise histories of wine-making families and corporate houses trading on family histories, all making technological wine branded as champagne but narrated in terms of terroir. We witnessed practices and artefacts of the technology in action, and we heard at length about how champagne was deeply embedded in place and designed to make the most of environmental conditions. We were invited into the sensory and discursive worlds of champagne and sought to engage with and understand them in terms of terroir. We were also introduced to the politics of wine in Champagne through a language of terroir. We heard at tastings not just about the quality of different villages, but also of champagne blending techniques. In all these sites and moments we observed the breaking of supposed terroir and branding, craft and industrial and the range of other codes, and we observed the active constitution of a complex regional wine world – discursively, in regulation, and in material practice.

Conclusion: towards a relational and performative reading of terroir in Champagne

The champagne story confirms that terroir is a malleable and political term. In this chapter I interpret it as a discourse of the territoriality of wine that relates the material relationships between environment, grapes, and human practices in the making and selling of wine, and their historical materialization in place to claims about quality, distinctiveness, and mystical but exclusive senses of place. Terroir is a master discourse of wine culture and practice that is co-constituted in the multiple spheres in which it performs – production (vine and wine), mediation, regulation, marketing, and identity building. Our experiences in Champagne confirm that in such contexts it is actively made and remade discursively and through wine-making/growing/ marketing practices, just as it makes regional meanings and practices. Terroir is a basis for performing the cultural and political economy of wine rather than a stable representation of the distinctiveness of particular places. It produces distinctiveness and claims of authenticity, scarcity, value, land rents, and cultural capital, which in articulation with a growing middle class and post-industrial aesthetics have generated the explosion of the wine cultural economy over the last twenty-five years. Terroir is deployed actively in measuring, articulating, mediating, regulating, and justifying quality, and in so doing produces that which it seeks to represent. It is a logic of quality that takes on meaning and purchase in its mobilization and brings into being the worlds that it measures, thereby creating and adding value as much as accounting for it.

Champagne is defined by the interplay of distinctive human practices and regional environmental qualities. Through a complex set of relations between environment, production and marketing practices, identity building, regulation and representation, terroir reproduces champagne as a distinctive and exclusive, place-based product. Its appellation is differently scaled to burgundy and bordeaux, and claims of distinctiveness are made at the regional scale (at least by the champagne houses). While scale of production, blending, a regional emphasis, and the use of branding practices link champagne to New World production, champagne is regulated by the AOC, and continues to draw on the mystique of Frenchness and place, and to emphasize tradition and *typicité*. It is at the same time region and brand, terroir and industry, and *typicité* and blend. As a term 'champagne' represents the exclusivity of place (production practices in environment, social histories, and a carefully protected and marketed image), and a regulatory space of production. At finer spatial scales different environmental qualities are argued to create different grapes that are used to create different qualities in bottles of wine and which are narrated differently to tell different stories about different wines.

The examples in the chapter drawn from our academic tour take us beyond debates over definition to a focus on the work of terroir in articulating production to consumption, creating value, and the interwoven politics of knowledge and regulation. They highlight both the malleability and performativity of terroir in branding, regulation, and the articulation of qualities and values. The chapter demonstrates that champagne's wine actors put terroir to work to protect and enhance the cultural and political economy of champagne. Champagne's qualities remain narrated by reference to the distinctiveness of place, exclusivity, and defining technology. Small producers make *terroiriste* claims about the special quality of geology, soil, and climate, whilst all producers utilize images of place (environment and social history) and emphasize regional exclusivity in marketing. All producers continue to make the claims about place expected in the wine world, even if they are not central to a marketing that is based on notions of luxury and rarity. Industry officials present narratives of terroir to explain the Champagne AOC, whilst officials and producers alike mobilize 'terroir' to debate the major reclassification currently underway. Terroir forms the basis for making and evaluating claims in this regard.

Part III

Creating the myth and selling the wine

7 Champagne's mystique, or complexity and consumer confusion

Tim Dodd

Introduction

Consumers seem to view champagne with some confusion. On the one hand they wonder why such a relatively simple wine is priced so high, and on the other they are entranced with the history and sense of uniqueness that the wine brings. Both of these sentiments will have a significant impact on the future of both the wine from champagne as well as the Champagne region itself.

The word champagne enjoys a powerful reputation and a strong image with consumers. For more than a century, various entities within the Champagne region have battled to preserve and enhance that reputation and have done so very effectively. Today, champagne is known as a luxury item with several individual brands also highly recognized and usually included when there are discussions of living a life of luxury and decadence. Continued preservation of this image will likely be a challenge for all associated with the region and the goods that are produced there in the future.

Attempts by wineries across the world to emulate the success of champagne and to develop their own luxury sparkling wine brand on a comparable scale have been generally unsuccessful. These efforts have sought to capitalize on the innovations and product development leadership that were developed by growers, cooperatives, and wine companies in the Champagne region. These other regions (both New World and Old World) have also sought to mirror the marketing practices and exclusive nature of their region. In many cases the wineries in these areas wished to use the word champagne on their label or marketing materials and were attempting to provide consumers with a description of the process used and the type of wine that was in the bottle. However, champagne producers saw this effort as devaluing their product and infringing on their reputation.

The region of Champagne has protected its reputation in a number of different ways. On the international front they have fought to make sure that other regions that produced sparkling wines did not use the word champagne to describe either the type of wine or the production process that is associated with the Champagne region. These efforts to limit the use of 'champagne' to the Champagne region in France have been pursued through courts in various countries and the World Trade Organization. This had been a particular issue in New World wine regions where wine producers had been using champagne to describe wine that underwent secondary fermentation in the bottle. In the past few decades champagne producers have been very successful in limiting the use of the region's name, making sure it is kept exclusively for their wines.

Protection also has been sought against companies outside the wine sector that have tried to associate themselves with the quality evoked by the Champagne appellation. Legal cases have been fought and won against companies using 'champagne' in association with a variety of products including cigarettes, mineral water, and perfume. In some of these cases the concern was for the indirect competition where other beverages were involved and in other cases the misuse of champagne's reputation was at stake (CIVC, 2007b). These legal challenges have largely been won or settled, but in the future the biggest threat for the region may come from consumers' reluctance to pay the prices that Champagne asks and the marketing challenges involved with maintaining a luxury brand.

Despite the efforts to reinforce Champagne as a unique region with a unique product, there are also a number of struggles that the region must overcome. The success in limiting the widespread use of champagne also will mean that the various companies producing and marketing champagne will need to maintain a strong presence as a leading luxury product. Otherwise, producers from different regions may, instead of trying to use the name of champagne, potentially develop their own unique sparkling wine products that can successfully compete. Champagne also has a number of other problems related to perceptions of consumers in maintaining this leading position.

The purpose of this chapter will be to discuss some of the challenges faced by the Champagne region related to their reputation and the perception of quality and to examine some of the ways that they have overcome these issues. In particular, the focus of this work will be upon two powerful forces that are working against each other with respect to maintaining and enhancing the image of champagne. These two opposing forces are the mystique with which champagne is held and the way it is perceived as a luxury product and the sometimes confusing image that champagne has especially for consumers outside of Europe. These two forces may ultimately determine the future demand for champagne and the manner in which champagne can be positioned.

The mystique

Champagne holds a special place in the world of wine and luxury products. This position has been guarded fiercely by those associated with champagne and the international image of both the appellation and its associated brands is powerful. The notion that champagne has a certain mystique associated with it is not surprising given its long history. A wide range of well-known politicians, celebrities, and others have at various times been associated with champagne and its links with both luxury and celebration.

Mystique is defined as simply having an air of mystery. Two other words that are associated with the term include aura and charm, both of which correspond with the manner in which champagne is widely viewed. This mystique helps champagne producers to effectively market their products worldwide and retain substantial appellation equity. In fact two forces that often work together are the appellation equity of champagne and the very strong brand equity of the large champagne houses. These dual forces are inseparable and help new champagne brands become established in new markets while they maintain a relatively high level of prices. The mystique of champagne has allowed a number of smaller brands to develop substantial export success when consumption from their local market has been in decline. These exports tend to be priced substantially higher than local sales thanks to the two equity forces that have positioned champagne in the luxury wine segment for most consumers.

The complexity of champagne adds to the mystique which the region offers but it also adds to the confusion which consumers have. When seen from an objective view the premium pricing of champagne (and indeed many other well-known wines) cannot be justified. These wines are often rated by consumers and judges as substantially inferior to similar sparkling and lower priced wines when compared in blind tastings. However, the brand and region along with the experience of consuming champagne itself is a part of the value placed by consumers when they drink a glass of champagne.

History

A long history tied to a unique product can create a number of stories, legends and identities that add to the product's mystique. This history is often used to reinforce the product's status and to provide credibility to the company or the product. When these historical associations are also linked to iconic people, famous events, or personal aspirations to success and wealth, it further enhances the general image surrounding the product.

In fact, another beverage (Coca-Cola or Coke) has also used history in a similar way to develop a certain mystique and to effectively market its product. Just like champagne has used the myth of Dom Pérignon, Coca Cola has also used the myth of John Pemberton, a quaint inventor, as the person who started producing Coca-Cola over 120 years ago and then turned it into an international brand (Pendergrast, 2000). In 1990, Coke even spent $15 million to create their own museum so the story of Coke could be passed along. This attempt to provide a romantic link to a past figure who toiled away and eventually developed a product that is predominantly sugar and water has many similarities to the myths surrounding champagne and the early developer of this product. In both of these cases, linking the brand to someone with very pure motives, humble surroundings and an inventive spirit gives the product an almost mythical quality. Just like champagne, the Coca-Cola brand carries substantial equity. Blind tastings of store brand cola that sell for half the price of Coca-Cola show that consumers often prefer the taste of the store brand yet Coca-Cola remains the dominant brand.

The history of champagne is much longer than that of Coke and includes references to nobility, famous individuals who were associated with champagne such as Dom Pérignon, politicians such as Winston Churchill, actors and actresses, and various other celebrity figures. This long history dates back more than 300 years and insinuates a type of pedigree for champagne that other wine regions have not been able to match. In the minds of the champagne houses this is also something that other regions will never be able to duplicate and this gives them a certain protection from competition.

Brands

Brands are central to the success of champagne, especially internationally where one-third of all production is exported. Although in many ways champagne itself is marketed as a brand by the CIVC and then reinforced by the various individual brands, the wine is also intertwined with the powerful role played by brands such as Moët and Chandon, Laurent Perrier, Pommery, Veuve Clicquot, and Taittinger. In fact 66 per cent of total exports are from the champagne houses with a value of €1.7 billion (UMC, 2010). Even more powerful are the companies which include a number of the most highly recognized brands. The five leading groups account for nearly two-thirds of the annual turnover by the houses and these brands have successfully added to the mystique of champagne and reinforced the strong luxury image and unique place that champagne has in consumers' minds. The brands constantly reinforce this image through their advertising, public relations, and other marketing efforts.

Many of the brands within the Champagne region have managed to capitalize on the long history of wine-making in the region through references to aristocracy (Guy, 2003). This association with wealth and luxury provides a foundation for the success of champagne. When first established, these wines also were marketed through deliberate acts of putting wine into the glasses of opinion leaders of the time. These icons strengthened the image of champagne as a rare and special item that only the wealthy could afford and the middle class could aspire to have. This image was also attached to these brands as exporters began to travel to different shores to sell champagne, providing a level of credibility that could never have been otherwise purchased through advertising.

The leading champagne houses developed very strong branding internationally in a number of ways. Some of them initially focused on specific countries, such as Clicquot in Russia, while others tried to broadly market to countries around the world through a number of different marketing tactics. Special events such as the launching of ships were opportunities for champagne brands to be associated with excitement, unique events, and luxury. This enabled particular champagne brands to capture a position that they have yet to relinquish. Many of these large houses also quickly saw the opportunity to develop several different labels and levels to appeal to a wider variety of consumers. For those who can spend substantial amounts of money, the houses provided wines at prices to meet the need for prestige and exclusivity. For those consumers with more modest means champagnes were still provided that could be purchased for occasional special celebrations.

Education

The CIVC and the major champagne houses have to date been very successful in educating consumers about champagne and the uniqueness of the product. In fact, substantial expenditure on a wide range of advertising and promotional items has continued despite the high demand for champagne during the past decade. A large number of educational brochures, maps, CDs, videos, and websites all bring the same message of elegance, luxury, and celebration. These materials also highlight the history and uniqueness of the region and educate consumers concerning the high quality of all parts of the process from the unique chalk soils, in which the vines are planted, particular vineyard locations, to the handpicked grapes, the extreme care during the wine-making process, and the innovation and distinctiveness of the various wines.

Another important aspect of the educational process is to teach consumers about the expensive process that champagne producers must go through to produce sparkling wine. Initially, considerable focus was on the individual hand care of each bottle, especially through the riddling process. As mechanical riddling has substantially overtaken the hand process, the focus has shifted to other unique aspects of champagne.

Educational materials also serve to reinforce both the celebratory and emotional aspects of champagne. Emphasis is often on romance, special occasions such as weddings, and associations with art and other symbols of culture. One champagne tasting guide produced by the CIVC asks consumers to provide an overall impression of the champagne they tasted in terms of four categories – body, spirit, soul, and heart. The specific emotions that the champagne inspires include sensuality, passion, tenderness, romanticism, mysticism, and charm. This evoking of an emotional link with champagne is central to the premium role that champagne tries to maintain in the various markets around the world. Providing education is also seen as a way to send out messages without advertising excessively. In fact some champagne producers are reluctant to engage in advertising but would rather focus on providing educational materials and being involved in promotional events where their brand can be exposed in a sophisticated manner.

Champagne producers also have realized that educating consumers regarding the special aspects of the region and the wines will help increase the involvement people feel with the product and reduce price sensitivity. An example of the use of education by individual brands was Laurent Perrier, which was in the middle of a major price increase during 2008. They were carefully trying to educate retailers and consumers that their previous prices were actually too low and the wines had really been selling at a discount. Their goal was to move the brand away from a value champagne brand into the top group and not be associated with the least expensive of the major brands.

Distribution and positioning

Distribution plays a role in maintaining the mystique of champagne through the types of distributors chosen to handle the wine in new regions. Champagne houses typically search for a distributor with a reputation of dealing only with top quality brands and will often avoid high-volume distributors even though it may initially cost sales. This association with distributors provides assurance for retailers that the product has been carefully handled and stored and also that the efforts to place the brand as a luxury product will continue. In some cases the champagne houses have seen poor storage of their products in some international markets tarnish the image of their brand; now owners carefully monitor every step of the process from the time it leaves France until it is purchased by the consumer. Strict attention to all phases of the product-to-market process is one of the hallmarks of quality assurance.

Active involvement by owners in the distribution process also carries over to appearances with distributors. Owners often have an almost celebrity status with wine buyers and retailers and will often travel around the world to be with distributors and attend various events where key retailers are present. The appearance is often linked with a celebration of an event that has a certain element of fun and excitement, which also goes hand in hand with the brand image. By working with the distributor the celebrity owner brings credibility and excitement to the brand and to champagne in general. This link with distributors helps to support the image of a special product and the prestige that goes with it.

Distribution also helps to guard the mystique of the champagne name and in preserving its place as a premium product. With many products the type of distribution outlets used are also linked with the image of that product and champagne brands are very sensitive to this relationship. When entering a new geographical market, leading hotels and restaurants are the preferred initial target to establish linkage between luxury accommodation, fine dining, and champagne. Part of the reason for this focus is that this is obviously where they can sell their product but it is also a way to position their brand with the leading local iconic hospitality brands. This positioning continues to build upon the mystique of the particular brand and upon champagne in general as the wine continues to be associated with special occasions, celebrations, and success.

A relatively uncomplicated wine

During the 1970s and 1980s many producers from New World regions began selling wine to consumers based not only on the brand of the winery but by using the grape variety as a primary signal for the type of wine they could expect. Regions remained important and were still part of the decision-making process but grape varieties also were a critical characteristic that consumers began using when deciding on a wine purchase. In addition, as wine consumption increased, consumers started to learn more and more about wine. They began attending wine education classes, reading wine books. Newspaper and magazine columns about wine sprang up in multiple markets around the world.

Consumers in these New World regions became familiar with grape varieties such as cabernet sauvignon, merlot, pinot noir and chardonnay. Champagne is fortunate that there are only three grape varieties used in the production of the wine and two of these are well-known iconic grape varieties. In many respects, chardonnay became almost synonymous for a dry white wine. Chardonnay is known throughout the world for a variety of styles of wine, and pinot noir has in the past few years become one of the most well-known and fastest-growing varietals in the international market. This helps champagne to immediately foster a consumer connection with varieties they are already familiar with as well as provide a foundation for them to learn about the Champagne region.

The use of these varieties, and often the blending of them, strengthens the reputation and aura surrounding the various champagne brands and allows consumers to feel comfortable about purchasing wine from a known variety. Even the *blanc de blancs* and *blanc de noirs* designations help provide consumers with a simple guide and enable them to understand the kind of wine being purchased.

The production method also adds to the mystery surrounding champagne. Trying to explain the various steps and processes can be a little hard for the average consumer to understand. For instance the way bubbles are actually developed within each bottle and the process of extracting the dead yeast adds to the intrigue and charm.

Internationalisation of champagne and sparkling wine

One of the initiatives developed by the champagne industry has been to purchase sparkling wine businesses around the world. Several notable companies were started in California, Chile, and Australia during the past few decades. These purchases enabled the houses to broaden the acceptance of sparkling wine and to familiarize themselves with local markets. The champagne producers do not believe they compete with sparkling wine and that the purchases simply broaden the overall market. Champagne, they believe remains in a special category that is not part of this product set.

This effort to expand the sparkling wine market may have been a positive step in two ways. First, it has enabled the champagne houses to have some control in positioning sparkling wine as a separate product to champagne rather than as just a competitor which has better value. Second, it enables them to teach consumers about the process of making sparkling wine. This helps to reinforce the history of champagne and the originality and authenticity of champagne over sparkling wine. As consumers gain knowledge of the process of growing and making sparkling wine it is hoped that the premium production methods employed by champagne will be recognized and appreciated.

Complexity and consumer confusion – forces against the luxury image

Although there are a number of elements working to sustain and enhance the luxury image enjoyed by champagne there are also forces and pressures working to decrease the equity of the region. Some of these issues are being addressed and managed by the large champagne houses, while others are outside forces which attempt to eat away at the reputation the region has enjoyed for centuries. Some of these issues are also paradoxical in that in some respects they keep enhancing the mystique and respect for champagne, while in other ways they bring into question the foundation that the name rests upon. The following discussion highlights five areas where champagne is vulnerable to consumer confusion and consumer rejection of the foundations that champagne rests upon. While there are several other issues that will likely place pressure on the willingness of consumers to pay a premium for these wines, the five outlined are certainly imminent dangers. Although champagne producers may believe the wall of protection they have created is impregnable, consumer demands may change which would make the region susceptible. No practice or product is safe from changes in technology and consumer acceptance of products, as the Portuguese have learned. In their situation very-long-held traditions of cork closures have come under attack from screw caps and other wine closures. In some countries these attacks have successfully eroded the market share of cork as the preferred method of closure. Champagne too may face similar challenges in the coming decades.

Characteristics of the wine

The subtle taste of champagne, which is often touted as a unique strength, has a potential to cause a devaluation of the brand. Other sparkling wines which may taste similar can seem to be good substitutes for champagne at a fraction of the price. Consumers interested in value may increasingly turn to these substitutes during various types of celebrations especially as an increasing number of countries are producing sparkling wines and improving the quality of that production.

Champagne producers generally do not like blind taste comparisons between their wines and sparkling wine from other countries. They believe that the purchase of their product has more to do with a whole range of other aspects than just the taste. The experience of being associated with a luxury brand and the feelings that come with this are often reasons to purchase an item beyond the functional or objective benefit that it brings. In fact, several high-profile blind tastings seem to show that judges will often prefer a Spanish, Australian, Italian, New Zealand, Chilean or even an English sparkling wine which costs substantially less than one of the expensive champagne brands. Moreover, a number of store brands produced from champagne and sold for around 20 per cent of the price in blind taste tests have outscored the flagship branded wines.

Two other characteristics of champagne also hinder the potential prestige of the wine and add to consumer confusion and resistance to paying large sums for one bottle. The first is the non-vintage nature of quality champagne. In most other types of wines, blended and non-vintage wines are typically viewed as inferior and of lower quality. With champagne, however, non-vintage wines are the standard for most large champagne houses as they try to maintain a consistent product. Consumers who are not knowledgeable about this practice may resist making the purchase because of this association. Education by the champagne producers can help to overcome this perception but it still may be difficult to resolve.

The second issue relates to the production process, which can be relatively easily repeated by other sparkling wine producers. Champagne has tried to limit the use of words on labels that would mention anything related to their production processes but consumers have generally recognized that the method of producing the bubbles in the bottles is the same for a $10 cava as for a $250 bottle of champagne.

Value and competitive pressures

While champagne producers claim there is no substitute for their wines, consumers may increasingly view champagne as an expense that does not have the value for which it is priced. This pressure on prices, and potentially on the brand equity of Champagne as a region, is especially prominent during economic downturns when consumers turn from luxury products and seek value in their purchases. During the most recent downturn for instance, the CIVC reported that champagne sales declined by 9.1 per cent in 2009 over the previous year and the downturn was mainly in the export market (CIVC, 2010). Outside the European Union, exports were down 25.1 per cent as consumers in these countries reduced their spending. A long economic downturn may push champagne companies to reduce prices therefore undermining the image of their products as a premium product.

There are also efforts by producers to expand into new markets such as India, China, and Russia where conspicuous consumption by consumers with newly found wealth is prominent. However, with the slowdown in the worldwide economy, this type of consumption that is heavily dependent on price and brand has borne the brunt of the slowdown. These new markets also offer other challenges for brand management. In many cases problems with distribution and storage may impact the quality of the wine and create a backlash towards the image of quality held by consumers.

A large number of brands

Although just a few large houses dominate the image of champagne there are thousands of companies and individual producers that are involved in the industry. This provides problems for maintaining quality and protecting the image of champagne. Strict production regulations help to limit potential problems but the actions of a few producers could potentially tarnish the reputation of all.

The other issue related to the size and number of brands is somewhat paradoxical in the wine industry and may eventually cause problems for champagne. In most wine regions the most expensive wines tend to come from small producers who only produce a very limited quantity of their product from a special area or where there is some other unique characteristic which makes the wines sought after. These wineries are able to garner a premium price because of the image they have established in wine shows, blind taste tests, etc., and consumers clamour for the wines and push prices up. This in turn adds to their growing reputation and establishes their brand as unique. By contrast, in champagne the highest-priced wines are those that come from the largest companies producing enormous quantities (almost in a mass-produced fashion) with mechanized processes and huge warehouses and factories. Thus, the brand itself is setting the price and establishing itself in a luxury niche rather than the uniqueness and rarity of the wine being pushed up in price by wine trophy hunters.

Labels and restrictive French laws

Most of the labels for the champagne houses focus on the brand with very little supporting detail or information. For consumers who are familiar with these brands this is not a concern. They typically are not interested in learning additional information about the wine such as the type of grapes it is made from, the particular region, or serving and cellaring suggestions. This is also true for other iconic wines that have such a strong brand presence that they see little need to 'educate' consumers concerning their wine. So long as there continues to be strong support for these brands and consumer willingness to pay significant prices for the product, this strategy will be successful. Some houses have developed a vintage line that along with the year of production also gives consumers some additional history or other information to help support the mystique of the brand. Interestingly, smaller grower brands will often provide greater detail concerning grape types, history of the vineyards, and specifics of the vintage or location. This is particularly true for smaller champagne companies looking to establish niche markets internationally. Many consumers in international markets have only been exposed to perhaps five or six leading champagne brands and have little or no knowledge of the thousands of other producers who make similar quality wines but who cannot command the type of price obtained by the leading houses.

Restrictive French advertising laws also may be undermining the power of the champagne brand in the home market which still accounts for over half of total champagne sales. The inability to effectively promote in the home market may have two potential impacts. First it discourages opportunities for the companies to learn what types of advertising work most effectively in their home market before taking these same ideas and potentially adapting them in the international environment. Second, it may hinder the ability to maintain brand equity in the local market. With potential international competition and continued declines in wine sales, along with economic pressures, consumers may consider switching to other products and be interested in looking for value brands outside the major houses.

Regional confusion and the expansion of Champagne

The planned expansion of the Champagne region also has the potential to tip the balance and place downward pressure on brand equity and pricing. This expansion will potentially increase production by up to one-third and the number of new grape-growing villages would increase by 40. At present there are 319 villages currently deemed to be worthy of champagne production and with these 40 new ones (less two current villages which will in future be excluded), the area will expand substantially. This is all occurring at the same time that sales are plummeting around the world due to the economic downturn. Although the new production will not hit consumers for another decade, it is possible that this expansion will encourage producers to begin to lower prices and look for alternative markets. Already a number of wine-writers have written scathing articles concerning the plans to expand the region and wine blogs have also featured consumer scepticism about the motives for the expansion. Arguments to support the claim that the reclassification will increase quality have generally been ridiculed due the fact that only a tiny portion of existing grape production is actually being removed. In addition, suggestions that this is really just a move to correct an old injustice and that the land should have been originally included in the champagne appellation have not been widely accepted. In fact, many writers have claimed that the move was orchestrated by the large champagne houses in an effort to increase profits during the boom period for champagne sales when demand in new markets across the world pushed local production to a straining point. The new area would allow producers to increase production while at the same time putting downward pressure on grape prices.

This pressure on pricing has occurred with other regions. Overproduction of Australian chardonnay and more recently New Zealand sauvignon blanc led to these wines almost becoming a commodity. In both cases the wine industry in these regions became extremely concerned as prices began collapsing and bulk wine purchases by supermarket chains resulted in a loss of regional equity of these wines. The branded, well-known wineries also began feeling the pressure on their pricing and some have had to move off their previous premium levels. Especially during economic downturns and growth in production this scenario could also become a reality for champagne producers.

One of the overriding issues faced by growers and champagne producers is the issue of balance. All those involved in the value chain do not want to see this balance come under pressure. During times of high demand there is concern that champagne is being priced off the market despite the willingness of consumers to pay for their products. During downturns, the concern begins to focus on sustaining prices so that profit margins and livelihoods will not be negatively impacted. The emphasis for those in the industry is about trying to maintain this stability in the face of a changing market. If demand and supply actually get too far off balance then all of champagne becomes concerned. This imbalance may lead inventories to grow or prices to increase to unsustainable levels. The increase in production that will result from the expansion may well be easily absorbed if demand for champagne is strong. However, if this production comes in the face of a weak economic climate then this balance could be severely tested and the champagne brand could suffer.

Conclusion

Since wine producers first learned how to control the process of producing wine with bubbles, a certain mystique has surrounded this process and the wineries that produce these wines. Champagne has capitalized on the process and has managed to establish a brand that is coveted around the world. The number of lawsuits and actions taken by the CIVC to maintain the authenticity of the region highlights how much other wine and luxury item producers view the brand and the cachet attached to it. Perfume, mineral water, and a wide range of other beverages and food items have tried to attach the mystique of champagne to their brand to indicate that it is a high-quality, premium item.

For over 300 years the wines from the champagne terroir have been known as *vins de champagne*. The region has vigorously defended its name and has been successful in maintaining its uniqueness. Everyone in the area has also supported the fight as they realize that so much of the success of the region relies on the special and unique image associated with the wine. Even the many fights in the courts and international forums have only helped to enhance the image of champagne as a unique product. The mystique has been emphasized through the magical and unique region as portrayed by the protectors of champagne. Consumers are told that only this region has the terroir to produce the fabulous product and that they should pay a substantial amount for this wine.

The mystique of champagne has continued into the twenty-first century as people with new wealth from around the world have been willing to pay the premium for this product. During the rapid expansion of the world economy champagne sales skyrocketed. This may be partly due to the pleasure that people obtain from spending money on a product which costs a lot of money. A recent study by Plassmann *et al.* (2008) showed that people did in fact derive pleasure from wine if they were told it was more expensive. Thus the pleasure of drinking champagne comes from the relatively high price (compared to most other sparkling wines), the reputation of the region for producing quality, the association of champagne and success which people like to have attached to them, and the idea that this is a frivolous and almost cavalier way to spend money. Consumers make the purchase with little regard to the cost because there is something really worth celebrating. Champagne fills this need through the overall mystique it has with consumers. However, could this mystique begin to dwindle as new products are produced, as economies begin to mature, and as wine consumers begin to learn more about wine and wonder why substitutes could not be used during celebrations?

The production process is itself a mix of mystique and confusion. The large producers in fact have developed industrial processes for making champagne and even automated the riddling process. However, the mystique of hand-crafted wines from hand-selected and hand-picked grapes remains. Many consumers still have the image of small quantities of wine being given loving care by artisans and that the wine is produced almost on an individual bottle basis. The reality is that the wines are now produced by some of the large houses in an industrialized, mechanized fashion. As consumers see or learn more about this process the mystique of handcrafted products may fade.

A second challenge to the mystique of champagne is the large increase in production that will likely occur in the coming decade. Supermarket champagne brands, especially in the UK, may continue to expand. The image of the superiority and exclusivity of the leading house brands may begin to fade especially if blind tastings reveal that many consumers tend to prefer the taste of cheaper options. This erosion of equity will probably take many years but could begin damaging the mystique of the brands in the long-term.

Other eroding factors relate to consumer knowledge about wine which may lead them to seek substitutes that serve the same purpose. In new wine producing regions, some producers are experimenting with different grapes, production processes, and are also challenging the idea that great wines can only be made in the Old World. An increasing number of wine brands that capture the imagination of the wine-consuming public may begin to eat away at the exclusivity held by champagne as the only product appropriate for celebration. Sophisticated marketing campaigns and an exclusive image may begin to capture the imagination of a fickle public. However, although these influences may chip away at Champagne's reputation, the region is still on solid ground and the mystique remains, at least for the foreseeable future.

8 The future of the champagne brand

Larry Lockshin

The Champagne region has arguably been the most effective district in the world at marketing its regional identity and maintaining an exclusive luxury-based positioning. The average price that growers and producers receive is the highest among major wine-producing regions. However, champagne's position is under threat from a range of sources, some within the region itself, and some without. This chapter commences with a brief background review of the reasons why champagne has gained such a position within the global wine market. The next section focuses on the key threats to the continued maintenance of the champagne brand position, discussing the origin and possible effect of each in turn. The chapter finishes with some recommendations for actions to take to insure that champagne can remain at the top of the wine world in terms of luxury and high-priced positioning.

Introduction

As noted earlier in this book, the Champagne region managed to create a unique product out of a handicap – acidic and relatively unripe grapes. It turns out that these are the key ingredients, along with complex series of vinification and blending steps, used to create the beverage we call champagne. If we look at other well-known wine regions, we can also find they have united specific grape varieties, growing conditions, and vinification into something unique and prized among a certain group of buyers. Just like champagne, each of these regions' history combines the development of certain wine styles with the attraction of some group of often wealthy and influential buyers, who help create the demand and reputation for the wines. Why is champagne different?

Historical brand building

Champagne has some of the same factors working in its favour and some unique ones as well. The history of the region plays a major role in achieving its reputation. As the producers switched from still wines to sparkling in the mid-part of the eighteenth century, the need for greater capital and the potential profits attracted some of the wealthier families in France and in neighbouring Germany. Many of the names we associate with champagne, such as Deutz, Krug, and Heidsieck, are of German origin and their input helped build the champagne houses along with the French owners. These producers of champagne developed major brands with their house name, buying grapes and eventually some wines from growers and local cooperatives. The major difference from other traditional wine regions is that these champagne houses grew quite large and therefore developed a range of activities we now associate with brand building, which were not common among the small grower–producers in other wine regions.

Some of the characteristics of brand building that differentiated the Champenois were standardisation of a 'house' style and a range of sweetness levels initially developed for the tastes of different export markets, but later enshrined in the style names across different producers: *extra brut*, *brut*, extra dry, *demi-sec*, and *doux*. The standardized house styles blended from wines from different vintages and the relatively standard labelling of sweetness levels made wines from Champagne more akin to modern food brands where purchasers could be assured of a standard level of quality and flavour of what they bought.

Another characteristic that led to stronger branded wines from Champagne than other wine regions was the luxury focus, mainly of the large champagne houses. From the popularity in England at the end of the seventeenth century through the court of Louis-Philippe in France in the middle of the nineteenth century and the Napoleonic invasion of Russia at the end of the eighteenth century, champagne became a drink of nobility and royalty. There are stories of Charles-Henri Heidsieck riding ahead of Napoleon's march into Moscow with cases of champagne to sell to the victor (Kladstrup & Kladstrup, 2005) and sales agents were employed by champagne houses as early as the mid-eighteenth century to take their wines to the royal houses of Europe. All of these activities built the idea of a style of wine from a specific region as well the house brands themselves. From the beginning of sparkling wine production, sales were focused on high-end buyers and luxury positioning. Champagne as a style was not a labourer's daily drink as were the basic wines from the other luxury regions; there were no basic worker-level champagnes, they were wines for the rich. This very specific luxury positioning helped focus the status of champagne as a drink differently from the high-end wines from nearby Burgundy or Bordeaux, where the majority of the volume from the region consisted of lower-priced and less consistent wines.

Another facet of the brand building by the large champagne houses is still evident today. The major houses are export-focused and their sales lead the region in all export markets. France continues to be the largest market for champagne, but the majority of the sales domestically are from the smaller houses and grower–producers. This early emphasis on export, as far back as the mid-eighteenth century, helped develop a culture of serving different markets and viewing the sales of champagne as a way of serving customers, rather than the more inward looking production focus of many of the other regions. By the nineteenth century, the major champagne houses were adjusting the sweetness level and style for different international markets, another sign of how such a strong brand was developed.

Another key ingredient of champagne's successful branding was the link to celebration. No other wine or perhaps product, with the exception of diamonds, has been so closely linked to occasion-based consumption. It is not clear exactly how the first link was made and there is a range of apocryphal stories. The result is that the consumption of champagne is strongly linked in the minds of both consumers and non-consumers with celebration. The major houses and the CIVC continue to emphasize and retain this link through their sponsorships of major sporting events, key celebrations, and national festivals. It is interesting to note that the French consume more champagne per capita than other countries, and this is due mainly to their use of the wine as an aperitif as well as a celebratory drink, in contrast to most of the rest of the world. This specialized and focused positioning made it easier to promote champagne in key markets to essentially the same segment of buyers. Marketing campaigns could be developed and implemented by both the champagne houses as well as the CIVC, adding more synergy to their efforts than in other wine regions. This segmentation also serves as a good model to growing the champagne brand in developing countries as their socio-economic status reaches certain levels.

We have seen that historically champagne producers, especially the major houses, developed strong branding based on both the house name and the region/style of champagne. After the riots of the early twentieth century and the recovery from phylloxera, the growers and the houses came to an agreement to collaborate in the future development of the region and the wine. As noted earlier in this book (Chapters 1 and 3), production limits are agreed between growers and producers. These include limits on the land used for grape production as well as limits on the harvest each year to keep production in line with demand. Because champagne is the vast majority of the wine produced in the region, compared with other regions where multiple styles of wines are produced, these controls strongly aid the luxury positioning of the region. New discussions are taking place to enlarge the area where grapes can be grown to include land taken out of production after the phylloxera epidemic. This increase in production is one of the issues to be discussed in the following section on possible threats to champagne's long-term brand.

Possible threats to the champagne brand

Champagne seems to be unique among wine regions, because the overall name of the major wine produced has become a brand in itself and is strongly associated with celebration and luxury consumption. The result has been a high and more uniform price to growers and producers compared with other wine regions. All of the best-known international regions have key producers, which obtain high prices and have long-term brand recognition; in fact it might be said these high prices and recognition are a prerequisite for regional fame. Champagne has developed a unique style and a system which allows these benefits to be more widely shared than in any other region. However, it is possible that the edifice of controls, rules, and the resulting image are under threat from a range of sources. This section will discuss each of these potential threats in turn.

Reduced prices

The biggest threat to champagne's dominance and luxury positioning is the potential for reduced prices. Lower average prices for champagne will erode the luxury positioning and the long-term link to celebration and high-end consumption. Reduced prices could and to a degree already do result from several sources, each of which is discussed below.

Retailer pressure and low-priced entries

Around the world more and more wine is being sold through major grocery and discount stores, often called multiple retailers. In key wine-drinking countries, like the United Kingdom, the USA, France, most of Western Europe, Australia, and even in Asia, multiple retailers account for over 75 per cent of off-premise wine sales (Euromonitor International, 2010). In most countries off-premise sales are over 60 per cent of total sales, and in some instances (the United Kingdom and the USA) they account for over 80 per cent of total sales.

Multiple retailers are pursuing two strategies, each of which hurts the ability of champagne producers to maintain their market-leading prices, and thus their luxury positioning. The first strategy is discounting. The major multiples are able to buy wines direct from producers and gain volume discounts. On top of this, they are aggressive discounters, using a range of techniques to promote and sell wines at low prices, such as BOGOFs (buy one or two and get one free), bundling (multiple units for one low price), and the standard heavy price discounts especially around Christmas and other major holidays. Research shows that over time, discounted prices end up setting the perceived base price for a product. If champagne is advertised and sold at prices lower than those set by the producers (but not enforceable due to competition law), then buyers will soon expect these sales prices as the normal price. A spiral of discounting can then occur with the listed price no longer used and new discounts below the previous discounts being promoted. This strategy seemed to be used heavily during the global financial crisis of 2008–2009 (and continuing in some countries as this is written in 2010). Sales of champagne decreased dramatically during the pre-Christmas season in 2008, again in 2009 and producers and retailers responded with lower prices to maintain volume (Anon., 2010c).

There are two issues with such discounting. One is that regular buyers come to expect lower prices and become reluctant when prices are raised back to previous levels. Second, at low prices sales increase partly because buyers who are only willing to spend €10 or £10 enter the market. These buyers then leave the market, or more typically buy other sparkling wines, when prices increase. Both of these factors have long-term effects by increasing sales based on low prices, and then reducing sales when prices are raised in the future. Champagne producers cannot rely on sales volumes being maintained when (if) prices are raised. We will discuss in the final section some of the mechanisms producers can use to dampen these possible outcomes. However, it should be noted that nothing will change perceptions in the short run; sales volumes at higher prices will have to be built slowly over time.

The second strategy multiple retailers are using is BOB (buyer's own brands). Here the retailers typically approach smaller producers, either individual grower–producers or cooperatives and contract for champagne to be labelled with the retailer's own label. Sometimes this label bears the actual retailer's name and can be identified as such. More insidiously, the recent trend is for retailers to copyright a new name for their home brand, which sounds like a real producer and hides the fact that it is a retailer brand. Either way, these low-priced champagne brands create a lower-price perception to the consumer and add to the expectation that champagne can be bought relatively cheaply. The retailers have no incentive to raise prices or to maintain the positioning of champagne. They rely on the large amount of reserves of champagne sitting in cellars across the region. Since they usually buy from smaller producers, they can often play one against another to get lower prices.

Oversupply

A second driver of lower prices is a potential oversupply of champagne. As noted above, the CIVC meets each year to decide the amount of grapes that can be harvested and turned into champagne. This amount is mainly based on the known amount of wines sitting in the various cellars as well as predictions for sales over the coming few years. The ability to control production or supply to match sales or demand is a strong tool in the hands of the Champenois. It is not a completely accurate tool, as all the stocks are not known and predicting demand is not infallible. It is also a blunt tool, given the fact that reductions in production in one year do not affect supply for several years, so immediate reaction to market trends is not possible.

The potential oversupply of champagne is driven by two factors, one major and one more minor. The major factor is the huge and unknown amount of champagne sitting in the cellars of growers and small producers. As stated in Chapter 1, many small growers take some of their payments from cooperatives as wine, usually bottled and either on lees or already disgorged. These small producers hold the wine as a hedge against future downturns in prices, or as means of ensuring retirement, or just as general savings, all of which are safe from income tax in the short term. This unknown quantity of champagne seems to be most of the source of BOBs at this time. If the financial crisis continues or sales and prices of champagne do not recover, more producers might be willing to sell their stocks for quick cash. Because the quantity is not known, it is hard to project the long-term effects of this pool of unfinished wines. However, it is possible and perhaps likely that as grower–producers need some cash for personal use or the offer is too good, that these champagnes will enter the market and undermine the existing luxury pricing.

The more minor factor is the possible planting of new areas within the champagne appellation. This is likely to have a more minor effect because the land area will be well discussed and the implementation will be set over a period of time and closely monitored. Certainly the overall production of champagne will be increased, but this production is likely to be matched to global demand and not allowed to fluctuate as widely as the release of wines from existing cellars.

Increasing competition from sparkling wine producers

The next threat to maintaining champagne's luxury positioning is the world-wide growth of sparkling wine. This can be viewed both positively and nega-tively. First, we will be clear about these competing wines. Champagne is a sparkling grape wine produced according to specific rules in the Champagne region of France. Sparkling wines can be produced anywhere that wines are made. As noted in Chapter 2, there are three main ways of making the wine, two of which are cheaper than the champagne method. So competing prod-ucts for champagne can range from the cheapest wines with bubbles added, to medium-quality products made in bulk vessels, to wines produced using the same methods as in champagne but in different regions, and often using different grape varieties.

Recent research shows that the market for sparkling wines is growing faster than the market for champagne (Bainbridge, 2010; Euromonitor International, 2010). The compound annual growth rate of sparkling wine globally between 2004–2009 was about 3 per cent in volume and 5 per cent in value. During the same period, champagne volume was down about 0.5 per cent with value increasing about 2.6 per cent (Euromonitor International, 2010). Mintel predicts UK champagne sales to increase by 16 per cent in value to £853m between now and 2014, but with inflation this is only a 1 per cent increase. In contrast, the same report predicts that sparkling wine sales will grow by 40 per cent to £828m, which is a real increase of 22 per cent.

In a positive sense, a growing overall market floats all ships. If sales of all sparkling wines are increasing, as they are in Australia, it usually means that champagne sales are also increasing. One of the arguments for this positive outcome is that some of the people who try a product or a category become interested in that category and then look for more information and ways to interact. The significance of the concept of involvement has been demonstrated in the wine area (e.g. Lockshin *et al.*, 2006). Higher-involved consumers try more wines and develop a strong interest in regional wines. So, a logical outcome of more people buying sparkling wine is that some of them will be interested enough to try the 'original' sparkling wine and some of those will become regular consumers.

There are two downsides to this particular assertion. The first is that there is not necessarily a relationship between the number of people drinking sparkling wine and the number of people becoming champagne drinkers. The second is that competing sparkling wines are being trialled and developed in key wine-producing areas, so that some consumers may never look to 'moving up' to champagne, but merely up to the next stage in the brand hierarchy of a different sparkling wine.

The majority of the competing products from around the world are simple sparkling wines offered at commercial to premium prices (e.g. most would be under €5 and the rest under €10). These wines bear little resemblance to champagne and most likely the people that like these inexpensive sparkling wines would not like champagne even if offered at the same price. The marketing for these low-end sparkling wines is less about celebration than enjoyment in a social setting, which again is not similar to the marketing of champagne. However, producers of the next quality level up in sparkling wines are trying to develop some secondary flavours and complexity and also market their wines as a bit more upscale. It is more possible that consumers of these wines would also try champagne if the price differential was not too great at the lower end and could possibly become regular drinkers. The biggest impediment to directly competing with champagne is the price differential between the low and mid-priced sparkling wines and champagne. Of course, if the price of champagne stays down or comes down even further, the difference may be small enough to induce more trial and possible switching.

High-end sparkling wines are also being developed to compete directly with champagnes. Some of the biggest and most well-known producers are the major champagne houses themselves, which established production houses in key international growing areas, such as the western USA, Australia, New Zealand, and Argentina. They bring to their ventures a strong understanding of how to grow grapes and produce top sparkling wine. However, it seems to this author that for the most part these ventures have stayed away from making sparkling wines to compete at the top level with champagnes. Their wines are typically priced at about half the entry level amount for the same house in Champagne, and most of these producers have a top sparkling wine that is priced near to the entry level for the same house. Overall, they do not seem to compete at least on price for the same market.

Other regions also produce sparkling wines that aim to compete with champagne at least as a style. Perhaps the best known is cava from Spain, which uses similar production techniques, but indigenous Spanish grape varieties and some small production changes to create their own style. Other regions in France produce *crémant* (sparkling) style as well as these other countries: espumante in Portugal; Franciacorta, Prosecco, and Asti in Italy; Sekt in Germany and Austria; and Cap Classique in South Africa. Other wine-producing countries also produce high-end sparkling wines using the same methods and often the same grape varieties as in Champagne. This means that there is a lot of competition for sparkling wine drinkers everywhere. Many of the historical regional styles, either *crémant* or the specific sparkling regions listed above, are not aiming to imitate champagne, but to make an alternative sparkling drink with different flavours. However, many of the New World producers are specifically trying to emulate champagne and to copy as closely as possible the style and quality made there.

Again, we can look at this competition in two ways: either it is introducing buyers to more complex and expensive styles of sparkling wine, which might lead them to try and even regularly buy champagne; or it is perceived as equivalent in style and luxury positioning to champagne, but is cheaper and sometimes more available. One could look at this competition as similar to that developed by the Japanese car manufacturers to compete with the European luxury cars. Initially the Japanese cars were similar, but much less expensive. As their reputation and expertise grew, many buyers began to prefer the Japanese luxury brands for their own sake and not as an imitation of European luxury cars. The same could be the outcome for champagne without continual improvement to both production and marketing, as we will discuss at the end of this chapter.

Narrow distribution

Related to the competition from high-end sparkling wines produced in other regions is the issue of the relatively narrow distribution and sales of champagne. Today the majority of champagne, over 50 per cent, is still sold in France, although this share is dropping. Over a quarter of champagne is sold in Europe, which means that close to 80 per cent of sales are to France or other parts of Europe. The next biggest market is the USA with about 8 per cent of sales followed by Japan with only 3 per cent of sales. Looking at these figures we can see that champagne is mainly a European drink and that sales will be mainly affected by issues in the key European markets. During the global financial crisis of 2008–09, the United Kingdom and the USA were the most affected, and champagne sales reduced most heavily in these countries. Overall sales dropped from about 339 million bottles in 2007 to 322 million in 2008, and 293 million in 2009. Much of this is due to the narrow nature of the existing markets for champagne. Of course as the economies in these key countries recover so will champagne sales, which by the first quarter 2010 were above 300 million bottles. Most of this growth has come from the European Union and to a lesser degree Japan and Australia, while France only grew 5 per cent in the same time period (Anon., 2010c).

This emphasizes the major importance of only a few markets for champagne. One would expect the champagne producers to be working hard to remedy this situation. Asia, and China in particular, are growing quickly in sales for red wine, but champagne and sparkling wines are not keeping pace. India, Russia, Brazil, Mexico, Poland, Canada, Argentina, and Slovakia are another set of strongly developing wine markets, where champagne could take part. Not all of these are growing at the same rate, and all are growing from small bases, but they offer good opportunities for champagne producers to spread their market risk more widely. Especially with the aforementioned growth in sparkling wines, champagne needs to rely less on gaining more penetration in their existing markets and grow the number of consumers in developing markets. This will be especially important as the area for production increases over the next 20 years.

Ownership and structural changes

Probably less important for the short term, but already beginning to create rumblings within the region in the longer term, are the changes to the ownership of grape and wine production. This is occurring at two levels: the major champagne houses, and the small producers. During our visit to Champagne in 2008, several of the principals at major champagne houses as well as some of the growers discussed how important it is for all the players in the region to be able to meet and talk. This is undoubtedly an outcome of the fierce fighting in 1911 and through the mid-1930s, which resulted in the balanced organisation, the CIVC. We heard that growers, producers, and owners of the major houses regularly interact in local shops and bistros. We witnessed a phone call to the director of a major house, which resulted in him leaving the meeting a bit early to discuss an issue with one of his many growers.

This network of personal and community relationships is an important aspect of the strength of the Champagne region, and one of the reasons people and organisations, which are often at odds in other regions, are able to meet and come to terms for the good of the whole region in Champagne. Now, some of the major champagne brands are in the hands of large, publicly held corporations, like LVMH and Pernod Ricard, which are not headquartered in Champagne. Some people said to us that they do not see the employees of these public corporations the same way they see the owner managers of the other houses. There is worry that the fabric of the region will be changed when locals are no longer owner-operators. Perhaps decisions will not be made with the best outcomes for the region in mind, or long-term outcomes will be sacrificed for shorter-term ones. Nothing specific was claimed, but as discussed earlier, most observers agreed that champagne has built some special advantages with its unique structure and collaborative framework among all interested parties.

One could imagine a scenario (though this is strictly an imagined one) where one or more large corporations decide to produce more (or less) wine based on their own needs and profits against the wishes of others in the region. They may decide to buy and develop some of the land to be added to the appellation. They might decide to produce a wine that is a blend of champagne and other regional wines. Any of these or other decisions, which take them out of the agreed actions for the region, could start some rifts or even bring to the surface some that have started already and begin the destruction of this unique structure.

A different but related issue is the thousands of small producers. Many of these producers have children who do not want to continue in the business, or some that do and others that do not. The taxes on inheritance and the high value of land and property in Champagne make the transmission of land difficult. After speaking to some growers we understand that many owners do not live in Champagne, but hire others to manage their property. This problem is not unique to Champagne, but the ramifications could be more severe due to the close-knit structure, both socially and production-wise. A continual rise in non-resident ownership could interact with the issue raised about corporate ownership and management leading to less willingness to cooperate and collaborate.

To be clear, neither of these issues seems to have major effects so far, but they were mentioned while doing the research for this chapter. This means they are in the minds of the local growers and producers and could have effects down the road, which could reduce the effectiveness of the regional branding and production management that now occurs.

Climate change

This is a long-term issue and should not be surprising to anyone. The debates and discussions about the veracity or degree of climate change are far beyond the scope of this chapter. However, many authors and even a dedicated conference in 2007 have discussed the likelihood and impact of climate change on the wine sector. The areas of the greatest predicted change are mainland Europe (where Champagne is), California, and inland Australia. Since the style of wine produced in Champagne is only produced in cool to cold growing areas, the long-term effects of global warming or even local warming could make the region unable to produce the style of wines it is famous for.

Already good-quality sparkling wines are being produced in England in areas of similar soils to Champagne, but until recently they were too cool to ripen the same varieties of grapes. There are rumours that some of the champagne houses are buying land in southern England at 10 per cent of the cost of land in Champagne.

Whatever the truth to the rumours, part of champagne's style is the ability to get flavour from grapes that struggle to ripen enough for still wines. Changes to the climate will certainly affect the ability to make the same style of wine. In the short to medium term, it seems that slightly warmer years are resulting in more vintage-level champagnes and overall better quality as the grapes can ripen just a bit more than in a normal year. If warm years become more commonplace, there will be less wine to blend into these vintages to ensure an appropriate level of acidity and maintain the various house styles.

Possible strategic actions

The conclusion to this chapter is not a set of hard and fast recommendations that will solve the problems of the Champagne region. Most of the issues raised here have been raised in bits and pieces elsewhere and the CIVC and individual players in the region's economy certainly have their own strategies and tactics in place. However, the long-term problem of the slow erosion of the luxury status of the champagne brand, due to price reductions and competition, is the key issue that must be faced. This will be the major portion of the strategy discussion.

There is not much control the CIVC can have over individual grower sales of hoarded bottles to major retailers or even as their own discounted brands. The best action for the region is to maintain the luxury status so that everyone continues to receive good prices for their production and even BOB and the lower-priced grower brands maintain their high perceived value. The expansion of the market for champagne is a given, and one the CIVC and the major houses are already developing, though perhaps a bit too slowly. It is always easier to keep knocking on doors that are already open, where you have distribution and partnerships, than to develop new ones. More effort needs to be pushed into the whole range of alternate markets for two reasons: one, it reduces the possible effects of economic or other events in the major markets of Europe and the USA; and two, growing the base reduces the surplus and provides upward price pressure across all markets. With more markets vying for a limited supply, the luxury status and high price for champagne can continue.

As this is a marketing/branding chapter, we don't have much to say about climate change or structural issues in Champagne. Obviously these could become major issues if not monitored and dealt with early rather than as emergency measures. The CIVC and the major houses need to be very aware of the social and political networks that make the region able to act as a unit in most situations and make sure it is maintained. The continued collaborative structure of the region is necessary to implement the ideas that follow in the section on maintaining the luxury status for champagne.

Growing the market for champagne

Numerous empirical studies in brand purchase and repeat purchase, i.e. loyalty, show that increasing penetration is the only way to grow market share and overall sales (see Sharp (2010) for a list of references and a good summary of the research). There is little support for growing sales and market share by getting already heavy or regular consumers to buy more. There is a lot of evidence that shows the vast majority of growth comes from gaining light or irregular buyers and non-buyers to purchase. This may seem self-evident, but many producers spend too much effort and money trying to maintain or increase sales by regular and heavy buyers, rather than focusing on new or light consumers. Champagne needs to follow this path, if they want to increase overall sales.

What does this mean specifically? As noted in the section about narrow distribution, it means the CIVC and the producers selling directly to the market need to increase the number of countries or areas where champagne is promoted. If budgets are tight, it means reducing some budgets from existing markets and allocating it to newer and developing markets. In some areas it will mean gaining distribution, or revising distribution to partners that can increase the breadth of availability. This does not mean entering low-end retail channels as will be discussed further below in the section on pricing.

From a target market perspective, growing the penetration means working to ensure more of the types of drinkers that fit the champagne profile are engaged and contacted. We are not advocating mass media campaigning, but still communication needs to be extended in both existing and developing markets to the eligible target market. Specifically this means reducing media efforts that focus on loyal existing consumers, such as direct mail, email, social media, and websites. These are basically reminders and enforcers of awareness and recognition among regular consumers. If they are inexpensive, keep them. If these are too costly, use the money saved to widen the promotion targets.

An interesting area to consider is the long-term focus of champagne on occasion-based celebration. It is evident that the CIVC and major houses are trying to move champagne from being associated only with celebration to a broader positioning as an aperitif or even as a food wine. This change of positioning could be even stronger. Certainly some of the sparkling wine competitors are trying to expand the usage occasions for the category and this could help champagne as well. Enlarging the usage situation plays to the fact of increasing penetration, which is the only way to grow the champagne brand. One example could be to spend some efforts on increasing the image of aspiration and the collectability of champagne to have it compete more directly with Bordeaux wine in China. Focus could be made on five-star restaurants in key cities to promote the wider use of champagne and perhaps even link it to Chinese foods, which may be an easier match than with Bordeaux wines.

Perhaps champagne and major houses can take some hints from how other luxury brands promote and communicate. Mercedes Benz, Rolex, and many other top-end brands use a lot of mass media aimed at high-income markets, such as glossy magazines, airline magazines, art and theatre sponsorships. They don't advertise in specialty trade magazines, and this makes sense for champagne; don't focus on wine or wine-based communications, but expand the reach to high-income earners as broadly as possible. Some of this broad reach will serve as reminders to existing consumers, but mainly it will hit light or irregular buyers of champagne. Of course there will be a lot of leakage in expanding the communications platform to a wider base of potential consumers, but as long as the image portrayed is of luxury and high-end, it will only reinforce the long-term position and growth potential.

Pricing issues

It is simple. Champagne must retain and even increase its luxury pricing to retain its long-term brand image and position. If the producers and the CIVC merely want to sell more champagne and super-premium pricing is not the long-term objective, then reducing the prices will increase overall penetration and usage. Champagne does have a unique style and taste, but research shows that many consumers are not very good at tasting subtle or even not-so-subtle flavours (Mueller *et al.*, 2010). They react much more strongly to price and packaging cues. The CIVC and champagne producers cannot expect consumers to buy the wine merely for the taste. This is in line with current practice, but as noted above there are worrying signs of discounting and 'temporary' price reductions.

Pricing research shows that consumers quickly adapt to price changes and that discount prices soon become the expected price. Producers should resist as much as possible retailer attempts at discounting and special promotions. Unfortunately so much wine is now sold through multiple retailers that it is nearly impossible to ignore this channel if producers want to increase penetration in existing or developing markets. However, if champagne is to retain its image, then any type of price reduction is going to erode it. Of course this is easy to write and much harder to enforce among producers, especially any that are facing short-term cash-flow problems. Perhaps some seminars and empirical evidence showing the deleterious effects of price reduction could help sway producers to be more circumspect.

Some producers may argue that they have high-end brands within their portfolios and are expanding penetration by launching lower priced champagnes or even providing wine to retailer's BOBs. However, at the lower end, champagnes are now coming too close to other sparkling wines in price and soon there is a real danger of the difference being lost. In the long run, champagne has to decide what its international positioning is before it can develop the proper strategies.

Conclusion

Champagne has perhaps the strongest and overall highest-priced territorial brand among all wine-producing regions. This is the result of a long history of luxury promotion accompanied by astute management and a bit of luck. However, the rest of the world is catching up at the same time that the financial recession and retailer power have begun to force some prices down. It is possible to have a relatively small number of super high-end producers and a majority of lower-priced offerings in the regional portfolio as in Bordeaux. This is relatively easy to develop, but most likely it would result in lower average prices along the whole production and marketing channel. The Champenois need to decide what the future positioning is for their regional brand. The future decision on opening new land will decide how big production will become, and then marketing will have to work with this level of production to either maintain exclusiveness or sell some wines at lower prices. Maintaining the exclusive position and price for champagnes means growing the market enough to absorb increases in production at existing or higher prices. Champagne must retain slightly more demand than supply and the only way to do this is to expand the number of consumers in existing and developing markets. This is entirely feasible because champagne sales are still focused on a few countries and a relatively few regular consumers. Extending the usage occasions and the countries accepting and demanding champagne as a luxury good is the way forward.

9 Distributing champagne

Olivier Dusautoir and Steve Charters

Introduction

The distribution of champagne is the link between the place of its preparation and where it is consumed. In this chapter, we will examine not only different distribution channels but also the role of the different intermediaries who control the channels by answering the following questions:

- Where can you obtain champagne today?
- Who are the stakeholders which enable the flow of champagne from a cellar in the region to the consumer?
- What are the criteria by which the producers of champagne choose their distribution system?

We will also examine how the distribution channels used by growers often differ from those used by the houses and the differences in what makes a French distribution network compared to export. However, there are two preliminary issues which are significant: first, the relationship of champagne to wine in distribution, and second how its role as a luxury product affects its distribution.

Champagne and the distribution channels for wine

Does champagne benefit from a specific form of distribution of its own, or can it be distributed like all other wines? Because of its reputation and image, champagne has particular symbolic meaning and characteristics. So do champagne producers adopt different networks and distribution channels from those used for other wines? Effectively the answer to this question is 'no', nor has it ever been the case in the past. However rich or famous the consumers of champagne may be, its method of distribution is the one traditionally followed for all wines.

In the eyes of many consumers throughout the world, champagne remains the essence of France, a unique and magical symbol of contemporary French elegance. Nevertheless, its privileged status linked to its history, its geographical origin and method of preparation, all of which have been maintained for a long time by the different actors of the industry and the region, changes nothing about the way in which it is distributed. There are several explanations for this.

First, in the past, champagne producers, négociants, cooperatives and independent growers have always used the same commercial intermediaries as other wine producers to sell their bottles (both in France and abroad), and the same means to promote the wine that the other producers employ.

It is true that for the wine trade champagne is regarded as a product apart, because of the image it projects, but it does belong to a category of wines which includes direct and indirect competitors. Recent years have seen the development of the category, with Italian, Spanish and New World sparkling wines of high quality, carefully presented in attractive bottles, offered at high prices and positioned without hesitation in the same market as champagne has always sought. This has reinforced the trade perception that champagne is only the first amongst equals. The appearance of these new competitors and their undeniable success in challenging the sense of the privileged place of champagne means that increasingly demanding consumers (and the wine industry) are becoming more fluid in their choice and less loyal. Additionally, in France the growth of some of the sparkling wines traditionally regarded as 'under-champagnes' (*crémants*) has only served to distort further champagne's image. It is now the case that some champagnes can be found at lower prices than these other wines. Although these low-priced champagnes may only appear at certain times, and whatever the reasons for such a pricing policy – which may be entirely reasonable – the impact on the consumer's perception of the status, function and quality of the product is problematic. This begs the question of why the wine trade continues to treat champagne differently from all the other items in the product category in such a competitive market.

For these reasons and others, and despite the significant and continuing communication programmes on the part of all the actors of the region and especially the CIVC, champagne follows the same channels of distribution used by other wines, both renowned and unknown.

Champagne and the distribution of luxury products

There is a debate between those who consider that champagne is a luxury product and those who feel it is no more than a wine – even though it may be an exceptionally good one. The aim of this chapter is not to determine this issue, but it is clear that this disagreement does not have a major impact on how champagne is distributed. It is also worth noting that whilst it is not universally accepted in the region that champagne is a luxury good, the majority of actors there, including vignerons, do believe that it is (Charters & Menival, 2009). This belief is mirrored by consumers, at least in France (Anon., 2003), and almost certainly in other markets.

We can start with a general comment about distribution of luxury goods generally. Authenticity is one of the key elements in the positioning of luxury products (Beverland, 2006). As Beverland (2006) has noted, one of the aspects of authenticity with wine is the renunciation of the typical industrialized techniques and crude commercial motives of the modern age. Yet slick distribution may contradict that story and appear coarsely profit-focused. In this way distribution may be an aspect of dealing with the product that runs counter to its perceived prestige and its exclusivity – so distribution needs to be handled carefully to ensure it does not undermine that image.

It has been suggested that – at least in the wine industry – luxury distribution strategies have been emergent, so that companies have taken advantage of situations as they arise (Beverland, 2003). Certainly the energetic promotion of the wines by past brand heroes, such as Charles Heidsieck, have operated in this way. Historically the positioning of champagne moved away from being a mere commodity to something sold in 'enchanted places' – linked in part to the rise of the specialist and department stores which were designed to provide customers with an experience rather than just access to products (Williams, 1982). This association with specialist retailing underlined the separation of the product from the everyday and the mundane; in this way distribution has been used to reinforce the overall brand image, and the wine's association with situations and experiences rather than mere liquid refreshment. It is interesting to ponder how this will be affected by the large-scale move into supermarkets which has taken place over the last few decades (see below). Linked to this is the comment by Vigneron and Johnson (1999) that luxury brands face an internal contradiction when they increase awareness of their product and sales. Luxury is based on scarcity; the more successful a luxury champagne is, the more that is produced, and the less scarce it is. Brands which once targeted the richest consumers are now very widely distributed. The development of Dom Pérignon over the last decade is testament to this; it has been estimated that at least five million bottles are made each year, it is now ubiquitous in airport duty-free shopping, and can even be purchased in French supermarkets – yet retains its reputation as one of the most luxurious (and thus scarce) and high-class champagnes available.

It is also clear that luxury wines operate a highly targeted distribution strategy (see, for instance, the focus on duty-free shopping over the last few decades). This targeting means that champagne uses very specialized distribution channels (Beverland, 2004).

However, it is possible that there is a conflict between various types of champagne and the way that they are distributed. It has been suggested that consumers may focus on either 'package recognition' or 'product recognition' of luxury wines (Muraz, 2010). The former is appropriate for high-volume brands targeted at a general audience, and needs to be attractively packaged but not necessarily memorizable. The latter is suitable for specialist products aimed at the connoisseur, and will benefit from being discreetly packaged (in line with apparent authenticity). Which of these is adopted will have an impact on the distribution policy of the brand owners and how consumers respond to the product on the shelves (ibid.).

Categories of distribution

Distribution operates, both in France and export markets, within two primary channels: the retail trade where you buy champagne to drink at home, and also consumption outside the home where champagne is consumed on the spot. To talk of the distribution system for champagne thus includes terms such as 'distribution channels' and 'distribution networks'; 'off trade' and 'on trade'. It is essential to distinguish between all of these terms.

- Distribution channels correspond to points of sale where the consumer can obtain champagne. Chains of hypermarkets, restaurants and independent wine merchants are all distribution channels. Each champagne producer decides whether or not to be present in each of these based on criteria defined in their strategy – including positioning and targeting.
- Distribution networks include all intermediaries, people and companies, chosen by a producer to commercialize its champagne in different circuits. Agents, distributors, importers, subsidiaries and joint ventures abroad all form this network. Here again, négociants or producers choose to use a particular intermediary to sell their champagne for their size, their strategy and their financial means.
- The off-trade market refers to the set of points of sale where you buy a bottle for consumption away from the point of sale. This includes supermarkets, retailers and the independent wine merchants; this is known as the retail trade.
- The on-trade market defines the set of points of sale where the champagne is purchased and also consumed on the spot. Restaurants, bars, hotels, night clubs and cabarets all form this market, where consumption occurs outside the home. Further, as with any product which is marketed these days, champagne can be marketed business to business, from a business to a consumer or from one consumer to another – which tends to be online sales and is very significant for the exchange of champagne and in the secondary (auction) market.

The markets for champagne

The domestic market is the most significant for champagne, representing 61.7 per cent of total sales in 2009 (although some of those sales will be to foreign visitors who take the wine back to their own country, including at least 3 million bottles which go to Belgium). Whilst there are some figures for France, it is difficult to know the split of global sales of champagne by distribution channels for export. Each champagne house which has that information through its distribution network jealously guards the details. In France, in 2007, the champagne market was segmented as follows: 37 per cent of sales were direct to individuals, 30 per cent direct to retail, 9 per cent Horeca[1] circuits, 8 per cent in wine shops and other specialty stores, 9 per cent to wholesalers and 7 per cent directly to businesses (CIVC, 2007a).

Champagne is distributed in most countries throughout the world – but sales are concentrated in a few major markets, with almost 78 per cent of shipments to the ten most significant of these (see Table 9.1). The period from 2001 to 2008 saw a boom in sales, with a record number of 332 million bottles shipped in 2007. This growth was powered by a strong performance in the major importing countries, (e.g. shipments to the United Kingdom rose from 25 million bottles to over 39 million in 2007). At the same time there was a dramatic rise in consumption in new markets. China and Russia are regularly quoted in this context as examples of this growth but they are not alone. In 2007 countries as diverse as Argentina, New Zealand, Angola and Slovenia all registered a rise in imports of over 70 per cent compared with 2006.

Retail distribution and home consumption

Multiple supermarket chains

In France and export, retail remains the most important form of sales of champagne. In France, approximately 34 per cent of the volume of champagne is sold in supermarkets (hard discount included). In this channel, négociants

Table 9.1 The ten major export markets for champagne, 2008–2009

Country	2008 (bottles)	2009 (bottles)	Change (%)	World share	Export share
United Kingdom	35,984,574	30,523,359	–15.18	10.41%	27.16%
USA	17,193,526	12,552,070	–26.99	4.28%	11.17%
Germany	11,573,597	10,947,967	–5.40	3.73%	9.74%
Belgium	9,910,581	8,168,385	–17.58	2.78%	7.27%
Italy	9,438,811	6,803,419	–27.92	2.32%	6.05%
Japan	8,332,233	5,133,802	–38.39	1.75%	4.57%
Switzerland	5,439,009	4,846,500	–10.90	1.65%	4.32%
Spain	4,090,505	2,979,997	–27.16	1.02%	2.65%
Australia	3,648,022	2,931,941	–19.65	1.00%	2.61%
Netherlands	3,511,889	2,735,858	–22.10	0.93%	2.43%

Source: Data from the CIVC.

represent over 80 per cent of volume, cooperatives around 15 per cent. Less than 5 per cent of the champagne bottles on the shelves come from growers, even though they represent nearly 40 per cent of French sales.

Almost all négociants seek to penetrate the various multiple supermarket chains in France and abroad either directly for their own brands, or by supplying BOBs. Their aim is to have widespread coverage and high visibility to ensure maximum sales. A few houses, however, prefer to avoid this circuit, either because they lack the volume that is necessary to maintain continuous supply or to preserve their image by avoiding such mass-distribution outlets. However, for the celebrations at the end of the year even the most prestigious brands are present on the supermarket shelves in France and abroad.

Access to supermarket distribution is not available to everyone. Beyond the constraints of volume, strict specifications and difficult negotiations are obstacles precluding the vast majority of small producers of champagne from entering this circuit. For those who do work with supermarkets and hypermarkets, where their presence on the shelves of these outlets usually guarantees their sales of a reasonable volume, they have to deal with the constant demands of their retail customers and often find it hard to control the final sales price to the consumer. Crucially it is important to remember that multiple chains do not share the same commitment to the reputation of champagne as a category and maintaining its overall image and value, especially when they deal with a single supplier. They are (quite reasonably) only interested in optimizing their profit. With this goes a fairly short-term focus – not the long-term development of brand equity for one brand, nor for the region as a whole. There is therefore a potential conflict between not only the positioning of one individual brand and the aims of the distributors, but also between the retail outlet and the image and reputation of champagne as a whole. The multiple grocers, because of their buying power (deriving from substantial economies of scale), thus have equivalent power to shape the long-term position of champagne as the producers and the CIVC themselves.

The champagne houses and large cooperatives use their key account managers, the specialists in dealing with important clients such as the large retailers, who are responsible for negotiating with the buyers of each outlet. In a more modest enterprise, it is often the owner or manager who deals directly with the customer. Negotiation can be done at both national and regional level depending on the internal organization of each brand.

It is important to note that cash-and-carry stores, although designed to supply retail stores and restaurants, are commercially processed by the houses like other retailers and are managed by the same account managers. The business approach to these outlets is substantially the same.

Hard discount

In France hard discount stores account for more than 10 per cent of large volume distribution, and they are often very significant elsewhere, such as in Germany. While, generally speaking, the major brands do not want to be stocked in the discounters for fear of devaluing their image with consumers, it is possible to find bottles of champagne there. These outlets are essentially the domain of a few, very cheap, private labels (BOBs). In terms of the commercial approach, it is also the key account managers of the négociants who manage the negotiations with the hard discount retailers.

Note that in tough economic times, sales in this segment of distribution may increase significantly (see Chapter 4 for the economic and reputation impact of this). In export, the hard-discount chains are also targeted by those operators looking to destock surplus wine at low prices, again most often through private labels. The consequent reduction in price is a key issue affecting the image of champagne – and indeed, the presence of champagne generally in hard discount stores and its impact on the overall reputation of the product must be considered as an uncertain element in the future success of the wine.

General retail

This includes all stores or shops where you can buy champagne. They are of several types, including wine merchants, high-end food outlets (delicatessens), grocery and convenience shops and department stores.

The wine shop, vintner or merchant is a specialist outlet dealing mainly in wines and spirits. All such wine shops offer champagne. The vintner is sought not only by the big brands but also by the small champagne producers – especially growers – whose wine they tend to prefer. The vintner wants to differentiate itself by offering a champagne which is more original, more authentic and more rare than the large brands which are also available at lower prices in supermarkets. The independent merchant is supplied either directly by the producer (in France and some surrounding countries) or through a wholesaler. Wine merchants offer wine, but more importantly they advise and inform their clients – a key area of added value. For this reason, suppliers of champagne attach great importance to staff training and information supplied to such stores, and have to visit them regularly. It is in the independent merchant that unusual champagnes are most often found, particularly vintage wines. Inevitably, because of the lack of economies of scale, the price of champagne in these outlets is higher than in supermarkets. Consequently, and to tap into this specialist market, some houses develop one or more champagnes in their range, which are destined only for these independent merchants.

The delicatessen, like the wine merchant, selects its champagnes on criteria of image, but equally based on notions such as terroir and authenticity. The concept of service and advice is just as important. Delicatessens are clearly less significant an outlet for champagne overall than merchants, but they still supply the rarest and most expensive vintages. In France and other countries, the delicatessen can be independent, or be part of a chain or be housed within a department store such as the famous Bon Marché in Paris, Harrods in London, or Takashimaya in Japan. Besides the major brands of wine and champagne, gourmet food stores often offer BOB champagnes as well – for example with Hédiard or Fauchon in France or Harrods in the United Kingdom. Because of the margins, as well as the impact on the wine's image, just as with the independent wine merchants, this type of outlet is cherished by its suppliers.

In all major western cities the traditional grocery store has been disappearing for many years, being replaced by convenience stores, which generally belong to large retail chains. The grocery usually buys from a wholesaler or directly through cash-and-carry. Meanwhile the convenience store is a distribution outlet that has grown rapidly in recent years, especially in big cities. In Tokyo, for example, strings of 'combined stores' (such as 7/11, am/pm, Family Mart), compete openly on every corner. Around the world these small shops are owned mainly by large distribution groups. For these types of stores, negotiations take place with the buyers of each of the groups. It is the task of the key account manager of the house in France, and that of the importer abroad. Traditional groceries and convenience stores generally offer very little champagne, most of which is limited to a few well-known brands (at least outside France) whose price is relatively high.

The presence of champagne in department stores is beneficial for major brands but also for some of the growers who can access them more easily than the supermarkets, at least in France. The offer is substantially the same as in delicatessens, and the features of distribution are quite similar. Prices are again relatively high but this type of outlet is frequented by a clientele whose purchasing power is substantial, so that price is less of an issue; indeed, as suggested in Chapter 2, a high price may actually be beneficial, as it enhances the reputation of the brand.

Direct sales

With direct sales to customers, we address a market segment and distribution process which is radically different from those we have previously considered. In France this market represents almost 40 per cent of sales of champagne but mainly involves the growers, whose business focuses primarily on this segment, through direct sales or mail order as well as that of sales at the property resulting from the growth of wine tourism in Champagne. The growers therefore use their address lists to sell their output at prices which are often more attractive for the customer and still profitable for the producer. Additionally they may complement these direct sales by also dealing with restaurants and, a more recent phenomenon, with online sales.

The houses also have their records of important customers who they contact regularly and especially at the end of the year to make specific offers of wines at attractive prices. It is worth noting that the houses, as well as some smaller producers, actively look for companies to target to offer their champagne for parties, canteens and end-of-year gifts, etc. However, it is important that the houses are not seen to undercut their other distributors. It is interesting to note that Moët et Chandon non-vintage champagne, for instance, is more expensive to purchase at its cellar door shop in Epernay than in most of the supermarkets to be found within a radius of a few kilometres in the same town. Direct sales are generally less well developed for export markets however, for the same reason – most producers cannot afford to bypass the local distribution chain by selling directly; their importers would object to being undercut, and end the relationship.

For the small producers, the individual customer is the core of their business. To become well-known, they have to devote their personal energy to maintaining their existing customers and working tirelessly for new clients; this is often by participating in trade shows at a regional, national or international level.

Online sales

Distance selling, as traditionally practised through mail-order or catalogues, now includes online sales, which are growing in importance every day. The wine market on the internet continues to rise with a growth rate of 31 per cent in 2007, 34 per cent in 2008 and 35 per cent for 2009. In France alone it was projected to become worth over 300 million euros by 2010 and there are nearly 300 organizations concerned (Findawine, 2009). No reliable statistics are available for measuring the volume of champagne sold on the web, but no doubt the trend for champagne, as for other wines, will remain on the rise.

The consumer can buy champagne online in several ways:

- Directly from the site of the producer if it sells online. Few large houses engage in direct online sales for two major reasons: logistics and price. Logistics, as quantities are often modest and the company ill-equipped for the delivery of such small volumes. Paradoxically, small producers know how to manage this better because they have become used to delivering just a few bottles or cartons to individuals. Price is again a deterrent because of the risk of upsetting other distribution channels which the company uses. It is important to remember also that a website crosses borders and may have an impact on distributors in other countries.
- From the websites of major stores. Most major supermarkets have their own site, as do some chain stores and many wine merchants.
- From online sites which were established independently of any real-world outlet. These may be general retailers or specialized wine sellers, some of which have existed for several years and offer a wide variety of champagnes.

Finally, there is the recent appearance of several sites dedicated solely to champagne, and from which it is possible not only to buy but also to engage with a community of champagne lovers and to learn and participate in discussions. See, for example, the Champagne Gallery in Australia (www. champagnegallery.com.au), or Madaboutbubbly in the United Kingdom and France (www.madaboutbubbly.com).

As well as consumers, the wine trade also has the option to buy champagne at commercial sites, some of which are reserved only for professionals. These commercial sites are naturally in contact with the champagne houses from whom they buy, often only small volumes. Essentially, however, these enterprises operate in exactly the same way as other intermediaries.

Consumption outside the home

This market is essential for any producer wishing to develop its brand image by giving maximum visibility to their label. As far as the domestic market is concerned, whilst it accounts for less than 10 per cent of the volume of champagne sold, it remains key. Internationally, the approach is exactly the same although in many countries (especially emerging markets) the volume sold on-premise is much more substantial. Each importer must place the champagne for which they are responsible in this area of distribution based on the brand strategy they have developed, although certain labels are primarily intended for retailers and will never get on a restaurant or night-club list.

At the high end of the Horeca channel the approach of the producer or importer is often the same as that used with independent wine merchants. They suggest vintage champagnes or special *cuvées* that are not found elsewhere, especially important at this level for promoting the image of the wine. This channel includes restaurants, hotels, cafes and pubs as well as discotheques, night clubs and other bars. These are attractive for champagne producers because of their wealthy and opinion leading clientele – even if they may exist in a world of bling-bling.

Restaurants – of various types

Everyday restaurants, bistros and coffee shops often offer one or two brands – particularly in France. They may buy grower wines directly from the producer, while for more traditional brands, they take either a wholesaler or they buy at cash-and-carry. Pricing policy will be in line with the price level offered by the restaurant for meals generally. Restaurants with a more traditional or classic approach in which wine is an integral part of the total product, offer a wider selection. Négociant wines and grower champagnes may be included together, including some vintage and special *cuvées*.

The most prestigious restaurants, are obviously a target for all the *grandes marques* (best-known most-prestigious brands), which aspire to be well placed on the wine list. If this segment is less buoyant in times of economic crisis it remains highly coveted because it is an obvious vehicle for reinforcing the brand's image of prestige. The prices are mostly high; indeed, the sector has been accused of wanting to make margins on champagne so high that sales suffer significantly. On wine lists of this level of restaurant one can find most major brands with vintage wines and special *cuvées* being especially important. The sales manager charged with these customers has to work very closely with them, given their value, by visiting regularly and organizing training sessions and tastings for their staff. They do not take the same approach as those who sell to supermarkets, and are trained to adopt different sales methods.

Other on-premise outlets

Hotels follow similar types of classification. There are 'small' hotels without food and only a bar, which must have at least one champagne on offer. Additionally there are hotels with restaurants which follow the same processes for supply as traditional restaurants. Finally there are the prestigious, international chains for business people, or luxury hotels located in the most famous resorts in the world. As with the top-level restaurants, they are courted in the same way by the vignerons and the houses, not just to be listed in the hotel bars and restaurants but also the mini-bars.

Both in France and other countries the major suppliers pursue the same approach for these categories. There is fierce competition to be the champagne of the week or month and to get special promotions. However, obtaining this visibility is time-consuming and the negotiations are hard. This highlights one of the key problems with the distribution of champagne – the time-intensive nature of maintaining the product's image and reputation. To succeed in being the 'house champagne' of a very-high-class hotel is not simple and is not necessarily very profitable because the negotiations are tough. The brand has to choose between volume, profitability or the visibility and image that can result from such a deal.

Champagne works hard to promote the idea that there cannot be a party if there is no champagne. Again, this sector – clubs and late-night bars – is highly coveted by the brands of champagne, yet again there are different types of institutions that will not be 'worked' in the same way.

Discotheques frequented by a young clientele tend to provide a limited selection of champagne by the bottle. These establishments are the object of hard-sell tactics by those seeking exclusivity. A different type of business is the night clubs and bars which are frequented by a clientele which may be young but has high spending power who often do not count what they spend. Again the major brands target these places, with a range of styles. The danger, however, is that mass consumption of such good wines by a client group who pay little attention to what they are drinking other than the status it affords will undermine the brand's long-term position, in comparison with more careful consumption by connoisseurs. Finally, there is a category of ultra-trendy night clubs where for many years only the best champagnes have been drunk. All these kinds of clubs and bars are naturally reserved for large-volume brands whose fame transcends borders. Few small producers have the time or means to provide the support needed to sustain their wines in such establishments – nor would vignerons, for example, have wines of such prestige that they would naturally appeal to such a clientele.

The 'Horeca' market is in general a difficult market for champagne houses. As we have said, the time spent exploring, visiting customers and convincing them to buy and promote the wine is substantial and often only small quantities are involved. In addition, the customer is fickle and establishments open and close at a rapid rate. Finally, delays in payment are sometimes long and the risks of non-payments more frequent than with other outlets. Yet, for the region as a whole it is significant that one cannot imagine a restaurant, bar, hotel, nightclub or private club without champagne – and it is crucial for the image of the region and all champagne brands that the larger houses especially continue to work this market.

The market for travellers

Travel is increasingly associated with champagne. Either travellers tend to be tourists, seeking an experience (and not a mere service) which a perceived fine wine can enhance, or they tend to be business people who may have good expense budgets, the need to feel pampered whilst they are travelling for work and are very often high-income earners (and therefore attractive long-term customers). Dealing with this market is again about reputation, image and position more than merely just one more outlet to sell additional champagne.

Duty-free sales are an integral part of champagne distribution. Airports around the world have now become tax-free shops; passengers are captive yet at the same time the development of travel as an experience rather than merely a service (Gilmore & Pine, 2002) means that travel companies are keen to offer more than merely a waiting or stopover point. Passengers with time on their hands are thus encouraged to focus on the most prestigious brands – including, given its luxury connotations – champagne.

The duty-free outlet is a marketplace for the biggest brands, and thus closed to most small producers. Due to space reasons, operators limit their offers to a few brands chosen from amongst the most famous – this being the best way to maximize sales given a short visit. Moreover, this area is not always profitable. Operators at airports often pay a high rent so they are trying to recover costs from the margin of the products they sell. In fact they can sell at a higher price than that charged 'in town' – despite the supposed duty-free nature of the sale. Further, when the purchase price is set it is often at the expense of producers and other suppliers who, feeling the need for visibility, want to be present on the shelves of these luxury shops.

Within airports, the champagne houses also negotiate their presence in airline lounges, where travellers in transit or waiting will sometimes spend several hours. These can be real showcases for brands and all lounges tend to have a champagne bar.

Listing by airlines is also highly coveted. The approach taken by a brand manager is often the same as the development of a house champagne for a great hotel. Two factors drive this line of business: the volumes and again (as always) visibility – especially as the airline will probably only stock one champagne in business class, and there is therefore a captive market. The process of negotiating with an airline is relatively simple. The carrier calls for tenders from various houses it has targeted as being 'worthy' of being on board their aircraft. The tender can relate to the 'first class' and/or 'business class' or occasionally 'economy class' for small bottles, although this is increasingly uncommon. The champagne house prepares a tender based on the criteria requested. If selected, the wines will be evaluated by the company's tasting panel (usually featuring some eminent wine tasters and critics). Following their recommendations further negotiations take place between the airline's buyer and one or more suppliers (e.g. over price, volume, availability, frequency and locations of deliveries). The advantage to a supplier of this listing is that volumes are generally consistent and run into tens of thousands of bottles; however, profitability is not always high. For these same reasons, this market is totally closed to small producers who have in any case neither the volumes nor the reputation necessary to be eligible to be listed.

The principle is similar for the railways, cruise lines and luxury ferry companies. Champagne is present in any travel enterprise which has pretensions to offer a quality service.

The structure of champagne distribution

As noted in the introduction, the distribution of champagne follows the same lines as wines and spirits and has no reason to seek alternative channels or processes, but the AOC champagne is certainly the only wine to be distributed in all outlets available, as detailed above. Who, then, are the stakeholders that enable the flow of champagne from a cellar somewhere at the foot of *Montagne de Reims* or the *Côte des Blancs* to a café in Paris, a restaurant in New York, a London supermarket, a wine bar in Milan or just the consumer's own table?

The distribution network, that is to say the business or individuals used by the houses or growers, varies depending on the size of the producer, the position it wants to have, the target market it has chosen and of course the determination and the means it has to grow. Moreover, while many small or medium-sized producers cannot or do not know how to handle exports, some of the others have quietly developed their own niche alongside the major brands.

The large groups, with their own négociant businesses and certain cooperatives or unions of cooperatives with their own brands, generally have a commercial network consisting of their own sales representatives, specializing in certain sectors of activity (retail, Horeca, duty-free, business and private clients). In France, in certain geographic sectors, they may use the services of an agent, often exclusively, to represent their brand. Meanwhile, in export markets the major groups have long-installed distribution subsidiaries in key markets. These subsidiaries source champagne from the parent company to be sold locally.

Négociants which have no subsidiaries (which may include some of the largest houses) will use their export managers to find one or more distributors in each country targeted for exports. The importer will be identified and recruited according to criteria and strategy developed by the manufacturer or brand. This is also the method generally adopted by the growers, although for the small vignerons the wine-maker–proprietor is often left to do everything involved in distribution – as well as making and marketing the wine.

To cover the so-called second-tier markets (that is those of less significance and taking lower volumes), most use agents to cover the territory for them, who are paid by commission. Meanwhile some houses, whose structure, strategy and resources permit, form joint ventures for distribution with a local partner or with other producers of wine or spirits whose products, business strategy and positioning are especially aligned to theirs.

It is thus clear that in the world of champagne all possible scenarios exist. Some groups have moved from a policy of subsidiaries to a joint venture with other brands and then later return to the system of subsidiaries. A house may even base an export manager overseas in order to facilitate better contacts with the local trade. However, it is also the case that because champagne has global coverage, all types of distribution must be dealt with. A large champagne house cannot pick and choose its markets; if it wishes to maintain its global image then it has to be in the USA, where there is a complex three-tier distribution system in each state, in Japan where personal relationships can make or break effective importing and in other key markets each with their attendant complexities.

Problems with the distribution of champagne

In order to provide a comprehensive overview of champagne distribution it is necessary to mention some of the more unorthodox and problematic routes that a bottle can take. These problems occur in part because of the value and perceived luxury status of champagne, which make it desirable and therefore encourage people to find ways of obtaining it legally and also because as a wine and a luxury product it is often subject to high levels of taxation which inevitably encourages evasion.

Smuggling, which involves passing the champagne across the border illegally without paying import taxes has been common in the past, and still exists in some tightly controlled markets. More significant for the producers is the parallel market, which is used to bypass established distribution channels. Broadly this involves an importer sourcing the wine not from France but from a third country where controls are laxer or duty lower, and then offering the wine to other outlets or direct to consumers. This has been a particular problem in the Australian market over recent years, with supplies of cheap champagne sourced by unlicensed agents from Asia or Europe. Local distributors have been putting pressure on their principals to end this by taking action against the importers in the third countries who have allowed the wines to be sold on to Australia.

In addition, there is also counterfeit champagne. In 2009 a mafia network in Italy was discovered to have been producing false bottles of champagne, some of which were sold in the United Kingdom. Over 25,000 bottles of fake champagne were confiscated but it was estimated that 300,000 had been produced and sold, even though their labelling was evidently not that of traditional champagnes (Anon., 2009). However, whilst this is fraudulent and annoying for the Champenois, it can also be seen as the price of success.

A further problem in a similar vein, yet nevertheless legal, relates to the sale of sparkling wine labelled as champagne in the USA. The USA is one of the few important countries in the world not to protect in full some European territorial brands (amongst which a number of wines feature, including champagne), and refuse to force their domestic producers to give up the use of those generic titles. An agreement between the USA and the European Union allowed an exemption in the use of these names to businesses which had a pre-existing brand labelled generically. The CIVC responded with a campaign attempting to explain why territorially based products should be protected. In addition, the European Union has at times impounded and destroyed bottles of sparkling wine labelled in this way at European ports when the wine was in transit to third countries.

Conclusion

By what criteria do champagne businesses choose their distribution system? How do they run a distribution network? The champagne producer must have a consistent strategy from production, through marketing to the consumer which is in keeping with its position in its choice of target markets. In following this it needs to employ a network which shares its strategy, and can manage the brand with image, commercial policies and communication that are always coherent. When hiring an agent or importer, beyond checking its history and solvency, a brand of champagne must check that its portfolio, method of operating and communication are in line with the brands positioning. For this reason houses often develop long-term relationships with importers they trust. Champagne Bollinger, for instance, has used the same importer in Australia for over 150 years.

The activity and dynamism of a distribution network is paramount. Beyond the fact that the relationship with a customer, agent or importer must be maintained all these actors have to be treated as partners and thus more than taken care of. However, a major concern for the future is the perspective of all of these intermediaries. As noted at the commencement of this chapter, champagne is distributed along with wines. It is an exceptional wine, but still one amongst many. Whatever the current outlook of the consumers, it is these intermediaries who are in part responsible for shaping the image and meaning of champagne. If, more and more, they see it as one sparkling wine amongst many, competing with cava and prosecco, then they may project its symbolic uniqueness less and less.

Between the message created by the brand manager in an office to promote their champagne and the sommelier, the salesman in the wine store or restaurant waiter, the road is long and the risk of dilution, distortion, or disappearance of the message is great. This is why the brand, large or small, must take care of all levels and all stages of its distribution network by providing information, training, tasting and each element that will ensure the final interaction with the consumer will be perfect.

Note

1   Horeca is **Ho**tels, **re**staurants and **ca**fés – thus the major on-trade outlets.

Part IV
Managing the industry

10 Creating and sustaining a competitive advantage over time

Managing the delicate balance between value creation and value appropriation

Martin Kunc

Introduction

The region of Champagne has achieved enormous success in the wine industry. The champagne brand is a synonym and a reference for many people, of luxury consumption. While there are strong-brand companies behind the marketing of champagne like Moët et Chandon (part of LVMH) or Vranken Pommery, the sparkling wine produced in more than 34,000 hectares in the area of Epernay-Reims is globally known. However, there is not much information about the actors behind this success. In terms of the sparkling wine industry, the region of Champagne is constituted by a number of key figures. Many of these (e.g. the number of people employed, numbers of houses, vignerons and cooperatives, yield, etc.) have been noted before, but other factors relevant to the value created by champagne include the following.

- Champagne accounts for 12 per cent of sparkling wine sales worldwide.
- The average price per bottle globally is €20.
- There are 200 companies located in the region performing activities related to the industry: machinery, laboratories, glass, cardboard, printing, corks, etc.
- The average price of grapes per kilo is €5.50 which is substantially higher than other wine regions.
- The price of land is at €850,000 per hectare compared with the average value of AOC vineyard in Alsace of €120,000, Languedoc at €11,000, Bordeaux at €64,000, and Burgundy at €87,000 per hectare.

The main producing areas in France are: Bordeaux 134,800 ha, Provence 67,900 ha, the Rhone 39,600 ha, Burgundy 30,000 ha, and Champagne 30,000 ha. However, only champagne has become synonymous with luxury.

This success story can be summarized in a simple phrase: 'a delicate balance between value creation and value appropriation'. This delicate balance, which evolved from learning processes between the social and economic actors in the region, recognizes the intrinsic complexity of social systems and the capability to sustain a competitive advantage in the wine industry over 200 years. In order to identify the factors behind the success of champagne in terms of value creation and value appreciation, I will employ the analysis of Pommery's managers about the success of champagne:

- *History*. Most of the champagne houses were created in the eighteenth century. This is an important differentiating factor with current sparkling wine competitors and one of the most important generators of value.
- *Quality guarantee based on expertise and terroir*. The tradition existing in the region and the unique terroir are responsible for constant quality. Throughout the years, cellar masters, who may work for the same company until retirement, are responsible for the *assemblage* of three different grape varieties: chardonnay, pinot noir and pinot meunier. Each year, the new wine is assembled with wine reserved from previous years (sometimes seven years) to maintain the uniqueness and the concept of each house's sparkling wine. For example, the current cellar master in Pommery is only the ninth since 1856.
- *Real creativity coupled with genuine innovation*. Ongoing R&D with traditional know-how where the cellar master is a key value creator. For example, processes of new yeast development and new styles in champagne are usually developed in the region by diverse actors, from small vignerons (grape growers) to large champagne houses.
- *International recognition, flanked by an expensive marketing budget*. The champagne industry invests 400 million euros in marketing to sustain the brands of their wines. Names like Moët et Chandon, Pommery and Mumm are globally recognized as luxury wines.
- *Controlled appellation of origin*. There is only one sparkling wine that can be named 'champagne'.
- *Premium price*. On average, the price of a bottle of champagne is €20 even including small houses without expensive marketing budgets.

The initial factors are responsible for the creation of value in Champagne, while the last two factors are related to the appropriation of the value created. While this is the current situation, the next section explains how champagne learnt to balance value creation with value appropriation.

Value creation

Value refers to the specific quality of the product as perceived by users in relation to their needs. Such a judgement is subjective and individual specific. Value creation depends on the relative amount that is subjectively realized by a buyer who is the focus of value creation and that this subjective value realization must at least translate into the users' willingness to exchange a monetary amount for the value received (Lepak *et al.*, 2007). Champagne generates more value than other wine region in France and worldwide. The luxury image of champagne has clearly translated into an average price higher than the rest of the wine industry. How was this value created and how is it currently created? The answer to this question is the focus of this section.

History

The main group responsible for the creation of value throughout the history of champagne was the négociants. While they controlled small to medium-size champagne firms, their main interest was in the business of selling champagne (Guy, 2003). Communicating with different clients, from the nobility to the rich commercial social class, was a central occupation of négociants (Guy, 2003). It is interesting to observe the photographs of the English royal family in different activities with the house of Laurent Perrier as a testimony of the linkages between champagne houses and nobility. To ensure supply, the négociants transformed themselves from brokers into merchant–manufacturers, buying large vineyards and investing in bottling and storage facilities. The négociants of champagne offered not simply a fine wine, but an exclusive sparkling white wine (Guy, 2003). The négociants became champagne houses during the French Revolution and aggressively cultivated new clients through personal relationships throughout all Europe.[1]

However, the champagne industry did not become stalled with difficulties or even a pool of diminishing consumers like the nobility. They invested in new processing techniques, transportation and communication networks so as to expand their sales to the new social groups emerging in the late 1800s in Europe and North America (Guy, 2003).

Champagne value emerged as part of the new mass consumer culture generated at the end of the nineteenth century. Luxury prestige wines became part of the culture and national consciousness of France and, as the centre of the new bourgeois, to the whole world. For example, the UK market, and especially the City of London, is one the largest markets outside France. Guy (2003) suggested that champagne was central to a process of rapid change, which included the beginnings of the modern revolution in consumption, in the late 1800s. Champagne was used to delineate social boundaries and its consumption became a basic ritual for membership within certain social groups. As an integral part of numerous traditions and rituals, champagnes became a centrepiece of bourgeois society in every country in the world. Thus, Champagne's investiture with the cultural capital of luxury and success resulted from both its linkage to France's reputation as the pre-eminent capital of the bourgeois world and the wine's own evolving importance as the international marker of social distinction. Sales grew from 5.9 million bottles in 1850 to 28 million in 1900.[2]

While some activities for the creation of value are related to whole processes or activities at organizational level, it is important to understand the role of social networks that are externally directed to detect the needs of customers in some circumstances. In that sense, the social position of the champagne houses in different social networks in diverse countries and social classes allows them to capture and understand changes in customers' needs. The idea of client relationship was central to champagne marketing before any other wine region and branding the wines using the family name of the founder was broadly used as a tool to maintain the relationship with clients (Guy, 2003). The use of the family name was even more important than the appellation 'champagne' as a form of personal assurance of the quality and uniqueness of the product within a distinctive bottle.

However, champagne houses were not alone in creating value through history. The evolving social positioning of Champagne as a region was demonstrated in different ways. For example, Reims cathedral was the place where many French kings were enthroned; Epernay was a royal city with the patronage of Louis XIV. Other examples are the photographs of some members of the English royal family with the founder of Laurent Perrier (noted above) and patronage of the Russian nobility throughout the history of champagne.

Other actors have also been important creating value at different levels. In the following section, I will review the work of cellar masters or oenologists in maintaining quality and facilitating the work of négociants.

Quality guarantee based on expertise and terroir

Champagne offers to consumers a sense of continuity in taste and quality, which was an important innovation as wines usually differ from vintage to vintage. However, the ability to offer continuity, which runs against the idea of vintage and offers a different value proposition, comes from the tradition in the art of *assemblage*, which resides in one very interesting actor: the cellar master or oenologist. Cellar masters work for years with the same house (like the example of Pommery). There are a number of factors for this situation but the *assemblage* of reserve wine dating from many years ago may be one of the causes.

Another aspect is that the art of *assemblage* is transmitted only by apprenticeship. The different interviews offered a common perspective: the knowledge existing in Champagne about the key factor for success, the style of the sparkling wine, is highly tacit. For example, oenologists have to blend many different wines, in some cases from many years ago, in order to obtain a constant quality over time. The art of *assemblage* is very specialized and only in performing the task can it be learned. For example, Pierre Cheval of Champagne Gatinois, a small grape grower and champagne producer, has engaged his son in blending wines for five years and expects he will need yet more time before transmitting the business to his son. The cellar master of Dom Pérignon, who has been in the company for 18 years, has also been working with an apprentice for many years. The long delay in learning the production process is also an important isolating mechanism that avoids the slippage of value and creates a barrier to labour turnover. Cellar masters remain with the same company for many years.

Cellar masters or oenologists also create value by acting creatively to make their job more novel, launching diverse versions of wine. For example, Pommery's cellar master works with four more people who are responsible for each champagne brand style. An important innovation launched by Pommery in 1999 was POP. A new version of POP is launched every year (which includes a new label and a different wine) with diverse themes like 'of the world', 'collector', 'silver', 'gold', 'blue' and 'maxi'. Other new products are seasonal champagnes (Springtime, Summertime, Falltime, Wintertime). Even though they are quite innovative, Pommery still maintains its traditional styles like Brut Royal, Rosé and Grand Cru Millennium.

Real creativity coupled with genuine innovation

Innovations to create value are welcome but under an umbrella determined by the traditions established in the region. One interviewee suggested that people and history is what matters in the region. Strong traditions generated by generations living in the same area and producing the same product were key determinants for the adoption of some innovations generated by some actors and adopted later by the rest of the region.

Champagne was a result of innovation and it maintains this traditional approach even today. Dom Pérignon's purported 'famous discovery' was an incredible innovation for the region when its main consuming market, Paris, switched towards burgundy and bordeaux wines in the 1700s. The Dom Pérignon myth was later employed to distance champagne from the innovations that turned sparkling wine production worldwide into a huge-scale industry (Guy, 2003).

Blending allowed the Champagne region to be innovative. For example, at Champagne Laurent Perrier they claim that initially their champagne was assembled from pinot noir and pinot meunier, but a cellar master subsequently added up to 45 per cent chardonnay in order to improve the elegance, freshness and finesse. However, there is not a common formulation for champagne. Each producer (large or small) has its own style determined by the proportions employed of each grape in the blend. Before this innovation, champagne was drunk at the end of the meal as a dessert wine. This change in taste allowed champagne to reposition itself from consumption at the end of the meal to the beginning of the meal as an aperitif – or even to be part of a meal. This innovation opened a new market for champagne.

Interestingly, the art of blending originated from the complexity of grape production due to weather variability. Champagne is the northernmost wine region which suffers sometimes a late freeze in May. As was maintained by Laurent Perrier, this variability in grape quality led to the development of *assemblage* to maintain wine quality and made the cellar master's sensitivity to reserve wines important in order to maintain a constant quality from different wines and years. While there is variability in grape quality each year, the main value created by the cellar master is to maintain the concept of the product every year. However, tradition is accompanied by investment in R&D with, for example, the development of proprietary yeasts adapted to different type of grapes. Innovations in production techniques have also been very common. For example, the style of vinification changed when they abandoned the oak barrels for the concrete tanks employed by beer brewers (Laurent Perrier visit). Later on they introduced stainless steel. Another innovation in the production process was the introduction of *gyro-palettes*, an automatic process for riddling champagne bottles in large quantity, mainly employed by mass-market champagne producers. However, many houses still maintain their process of riddling manually inside large underground tunnels for many reasons: different bottle shapes, tradition or exclusiveness.

Other innovations like new bottles and packaging were common in the history of champagne. The development by Pommery of POP has already been noted. This is a small bottle of champagne (200 ml), with different and new labels every year. This innovation opened a completely new market segment in the youth market as it was sold through night clubs and disco-theques. However, some new types of champagne, like Rosé, took many years to become established but still offered new opportunities to the region.

Regional innovation is also supported by other actors, like one of the main banks in the area, the Crédit Agricole. The bank is a regional investor with its own equity as it is a shareholder in some houses: most notably aiding the Taittinger family to repurchase their family house. However, its participation does not stop there since it funds research in the cluster for 82 million euros in water, vineyard and environmental scientific research, as well as supporting academic chairs and programmes.

At the level of society, the process of value creation can be conceived in terms of programmes and incentives for entrepreneurship and innovation intended to encourage new entrepreneurial ventures to innovate and expand their value to society and its members. In Champagne, value creation also occurs through entrepreneurial actions encouraging the new generation of vignerons, the sons of the current landowners, to become small champagne producers. This process is still on a small scale because 80 per cent of the properties of small grape growers are rented for a percentage of the production, and most grape producers sell their grapes directly to the main champagne houses or cooperatives instead of producing their own champagne by their own facilities or through local cooperatives.

This new generation of entrepreneurial vignerons has been supported by the SGV. Among different actions of the SGV to encourage entrepreneurs is the launch of an umbrella brand in 2001 'Champagne des Vignerons' – a generic umbrella brand created in 2001 for 4,800 grape growers affiliated to the SGV. The SGV wants to build and develop brand awareness around growers; it unifies members around strong values and targets marketing segments with this brand. Among the values implied in the brand are quality and tradition, as well as the representation of the terroir. However, this marketing action is only targeted to France where most grower sales are made, but where more than 50 per cent of current customers are more than 50 years old. The new entrepreneurial vignerons tend to produce more than 100,000 bottles per year, understand the concept of marketing and position their champagnes in different distribution channels in France and abroad through diverse strategies: restaurants, and newsletters to hundreds of previous customers and to distributors. Moreover, they are aware of the danger of commoditization and work strongly to differentiate their champagne. One of the entrepreneurial vignerons said 'each village has its own personality and quality'.

In other cases, innovations came from the arrival of new entrants, like Taittinger in the twentieth century. Even though in 1932 Pierre Taittinger bought a champagne house founded originally in 1734, he brought innovations to the business model like the exploitation of historical assets such as abbeys or chateaux. However, Mr Taittinger did not remain as an outsider since he incorporated to his business model a social and political role and commitment in Champagne. Reputation and location matters to be successful in the region. In one visit, our interviewee said 'the secret of Champagne – we have to live here'.

However, new entrants do not fit well all of the time. Recently, large companies have bought traditional champagne houses, but the arrival of new management teams or the existence of headquarters outside the region has generated concern within the region. In one visit, the comment was made that 'the mergers [of local houses] with other companies are not good because they [the new managers] live out in Paris.' This situation highlights the importance of social networks in the Champagne region.

International recognition flanked with an expensive marketing budget

The position of champagne is different in France from the rest of the world. In France, champagne is perceived as the essence of France by every class so the market segments consuming champagne include the middle class. However, they do not consume only branded champagne but they are linked to small producers through traditional relationships, in some cases lasting generations, as Mr Cheval said. Pierre-Emmanuel Taittinger said that the positioning of champagne is 'an affordable luxury' so everyone can enjoy it at least once a year. Another interviewee said that champagne is 'an affordable luxury because is easy to buy since you can separate it into small units (bottles), and, in case of crisis, you can buy two bottles but may not change your car'. The industry employs good advertising to position the wine: royal patronage or participation in key events like car races – the wine of Champagne is a celebratory wine.

Most of the small producers target local markets and France, and champagne houses mainly operate export markets like Britain, USA, Germany and Japan. This is very interesting in terms of value creation and value appropriation since champagne houses have to invest additional resources, like branding and distribution channels,[3] to create value and appropriate it, small producers only invest in the production of grapes since much of their champagne is produced cooperatively and sold from their own cellars. Prices reflect these differences between investment and market segments.

However, there are some challenges for champagne in international markets. As noted in Chapter 4 (see Figure 4.4) champagne is particularly susceptible to economic downturns. There are many newer sparkling wines on the market, especially from New World countries, as well as sparkling wines produced by champagne houses in those countries. The promise of growth in the large markets of China, Russia and India will not make up for reductions in major markets, which are declining, since they are still small markets.

Champagne has been a very successful area generating value in the long-term through learning processes, highly innovative firms and strong social networks. However, the creation of value has to be accompanied by good appropriation strategies, otherwise the economic actors in the region will not keep the high standard of living that they currently have.

Value appropriation

In the strategy literature, two key concepts operate across all levels of analysis to determine which actor captures the value that is created: *competition and isolating mechanisms* (Peteraf, 1993). The creation of novel products often produces a situation where there is limited supply and high demand. Competition will follow, as other suppliers of the product seek to replicate the value created and participate in the profits. A consequence of competition (increased supply) is that exchange value (price) will decline to the point where supply equals demand. Competitors may also be unable to retain value as end users benefit from the lower prices brought by increased competition. Isolating mechanisms imply that competition is limited and supply is not above demand. Isolating mechanisms can be knowledge, or physical or legal barriers which prevent replication of the value-creating product by a competitor. In essence, isolating mechanisms operate to limit value slippage, thus enabling sources of value creation to capture the majority of the value created. The existence of an isolating mechanism raises the potential bargaining power of the creator of value to retain this value, although the nature of the isolating mechanisms may be quite different.

In the case of champagne, there is a key legal barrier determined by the AOC laws that control a wine's content and linkage with a delimited territory, but the best indicator of success in the appropriation of value is the price obtained for champagne. I will review both ideas in this section.

Price

Value creation requires more than simply understanding what the customer or society is willing to pay for (Lepak *et al.*, 2007). Instead the firm must recognize the existence of multiple targets – whether intended as such or not – that exist in concert and not in isolation. Champagne, as a region, has numerous ways of creating value for different customers that want a luxury product: large houses aiming at highly selective customers, large cooperatives targeting the mass market, or small-scale vignerons who target the French market through relationships lasting generations. However, the variety of offerings may not be sustainable if everyone feels that the appropriation of the value created is not fair. In the case of champagne, there is a delicate balance between value creation, the wine, and value appropriation, the price of the champagne. The higher the value created, the higher the price obtained as Figure 10.1 shows.

While the most important value generators are the champagne houses, which sell 66 per cent of the wine and command the higher prices, there are

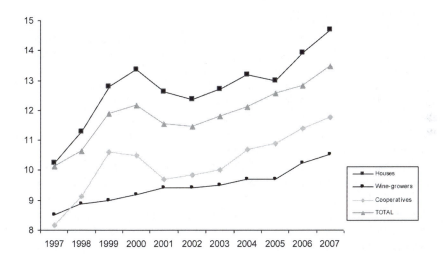

Figure 10.1 Evolution of average price in constant euros. (Source: CIVC/Crédit Agricole du Nord-Est)

gentleman's agreements with grape growers to buy their grapes at a fair price. One champagne house buys grapes directly from up to the fourth generation of grape growers in 17 villages using contracts lasting between 5 and 18 years. A manager of another champagne house said 'there is no competition in grape growers but a gentleman's agreement, and if a grower changes there are huge penalties'; another manager said, regarding the fairness of grape-buying deals, 'we have to live here'. The social fabric, which was generated by history and tradition, determines the categorization of the different actors into faithful or unfaithful. Therefore, social capital acts as an important restriction to free-riding behaviour for either houses or growers wanting to improve their appropriation of value. The price paid for grapes is €5.50 per kilo, which is one of the highest in the wine industry.

While champagne houses have all the resources, brand and distribution channels, to be able to appropriate the value from the French market, they target markets abroad. External markets are inaccessible in large scale for most of the vignerons unless they heavily discount their prices or ask someone else to manage their sales, which may erode the value of the champagne brand. Strong social capital has been built through resource investment by houses. One interviewee said 'Growers understand that the situation of privilege (in terms of grape value and income obtained) comes from the work of houses. For example, [when] phylloxera destroyed the vineyards, [champagne] houses subsidized the growers to plant new vines'.

Therefore, different actors in Champagne target different markets, avoiding price erosion in gentleman's agreements that may have lasted for hundred years.

Controlled origin appellation

The land devoted to grape growing under the champagne appellation has increased over the years as Figure 10.2 shows. However, the capacity of the region to grow grapes under the appellation has reached a limit in the last few years. As outlined in previous chapters, there is an extension of the AOC planned by 2015 but growers may be opposed to the revision and extension since new villages will be added to the AOC and the revision will add a lot of new people with the right to grow grapes, thus diluting the economic position of existing growers.

The history of the development of the AOC has shown the importance of the learning process which has occurred in the area amid conflicts between houses and vignerons. These conflicts occurred due to misunderstandings of the process of value creation and free riding by some actors during the nineteenth and the beginning of the twentieth centuries, as the following paragraphs describe.

The region of Champagne grew very strongly during the 1800s, altering the social fabric and economic relations of the wine community in the years leading up to the phylloxera crisis (Guy, 2003). By the time phylloxera

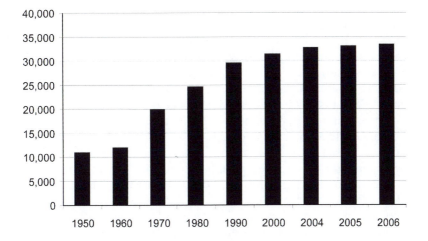

Figure 10.2 The growth in area under vine. (Source: CIVC)

affected the Marne region, vignerons were fully dependent on the négociants for the sale of their grapes. Radical fluctuations in the wine market showed vignerons the problems of economic hardship. Thus, the control of champagne was contested between vignerons and maisons as vignerons feared that house brands would be more important than 'terroir' (the vignerons' unique resource); in the process, village names like Ay or Sillery became replaced by a single territorial name – Champagne – and there was a need to set boundaries in order to guarantee the consumers' confidence in the product which was plagued with fraud from unscrupulous merchants.

Within Champagne, the fraud that required government attention consisted of three related issues: counterfeiting of names of manufacturers or brands; using the denomination 'champagne' as a generic label for sparkling wine; or labelling a wine 'champagne' when the grapes had been harvested or the wine manufactured outside of the region (Guy, 2003). The first two issues, which were fundamental concerns of champagne négociants, were strongly pursued by the French government using international laws regarding industrial property and French judiciary. While regional manufacturers obtained recognition of champagne as a denomination by the state, the boundaries of the region were ambiguous. The ambiguity was very useful for free-riding négociants that committed fraud (although it was not illegal at that time). Fraud included wine fabrication with grapes grown in other French areas; or bringing wines from Lorraine, Burgundy, Anjou, or even Germany (Guy, 2003).

For the vignerons, champagne derived its quality and prestige not from the firms in Reims or Epernay that bottled the final product but from the land and the Champenois vignerons who cultivated it (Guy, 2003). Vignerons intended to develop a powerful tool, through the delimitation of the Champagne boundaries, for punishing unscrupulous merchants who sacrificed the rural community for their profits. On the other hand, négociants considered that the best guarantee of authenticity for the public was based on maintaining the quality of their (named) wine and the prestige of their brands (Guy, 2003). With consumer preference for the authentic brands, the law of supply and demand would eliminate unscrupulous producers. The resulting stresses, which produced the riots of 1911, have already been outlined (see Chapters 1 and 5). Significant in all of this is the analysis of Guy (2003, p. 157) who said

> what emerges is a picture not of harmony and consent but of conflict and compromise; a glimpse of a dynamic rural society struggling to define the boundaries of its community and the position of that community within the French nation. Hidden was the friction of a community in transition . . . part of a long and recurring battle to define roles within the regional economy and the community.

She added that 'the cause that propelled them [vignerons] into the streets in 1911 was quite simple: to protect the connection between champagne, the wine, and Champagne, the land and its terroir' (2003, p. 161).

The battle over the control (appropriation) of the economic and cultural heritage of champagne (and more importantly over the value created) was based on different definitions over the issues and boundaries of the community. There are always tensions between economic actors in the appropriation of value. These tensions have come to be managed through institutions such as the CIVC, one of the key lessons from champagne for the other regions. Thus, the next section deals in more detail with the CIVC.

Achieving a balance between value creation and value appropriation: the role of the CIVC

In contrast to other wine regions, both growers and producers had achieved a balance between the creation of value and its appropriation through a third institution – the CIVC, with balance guaranteed by the co-presidents and a board of directors comprising five directors from the SGV and five directors from the UMC. The board usually meets eight times per year, and one of the key meetings is to decide the harvest dates as well as other issues related to the harvest. The CIVC can sanction a producer if its product is not under the rules of the AOC and can declassify a producer from the AOC label but the CIVC does not control the houses' operations outside Champagne.

Even though the institution seems to have a political role, its daily operations run by a set of commissions and professional managers are fairly independent and highly technical. The members of the CIVC have long-term appointments. The institution has a number of specialist commissions related to technical matters, communication and the champagne appellation, the equipment of the vine-growing area, champagne and health and after-sale quality. It employs many technicians and is composed of a vineyard department which defines the dates from planting to shipping, an export department which assists (they help companies and vignerons to export), a trade department which registers the labels/brands under the AOC, and an 'economic observatory'. Nowadays, the organization has a number of functions which include the following:

- registration of transactions between vignerons and houses;
- provision of statistical information and economic analysis to the level of a balanced scorecard for the chairs of the CIVC;
- performance of market surveys to evaluate quality and quantity; and
- at harvest time (jointly with AOC), the establishment of:

  - yield per hectare
  - pressing limits
  - minimum alcohol level potential
  - quality of the wine reserve
  - dates of vintage.

An important activity, close to the role of asset management in firms, is to register each land parcel in the region. By 2000 the CIVC had mapped the whole region in parcels of 50 square metres within the AOC Champagne. The CIVC also has regulatory missions closer to asset management such as:

- recording vineyard ownership from vines planted to shipping of finished product;
- delivering professional licences to négociants;
- developing certificates of origin for exports; and
- modifying the status of champagne négociants.

The CIVC does not only have activities related to controlling the adequate balance between demand and supply or the assets in the region, it is also responsible for innovations to improve standards in the region, including:

- raising of environmental standards to support a green strategy using fewer herbicides and pesticides;
- reduction of pressing yields to improve quality of must;
- increasing time in cellars after bottling; and
- the development of a particular yeast created for the region.

The area related to innovation is formed by a Technical Research and Development section with more than 45 engineers and technicians, a Viticultural and Oenological Department, which uses experimental vineyards

(30 ha) and cellars, laboratories and vinification equipment, as well as collaboration agreements with universities in applied research.

Finally, the CIVC is responsible for building the image of champagne in France and other major markets by controlling how the image is promoted through websites such as www.champagne.fr or www.champagne.com, providing educational brochures, maps, DVDs, etc., as well as contacting the press for neutral information and the protection of the appellation in the World Trade Organization and bilateral agreements with countries. Since champagne is not a generic noun, the CIVC is responsible for promoting abroad laws and regulations regarding the name, systematic surveillance and legal action against wrong use of the brand. In other words, the CIVC is responsible for maintaining the current delicate balance between value creation and value appropriation.

Final reflections and challenges

Champagne is a success story not only in terms of market positioning but in terms of achieving a balance between value creation and value appropriation. It is uncommon to see a balance between the process of value creation generated mostly by firms with distribution networks and the appropriation of the value from suppliers to these firms. This balance has to be obtained amid a highly complex business which includes the following characteristics:

- Large investment in real estate.
- Technical aspects of production:
  - purchase of grapes concentrated within 15 days during harvest each year;
  - *assemblage* of a large number of wines to obtain consistency;
  - purchase of bottles from diverse suppliers;
  - riddling and finishing the wine.

- Grape supply (89 per cent from grape growers) is determined by complex relationships (mostly social rather than commercial) affected by competition from other houses.
- Wines from different villages and different years.
- Long ageing process: two to ten years, which implies high levels of inventory.
- The costs are half of the selling price and production costing is very complex.
- Long delays between decisions and impact: the vintage from a good year like 1997 was on the market in 2005–06.
- Labour: restrictive legislation, salaried employees, and conflicting trade unions (three syndicats).
- Both agricultural and industrial activity.
- Both supermarket and independent retail channels.

- Both long and short distribution channels.
- Both distribution subsidiaries and importers: sales in 120 countries.
- Fast-moving consumer good resulting in high turnover of stock.
- Long time to market for innovation – three to ten years.
- The product is both wine (guardian of values) and luxury (high price, image, people).
- High level of social activities: there is a direct involvement in business function like buying grapes from growers due to social relationship.

Sustaining competitive advantage

Champagne, as a region, has managed to achieve the four cornerstones of sustained competitive advantage, which positions and sustains the region as a leader in the wine industry. The four cornerstones (heterogeneity, ex post limits to competition, imperfect mobility, and ex ante limits to mobility) are examined below.

Heterogeneity, which refers to the presence of superior productive factors that are in limited supply, is achieved by:

- A unique 'terroir' compared to other wine regions in the world. The combination of northern location and chalk produces high-acid grapes that make the unique taste of champagne combined with a cultural heritage that is impossible to imitate.
- Since there is no common formulation for champagne, each producer (large or small) has its own style determined by the proportions employed by each grape (pinot noir, pinot meunier and chardonnay) in the *assemblage*. This is an important aspect that may assure champagne's survival as champagne is not one homogeneous product but many heterogeneous products catering to different tastes and markets. There is a very fragmented supply with 5,000 individual brands under the champagne umbrella.

Ex post limits to competition, which relate to the forces that limit competition for the rents obtained from superior productive factors, have been conferred by:

- the legal protection for its regional brand: AOC 'Champagne';
- the existence of large firms responsible for marketing sparkling wine: Moët et Chandon, Vranken Pommery, etc., which create barriers to the development of stronger competitors in sparkling wine outside the region.

Imperfect mobility indicates the factors that are somewhat specialized and which relate to the specific needs whose opportunity costs are lower than the value of the product in the current strategy.

- The opportunity costs for employing the land located in Champagne in other types of productions are clearly lower than its usage in grape growing for sparkling wine. Therefore, the grape growers have an incentive to continue producing high-quality grapes and negotiate with houses for grape supply.
- The costs of opportunity for the brands developed by Champagne's houses are clearly lower when they are used in generic sparkling wine, or even in other countries. Therefore, Champagne's houses do not currently have an incentive to replace the sparkling wine production in Champagne with that from other regions.
- The historic relation of the region with royalty provides the region with a non-imitable intangible resource which enhances its reputation as a luxury product/wine drinkable on very special occasions.

Ex ante limits to competition, which limit competition for the establishment of a competitive position using the same resource, are obtained by:

- the existence of a centralized regulator for land transfers (SAFER) resulting in a limit to local houses and foreign firms buying land in Champagne;
- the social networks existing inside the region, which are effective deterrents to free-riding competitive behaviour.

These four cornerstones have not been achieved instantly; it was a long process of trial-and-error and reaction to opportunities and threats, as this chapter has shown. The achievement of these four cornerstones is related to the development of a capability in the region: the management of a delicate balance between value creation and value appropriation. This is one of the key lessons of champagne – the necessity to articulate institutions at regional level that are able to protect and nurture the capability of maintaining balanced relations among different actors localized in the same geographical region.

Challenges

Champagne is not exempt from challenges. The challenges are actions or events that may erode the pillars of its current success. This includes the fact that champagne houses lately have started being managed from outside Champagne. There may be issues of social capital and networks, especially with the relationships with vignerons and other houses, affecting the region in the future. Since most of these firms are listed on the stock exchange, they need to show steady financial results and this may affect social relations.

Further, there are two possible competing strategies for champagne producers: volume and value. Each may be attractive to cooperatives or houses (although the former may tend to go for volume and the latter for value). However, the adoption of one strategy by one group of actors will have an impact on those who choose the alternative course of action. Therefore, it may alter the current tacit actor–market segment arrangements as cooperatives may sell abroad in markets served by houses.

There is concern of the lack of enough supply in the short term which generates pressure on value appropriation actions between vignerons and champagne houses. The potential increase in grape supply by adding 40 new villages under the AOC is a step in that direction but it will take ten years to reach a productive level. Consequently, it may generate pressure on champagne houses run by corporations to expand capacity of sparkling wine production in other places, with the consequent risk for the Champagne region of losing its economic attractiveness for those houses.

The new generation of people may change the culture in the management in the medium term: prosperity vs *mévente* (lack of sales). The new generation has not lived through the learning processes which occurred in Champagne that achieved the current prosperity, especially *mévente*. Consequently, there is a danger that they do not recognize the existing delicate balance and try to move it towards their objectives. For example, new generations of vignerons are more entrepreneurial and prefer to sell their own wine in different markets, creating potential competition for the houses.

Global warming may affect the style of wines in the long term. This challenge is the most difficult to face and it may imply difficult decisions, as climate change may erode champagne's sources of differentiation and give new regions, such as the south-east of England, the possibility of producing wines similar to champagne. While champagne's success also resides in other assets, such as reputation and the AOC, the existence of new regions closer to Champagne with similar products that can potentially benefit from similar assets becomes a real threat.

Notes

1 Guy (2003) described many of the earliest champagne families' successes as the stuff of legend. Families like Moët and Clicquot became legends in the world of fine wines.
2 Currently, Moët alone sells over 30 million bottles of non-vintage champagne, and total sales from the region is around 300 million bottles p.a.
3 For example, Laurent Perrier, which is number three in terms of value and was created in 1812, has five subsidiaries established in the USA, United Kingdom (no. 1 export market), Belgium, Switzerland, and Germany to sell the product mainly to restaurants and cafes.

11 Strategic implementation

Accounting to accountability in champagne

Al Seaman

Introduction

As explained in Chapters 1 and 4, the business of champagne has evolved to a current state of relative success. However, this has not occurred without trials, tribulations and innovation. It is interesting and revealing to study these developments from an accountability perspective. Accountability in and of itself is not especially interesting without an understanding of the strategic implementation aspects of the business. A history of change and uncertainty has contributed extensively to the alliances and network forma-tions developed for the purposes of considering and confronting substantive industry issues. The creation of 'grassroots' movements out of this process of change led to an understanding that individuals and organizations in the region harboured knowledge and information that could be shared for the gain of all. From the initial sharing of information and exchange of ideas, the business of champagne continues to address the breadth and depth of concerns that shape the environment for this iconic product.

Complexity of managing and organizing has been understood for some time (Drucker, 1993). An array of stakeholders (producers, growers, owners, shareholders, financiers, regulators, consumers) contribute to the uncertainties in the dynamic environment of Champagne. Adding to the myriad of environmental uncertainties inherent in the champagne industry, the proposed expansion of the delimited area of Champagne introduces stress on both current and potential growers as well as the organizations of champagne. What pressures will the CIVC, UMC, and SGV experience with an increase in production of up to 30 per cent and an additional forty villages? Clearly, as the AOC authorities update and revise standards, intro-duce new technologies and transform systems, the management of the region and supply of champagne must continue. Importantly, evidence shows that many organizations are unable to capture and distil the relevant information from dynamic environments and respond in an opportunistic manner (Harreld *et al.*, 2007).

This chapter will review, interpret and explain the organization of cham-pagne in an accountability framework. In developing this framework, a model useful for the organizations of champagne to interpret and assess the status of their accountability systems will emerge. To show how champagne has progressed and succeeded from an accountability perspective, the current thinking in the strategy domain must be considered, otherwise without the development of goals and objectives accountability loses its usefulness. The chapter will continue with a brief history of accountability, accountability in champagne, and finally conclusions and recommendations.

Strategy, planning and uncertainty: a review

The many advantages of strategy in gaining competitive and other advantages have been portrayed in both the academic and popular press (Mintzberg *et al.*, 1998). Using a myriad of frameworks strategy is defined as the plans developed and actions taken to achieve an organization's objectives. Fundamentally, management uses a strategy to represent how the resources of an organization could be deployed to face the external environment in which it operates. The one caveat is that attainment of objectives will require good management decisions and execution of the plans.

Although there may be some slight variations in definition, 'strategy' is widely referred to as the plans and actions that organizations take to achieve their objectives. It is simultaneously a process by which plans for allocating resources are developed and the actions required to achieve those goals are identified. It reflects management's understanding of the firm's assets and position as well as the external forces it faces. At a very basic level, strategy is about making quality decisions and executing well on those decisions. However, as Harreld *et al.* (2007) suggest, there is a body of evidence that suggests that the strategic exercise does not simply translate to success.

Starbuck (1993) showed that strategic planning has insignificant contributions to profits. He attributes this finding to four ideas:

- the formality of planning can reduce contributions, i.e. striving for the wrong goals;
- barriers often prevent possible positive gains, i.e. many competitors see the world at least as well as you do;
- errors in managers' beliefs about their organization and the environment, i.e. reality often does not confirm the planning expectation; and
- the impossibility of accuracy in long-term planning.

All is not doom and gloom, however, as Starbuck suggested methods that would improve the result of the strategic process. Simply put, management should be building more alert firms with capabilities of response to changing environments. Interestingly, Weick and Sutcliffe (2001) help to reconcile management focus on strategic planning and the insignificant results often produced. Strategic planning provides the arena for actions in the organization and thus the generation of meaning. If planning stifles action, the organization loses the sense of motion and meaning.

It is not the strategic process itself that is especially difficult, rather it is the uncertainty and complexity in the organizational context that is problematic. As environments change with respect to customers, competition and markets, difficulties are created requiring a response from management. Successful managers continuously scan the environment for opportunities or threats, design responses and ensure that appropriate plans are implemented. Teece (2006) explained that information capture and analyses for the purposes of opportunity development demands a different skill set from those required for profiting from the opportunity. Strategy requires understanding of the information, developing and executing plans against that understanding, and more importantly being able to recognize threats as they develop and change quickly enough to avoid adverse outcomes. The idea that core competencies are developed and adapted to recognize and address the changing environment is described as dynamic capabilities. Eisenhardt and Martin (2000) suggest that dynamic capabilities have significant commonalities across organizations, and are homogeneous and substitutable. The business of champagne has, over the years, been able to harness and develop its core competencies in what might be called a classic case of the development of dynamic capabilities.

The structure of champagne as strategy: alliances and networks

Champagne has evolved to a position of some prominence in the wine industry through the use of strategic alliance and network formations as seen by the CIVC, UMC, and the SGV structures. Koka and Prescott (2008) provide some explanation for the use of strategic alliances. As an important component of a firm's strategy, alliance membership is used to access and acquire resources externally. Such relationships provide access to otherwise unavailable resources and capabilities. The strategic network participants share information, knowledge, and other resources. For the members of the network, they share all of the industry benefits accruing to the network. A firm's position or importance in the network may also affect the accessibility of network resources and potentially firm performance.

It would not be outrageous to suggest that alliance formations have contributed considerably to the success of champagne. Members have pooled and contributed resources to the alliances in an effort to enhance and improve the value chain of the champagne industry. Ultimately the growth and performance of the alliances has been fuelled by the integration of the motives and interests of the alliance members. Luo (2008) refers to this structure as the economic integration and interdependence of alliance members.

Accountability: linking strategy to operations

A well-developed strategy provides a pattern or plan for the integration of an organization's major goals, policies and action sequences into a cohesive whole. Such a strategy helps to marshal and allocate resources into a unique and viable arena based on its recognized set of competencies and shortcomings, anticipated changes in the environment, as well as the potential moves by equally adept competitors. What is really important at this point is the capability of the organization in its deployment of the strategy – that is, the strategic implementation.

With the strategy exercise complete, management must clearly demonstrate, identify and communicate the mission, vision and values, as well as success factors, that is, the things that an organization must get right in order to enhance the ability to be successful. This clear context will drive action planning, measurement and alignment throughout the organization. At this point, the importance of accountability as a natural bridging construct between the individual and the organization strategy must be stressed. Accountability relationships govern complex organizational relationships. Participants must answer to many others under a variety of conditions or ground rules. In addition, accountability relationships are often fluid and dynamic with each partner to the accountability relationship learning to anticipate reactions of others and develop patterns of mutual adaptation. A framework of accountability can provide the structure and meaning necessary for participants to understand the strategic implementation process.

The adoption of the framework methodology assists management in clarifying their strategic elements, that is, vision, values, goals and objectives, and the development of a measurement and performance system. With the framework as a reference, the action plan of organizational activities is always linked to the strategic direction. The action plan provides the basis for measuring organization activities in a scorecard fashion and determining the success of projects or the need to withdraw or revise the project activities. Strategic implementation using a framework methodology is developed on a foundation of values-based behaviours which support all activity within an organization and make visible the behavioural expectations for all organization participants. Accountability is more than a mere accounting (i.e. what we get done), it has an important behavioural dimension (i.e. how we get things done).

As noted by Lerner and Tetlock (1999), accountability can have both positive and negative impacts. One important negative implication is that decision-makers will provide the least effort to produce results that are consistent with the known views of their audience. The positive impacts are more appealing and include greater learning, increased cognitively complex decision and judgment strategies and greater effort towards task accomplishment. Schlenker (1985) suggested that accountability leads to improved information processing, a more thorough search for relevant information, improved recall, more complex judgement strategies, more data-driven information processing, and greater awareness of decision strategies.

What is clear in the research on accountability is that a wide range of issues have been considered with widely varying effects on those who are under pressure to justify their decisions. The ultimate conclusion has been that accountability is not a panacea for improving decision processes and, ultimately, the quality of the decision. The effects of accountability vary across a wide variety of tasks. It is clear that accountability is a logically complex construct that interacts with characteristics of decision-makers and properties of the task environment to produce an array of effects, only some of which are beneficial.

Champagne: strategic alliances – foundations for success

The broad spectrum of antagonisms and politics that have shaped the formation of the primary strategic alliances in Champagne are well documented in Chapter 1. Charters (2006) explains the methods and rationale of political involvement in the wine industry as ranging from social control, diplomacy, and economic to the control of production, distribution, and political conflict. The point of interest is that many of these circumstances and uncertainties led to the formation and evolution of the strategic alliances in Champagne. From this perspective we have alliances and an alliance of the alliances!

The SGV and UMC were formed to promote the interests of the members, all with commonalities that made alliance formation productive. As time marched on, the natural antagonisms between growers and houses led to the final alliance, the CIVC, which combined all the resources in the value chain, from vineyard to consumer. With time and success the economic integration aspects of the CIVC alliance evolved to include aspects of governance, trust, and justice – that is, the cultural aspects of champagne, how we do it. What is clear is that many of the troubling aspects of conflict and commerce in the value chain are managed by the alliances for the greater good of the champagne brand and more importantly the people of Champagne. Despite the alignment of the value chain through the alliances, the growers of the SGV still compete with the houses for sales while the houses of the UMC still compete with each other for inputs from growers and customers for the output of product. Importantly, both growers and houses understand that they need each other.

Champagne and strategy: an accountability perspective on what we observed

When viewed from the accountability perspective, champagne is indeed very interesting. Success is evident, it is difficult to argue with success and even more difficult to change if successful! Despite the success, there are obvious signs that accountability, both the performance and behavioural dimensions, is not well established. The question might be 'what is being left on the table?' Based on evidence garnered from a study of high-performing organizations there may be considerably more gains to be made.

Mankins and Steele (2005) conducted a study which suggested that, typically, organizations realize only about 60 per cent of their strategies' potential value. These losses occur from a few main factors resulting in a strategy-to-performance gap: results are not often compared with expectation so the causes of deficiencies cannot be identified; since multi-year results seldom meet expectations, planning becomes driven by error-ridden assumptions; and performance gaps are seldom identified, resulting in the inability of management to take corrective action. The consequence of these failures is the embedding of the performance gap in the culture of the organization creating a culture of underperformance.

Evidence gathered during the tour suggests that the possibility of a performance gap does exist. On a number of occasions senior executives of alliances and individual organizations were asked about performance reporting, for example the existence of balanced scorecards.[1] It would appear that such reporting does not exist. A senior banker responded that the managers of champagne are great 'strategic thinkers' but performance reporting did not seem to be prevalent. It could be argued that a lack of performance reporting would contribute to a culture of under-performance. With results relying primarily on the success of the brand, assumptions of planning are likely go unchallenged and opportunities for operational improvements unidentified. A senior executive of a house indicated that performance parameters are not required, as a bonus pool for the operational employees is being 'policed' by the employees themselves, that is 'pull your weight or the rest of the members will provide sanctions'. These examples suggest a disconnection between management expectation (the strategy) and the employees' performance, knowledge and innovation capabilities.

A remedy: a framework for accountability

Much of the industry is in transition as large organizations own and manage more of champagne. As new entrants to the business of champagne continue there are questions as to whether they understand the unique social fabric of Champagne. The result is perhaps a clash of big versus small, old versus new, and ultimately an issue of traditional versus modern management style. Faced with issues as noted above, in addition to the environmental uncertainties, adoption of an accountability framework could enhance performance by working on both the planning and execution of strategy. Such an approach would ensure clear linkages from strategy to operations and provide the alignment of operational activities to support the strategy directly. Closing the performance gap requires that operations and management understand and communicate with each other; that is organizational alignment.

On one hand, the craft technologies of growing grapes and champagne production call for a results oriented management control system (MacIntosh & Daft, 1982) using general data with frequent reporting and achievable standards. On the other hand, the large technical professional organizations use extensive budgeting and statistical techniques but report less frequently against difficult standards. The point is that no matter what the industry or size of the organization a management control system can be developed using an accountability framework system that promotes and enhances understanding of the goals and objectives of the organization.

Champagne in a high-performance context

A typical accountability framework is represented in Figure 11.1, showing a vision that should inspire, supported by the success factors that would assist in achieving that vision, all developed from a base of values. The framework provides an organizing point of reference for organizations as they strive to communicate to employees where the organization is headed so that operational levels will be able to develop executable plans and provide concrete links to performance. This is the domain of strategic implementation.

Mankins and Steele (2005) suggest the potential for substantial gains by ensuring that the strategy-to-performance gap is closed or narrowed. They found seven keys to successful planning and execution which allows an organization to quickly spot and minimize performance problems. The accountability framework of Figure 11.1 provides a visual explanation of the less concrete strategic implementation. Using the accountability framework and the seven keys to high performance, an analysis of management as understood from the study tour of Champagne is very insightful and could provide useful information and insights for future management activity.

Over the years champagne has successfully demonstrated its strategic capabilities. Careful negotiation has led to performance targets of the CIVC. The success of this planning has led to achievable targets (i.e. grape yields and prices) that have proven successful for both growers and houses. Constant vigilance and negotiation have challenged the assumptions of how the champagne industry conducts business, selling Champagne 'the district' rather than as a 'village'. The separation, challenge, and building of the business assumptions ultimately allow the high-level financial forecasting and price setting. This settlement at a high level allows the growers and producers to concentrate on what they do best. Conflict and other barriers to doing business are lowered, trust improved.

Strategy is often abstract and difficult to communicate and translate into actions. As a result actions at lower levels in support of the strategy are difficult to develop and perform. This is an area of potential improvement. We

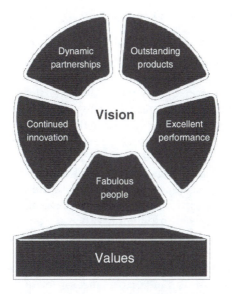

Figure 11.1 Sample champagne accountability framework. (Source: Kemerer Group, Inc.)

did not find an example of the linkage between strategy and performance, for example balanced scorecards. This link is often difficult to design as a result of the planning and execution of the strategy not being communicated in clear, understandable language. With many different organization levels, the front lines are separated from executive levels and understand the business in a different way. It must become clear to operations what they can do to support the strategy of the organization. This requires communicating the strategy in clear, concrete terms. When operations know what role they play in support of the strategy, actions can be developed and outcomes linked to a clearly understood strategy. This is the clarification of accountabilities to include both dimensions – 'what we do' and 'how we do it'.

As various levels in the organization understand and agree upon their role in supporting the strategy a rigorous framework of accountabilities is much easier to develop. An accountability framework allows the links from strategy to business performance. Role activities in support of the success factors become explicit, including linkages to financial performance. Just as operations may not understand the strategic language of the executive team, operations managers may be just as difficult for executives to understand. The developing and understanding of roles in the organization will facilitate determining what may be the cause of performance shortfalls. Such shortfalls could be a consequence of poor execution or unrealistic expectations. An accountability framework provides the basis for the identification and correction of difficulties as they arise. Individuals are strategically aligned when their behaviours correspond with and support their organization's strategy.

The discussion that arises from the creation of an accountability framework facilitates the deployment of more realistic and hence executable activities. With early discussion of the resource requirements, activity deployments will more closely match the understanding of the strategy and operations required to attain that strategy. Such discussion improves both the strategy and the resource deployment capability.

The accountability framework directs the implementation towards the activities which must become priorities in order to accomplish the success factors identified as being supportive of achieving of the vision. It also provides the organization with the answer to the question 'Why aren't we there yet?' With priorities each organization member will have a clear set of accountabilities derived through the processes of communication, negotiation and understanding. I believe that this is one of the main shortcomings of the management processes of champagne. Research is clear that those with accountabilities are aware of the views of their reviewers; they employ a low-effort solution to the performance problem (Tetlock, 1985). This is consistent with views of decision-makers as cognitive misers who prefer solutions that require the least effort. As a result, when the views of the reviewers are known, decision-makers will provide decisions or actions consistent with those views. Tetlock (1983) found that accountable subjects who were aware of the views of their reviewers shifted their opinions to be consistent with those views. The implication for champagne is that an 'understood' but not 'explicit' expectation most likely does not serve the best interests of the organization or the organization participants. The domains of creativity and achievement are unexplored.

High-performing organizations continuously monitor performance comparing plan to reality. Plans may be reset, resources redeployed. Of importance in this process is determining whether the plans or the execution might be flawed and then corrected. Without a solid accountability framework, the clarity and understanding required for monitoring procedures to reveal problems is not available. I believe that an accountability framework with subsequent monitoring could provide gains for many champagne organizations. An example is the constant attention paid to determining yields and harvest periods. The gains from such attention to detail could be realized throughout the champagne production process. Weick and Sutcliffe (2001) believe that anticipation of problems from constant vigilance produces more gains than having to deploy for resilience, in other words, prevent the problem then fixing it is not necessary.

The last area for consideration is the motivation and development of staff. An operational process is only as good as the people that make it work. Key to high-performing organizations is the selection and development of management. There is a cost, but the long-term rewards will be exhibited through excellence of planning and implementation. The champagne industry has a compelling product and has developed the relationships in the supply chain. However, as research has shown, firms with strong implementation capabilities are also strong in development. An accountability framework as an information and communication tool reveals performance gaps, including the needs for management development.

Discussion and conclusion

It is clear that the strategic endeavours of the managers of champagne have been a success. Research reveals that not only poor organizational strategies fail; strategic implementation research demonstrates that even good strategies can fail during implementation (Gagnon *et al.*, 2008). New strategy or innovative strategies often fail due to employee inability or resistance to commit to a strategy resulting in inappropriate behaviours for accomplishing strategic goals. Failure of commitment leads to strategic misalignment, or individual engagement in support of the organization strategic goals. Strategic implementation is extensively goal-directed, while strategic misalignment reflects the absence of goal-directed behaviour. Strategic misalignment has been described as a lack of achieving coordinated action, goal incongruence and non-alignment.

The study-tour evidence indicates a lack of accountability systems present in champagne management. Research evidence suggests that strategic misalignment and performance opportunity losses are potential consequences. Accountability research evidence suggests that commitment and engagement are enhanced with the presence of accountability systems. This evidence presents both challenge and opportunity for champagne management. The challenge is to believe that there is potential for substantial gains available in the presence of their current success. The opportunity is developing and implementing an accountability system to realize the potential performance gains.

An accountability framework provides a goal-based strategic implementation system which by necessity enhances communication and knowledge within the organization. As implementation and information exchange progress strategic knowledge spreads throughout the organization building individual trust and commitment to strategic goals of the organization. As a result misalignment fades (Gagnon *et al.*, 2008).

The study also revealed that the accounting systems of the champagne business are indeed highly developed. This provides the foundation for the 'what we do' dimension of accountability frameworks. Communicating and ensuring that the 'how we do it' behavioural or cultural dimension is understood and implemented would complete the accountability framework. As in most organization programmes or initiatives there are caveats. A programme champion is required to ensure implementation and survival of an accountability framework. Internal systems must be present or in development to continue use of the framework once developed and implemented.

This may be a challenge considering the current successes of the champagne industry. However, the implementation evidence has shown that account-ability-based systems provide a tool to align systems and make better use of limited resources. With increased alignment in organizations, enhanced focus and performance will show gains far beyond the resources committed.

Note

1 A balanced scorecard is a managerial technique designed to assess company performance against a range of criteria – not merely financial ones – to ensure the active implementation of strategic plans.

12 Exploding bottles

Exploring the work culture and human resource issues of champagne

Liz Thach

Imagine a work environment so dangerous that workers have to wear iron face masks and padded clothing to guard against exploding pieces of glass and fermenting wine. This was the common work in the cellars of late seventeenth- and eighteenth-century Champagne before the introduction of stronger glass bottles. Some reports indicate that more than 50 per cent of the wine was lost due to exploding bottles – an early factor in the high prices for a bottle of champagne.

Today worker safety has improved dramatically, and modern technology has entered most champagne cellars – reducing the need for some roles and replacing more tedious jobs with robotic disgorging and bottling machines. At the same time, quite a few champagne cellars still employ riddlers – a position unique to sparkling wine producers in which specially trained workers spend six to seven hours per day hand-turning bottles in a wooden rack. This continues for a period of six weeks so that the yeast particles in the bottle can be moved to the neck for disgorging. Riddling is usually reserved for the prestige *cuvées*, with mechanized gyropalettes performing the same job in a mere three days for the standard *cuvées*. Nonetheless, this embracing of both old and new is a good example of the unique culture which operates in Champagne. This in turn, impacts the work environment and the delicate balance that can be found between grape growers, the managers of the great houses, and the unionized cellar workers.

The relationship between workers, managers, and regulators is key to understanding the work culture. Some say it can be compared to the sparkling wine that ferments for so many years within the champagne bottle. Most of the time it results in beautiful bubbles, but there are still occasions when the bottle explodes, sending shards in many directions. Indeed as one company representative reports, 'Today, we still have one in every 2000 bottles that explodes during the first three months of secondary fermentation'. This tendency for explosion is reflected in the fine tension that still exists today between the various factions – but for the most part this seems to result in a more exciting product and a desire by most to maintain balance and creativity.

In order to understand this unique work culture and the human resource issues which surround it, it is useful to examine three areas. The first is a brief overview of the worker history of champagne in order to understand the dynamics of the region. Next it is helpful to analyse the major types of jobs and human resource practices. The third area is an identification of the components shaping champagne's work culture – based on history and current worker customs. Together all of these serve to provide champagne with a delicately balanced competitive advantage that is nearly impossible to emulate in any other sparkling wine region of the world.

Historical overview of Champagne's work environment

Though accounts vary, most historians agree that it was the Romans who brought the vine to the region of Champagne around AD 50. It was also the Romans who are given credit for digging the original tunnels under the city of Reims as a source of building stone. In the 1700s the tunnels were redis-covered by Ruinart, and were quickly adopted by other famous champagne houses as their 'original' cellars.[1]

Long, cold hours in the vineyard: AD 200 to the middle ages

Historically, vines were planted by the local workers in the old random *en foule* system with no rows or trellising. Instead the vines were very close to one another and grew along the ground in multiple directions. This actually created more work than the current planting density of 8,000 vines per hectare. In addition to the pinot noir of today, other ancient varieties were thought to include pinot blanc, pinot gris, and gamay among others. Vineyards became so important that a large temple to Bacchus was erected in Reims in the third century AD.

Perhaps it was partially due to its wine production that Champagne became a frequent target of the invading Franks and Alamans, who were said to have a strong liking for the delicate drink of the region. The Romans had to defend Champagne through several centuries of attacks, including the famous battle with Attila the Hun in AD 451 – where more than 200,000 were believed to be killed – an eerie foreshadow of the bloody Battle of the Marne which would be fought in the same area in the First World War.

As the might of the Roman Empire waned, the Franks took control of the region and Christianity was allowed to take root. In AD 496, King Clovis was baptized by the Bishop of Reims, and a new era of peace and order came to Champagne with the monasteries encouraging grape-growing and wine production. The monks became experts in understanding the differ-ences in quality between grapes from the various vineyards, and in slowly perfecting their wine-making – though during these years the goal was to make still red wines, not sparkling. Despite this vision, many of the wines of the time were described as a 'pale pink'. A French writer from 1320 said they were 'clear, quivering, and fresh' (CIVC, 2007b, p. 16).

Though the monasteries owned some vineyards, the vast majority of vines were owned and tended by local landowners, who were required to give a percentage of their harvested grapes to the Church as tithes. Disputes occasionally broke out regarding the actual amount of grapes, because both the locals and the monks produced wine for sale. The work environment during this time was similar to other wine-making regions during the Middle Ages with long hours toiling in the vineyards, as well as coping with the cold snowy winters of Champagne and concern with frost in the spring.

Progress continued until the devastating Hundred Years War in the fourteenth and fifteenth centuries where many of Champagne's vineyards were destroyed. However, production tripled by the end of the century when grape-growing returned to the region, and in the 1600s the reputation of the wines became so well known that they began to be referred to as *vins de Champagne*, versus *vins de France* or *vins d'Ay*. The name 'Champagne' stems from the original name of 'Campania remensis' from the sixth century near Reims.

The art of blending and export sales skills: 1600 to the French revolution

As the wine of Champagne grew in reputation, the Abbot of Hautvillers decided to increase production to capitalize on such a profitable product. In 1661 he enlarged the cellars, and in 1668 appointed Dom Pérignon as cellarer with a commission to expand the wine business. Dom Pérignon focused on perfecting the profitable still red wines of the region and became intimately familiar with all of the local vineyards. Through many years of trial and error, he realized that blending the grapes from different vineyards resulted in a more complex and long-lived wine. He also worked closely with the vineyard owners to harvest only ripe pinot noir grapes as intact clusters early in the morning; to keep the grapes cool; to use fractional pressing methods; and to protect them from oxygen as much as possible. It was reported that the workers were very exhausted by the long hours and exacting requirements he insisted on during harvest and crush. His wine-making methods of using pinot noir grapes allowed his wines to age longer. This paved the way for others to create high-quality sparkling wine. His efforts paid off in that wine from Hautvillers fetched almost double the amount of money as that from other cellars.

Ultimately, the sparkle in the wine became fashionable in Paris and by 1674 most of the aristocracy, including Louis XIV, were drinking these wines. This was great news for all involved in the production of champagne. The only downside was the danger of exploding bottles in the cellar, and the fact that in certain years, more than 50 per cent of the product could be lost because of this.

Finally in the 1730s a breakthrough in stronger glass design and improved cork stoppers allowed champagne to move into a type of early 'industrial age'. It was during this period and the following decades that many of the houses of champagne were established, including Ruinart, Moët, Louis Roederer, Lanson, Clicquot, and Heidsieck. Most started as négociants, purchasing grapes from the growers then producing and selling wine. However, over time, some of the large houses also began to purchase vineyard property.

Ancient assembly-line-type operations were set up within the old Roman quarries which became 'crayères' to produce, bottle and store the wine. As production became more sophisticated and streamlined, cellar workers were hired and trained to produce the wine for the houses, and the role of cellar master was created to oversee operations. However, working conditions were challenging, as the cellars were cold and the bottles frequently exploded – even with the improved glass. Iron masks became mandatory to preserve eyesight and avoid ghastly scarring of the face.

The French Revolution, which started in 1789, effectively wiped out many of the royalty and rich aristocracy to which the houses had sold their wine. It also reduced the power of the Catholic Church, and many of the monastery vineyards were taken over by locals. However, production and sales remained strong during this time, as many of the houses developed sales forces to travel abroad and sell wine. As described by Forbes (1967), the champagne sales traveller of the time had to have a 'strong head but a bold face, a voluble tongue, and an indiscriminate and inexhaustible sociability'.

One of the more famous exporters was the Widow Clicquot who assumed operational control of the house of Clicquot in 1805, and devised a method to sell her wine to the Tsars of Russia. She is also credited with creating the first riddling rack by cutting holes in her dining room table in an effort to get rid of the yeast particles which clouded up her wines. By inserting the bottles into the holes upside down and banging them lightly, the yeast slides to the neck. It was then much easier to extract the yeast and recork the bottle without losing as much of the wine. She is also attributed with adding a dosage of very sweet syrup and brandy to match the palate preferences of the Russian aristocracy. In the beginning, she was able to keep this process secret and use it to create a competitive advantage; however, eventually the other houses learned about and adopted the technique (Mazzeo, 2008).

Growing industrialization and worker resentment: 1800–1939

Napoleon's reign from 1799 to 1814 only enhanced the reputation of champagne, as he took it into battle and introduced it to new export markets. Accounts also indicate that by declaring war on Russia, he encouraged more consumption when the Russians, Austrians, and Prussians invaded Champagne in 1814 and stayed to drink the product. By the 1860s, champagne was so well known that it was drunk in many of the emerging New World countries, such as the USA and parts of South America. Indeed, the taste profiles of the Americans and British were different from other

Europeans, and their request for less sweet wines resulted in new break-throughs in the *liqueur d'expedition* and the styles of brut and extra brut were developed.

As noted in Chapter 1, the industrialization of the champagne process continued with new and more sophisticated equipment added to the cellars of the houses, and it became yet more evident that the wine could only be produced by those with immense financial resources. It was not a wine that could easily be crafted by growers with limited resources, and they became dependent on the price houses were willing to pay for their grapes. To make matters worse, there were no rules at that time preventing the houses from purchasing grapes outside of Champagne. Resentment and anger began to simmer in the workforce.

The history of this discontent has already been outlined (Chapters 1 and 5), but crucially some of the growers became so concerned about the power of the houses that they started their own cooperative in 1893, and then in 1904, started the SGV. A union to represent cellar workers and office staff was also created.

The First World War from 1914 to 1918 brought an unusual truce, with the front line running through the vineyards for three of the four years, and the sons of both growers and house owners fighting side by side in the war effort. The Battle of the Marne left the vineyard land covered in bodies, blood and artillery shells, but amazingly wine-making continued throughout the war, with some good *cuvées* created during those four years. However, many of the vineyards were destroyed, and the houses subsidized the replanting so that the growers could survive. This helped to repair some of the old resentment and created some new loyalties and mutual respect (Kladstrup & Kladstrup, 2005).

Global marketing skills and partnerships: 1940 to the present

It was not until after Prohibition and the conclusion of the Second World War in 1945 that the golden years descended upon Champagne again. Part of this may have been due to the creation of the CIVC in 1941 with a focus to enhance relationships and create positive dialogue between the SGV and the houses, including fair grape price negotiations. Clarity around Champagne AOC standards, established in 1935 by the INAO, also assisted in resolving long-simmering debates over appellation limits and quality standards.

As has been shown previously, from 1945 to 1975, champagne sales soared around the world, and the emphasis on great marketing and branding competencies was enhanced. Collectively the houses of champagne in partnership with the growers and CIVC helped to create and defend legally one of the most powerful territorial brands in the world. In addition, large sums of money were invested in upgrading wine-making equipment to create state-of-the-art facilities, and lavish promotions were implemented in major markets. Today, new discussions about expanding the appellation territory bring fresh controversy, and the relationship between the houses, growers and CIVC continues to exist in a fine balance of co-dependence. They all recognize that they need one another to exist, but minor changes in the strategy of one party can still cause explosive responses from another. In terms of work roles, the houses continue to focus on strategy, finance and marketing/branding competencies, whereas the growers concentrate on viticulture. Oenology falls under the joint tenure of the house's cellar master and the unionized cellar workers. Currently, according to the CIVC (Daniel Lorson, CIVC, personal communication 2008), there are approximately 31,000 workers employed in the production of champagne, divided amongst négociants, growers and cooperatives.

Key jobs and human resource practices in the Champagne wine industry

In reviewing champagne's employment situation of today, it is not that different from its past. Roles are still sharply divided by growers and houses, with the professional organizations (CIVC, SGV, UMC and the workers' unions) providing support and guidance to both.

When examining the value chain (see Figure 12.1), it is clear that the growers hold their dominance in land ownership and viticulture expertise. The houses work with the cellar and administrative union employees to produce a large majority of the wine; however, this is changing slightly with the growth of cooperatives and grower–producers (RMs), and the production of BOBs. Global marketing and finance is primarily held by the houses with legal protection of the brand 'champagne' as the responsibility of the CIVC. This is different from other regions of France in which many of the growers also produce and sell their own wine, and major producers own hundreds of hectares of their own vineyards, as in Bordeaux.

Viticultural jobs, responsibilities and salaries

The type and number of jobs held by each of the three value chain compo-

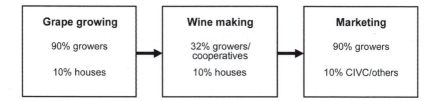

Figure 12.1 Champagne work–value chain and ownership.

nents also differs. With grape-growing, the majority of the 15,000 growers only have a small number of hectares to farm, with the average being 2.22 hectares. In most cases the family (father, mother, children) handle most of the job responsibilities during the year. According to the CIVC (2007b), these include pruning, tilling, spraying, tying up, de-leafing, pinching back, trellis maintenance, and weeding.

For harvest, growers will invite friends and neighbours to help with the picking if it is a small vineyard; however, for larger operations they will hire seasonal workers. In general, 100,000 seasonal workers are hired each harvest – most being students, the French who want to work in the vineyards and make some extra money, and seasonal workers from Eastern Europe. If travellers are hired, the landowner is responsible for providing an even field so they can set up their caravans for housing. In addition, they must be provided with water, restrooms and rubbish receptacles.

Work responsibilities during harvest are usually divided into: (1) pickers who carefully select only ripe healthy clusters and place them in five-kilogram buckets; (2) porters who drive small tractors where pickers can dump their buckets into larger bins of 45–50 kilograms; and (3) loaders who load the larger bins from the porters onto trailers. From there the grapes are transported to the press. Most of the presses are located in the vineyards so that transport time is kept to a minimum. Harvest generally lasts around three weeks.

Other vineyard-related jobs include vineyard consultants who may be called in to advise on disease or pest related issues, and finance/tax-related work to track harvest sales and complete required paperwork. In general it costs €10,000 to €15,000 per hectare for vineyard maintenance costs each year in Champagne.

In terms of salaries for vineyard workers, as with all grape-growing regions, producers in Champagne are required to pay the obligatory minimum French salary of €8.71 per hour for a 35-hour work week. In addition, employers must provide 10 per cent for holidays and 10 per cent for the end of contract. However, they are allowed to deduct money from the pay if they provide meals (deduct €1.41 for breakfast, €8.44 for lunch and €5.63 for dinner). Recent salaries for harvest workers are illustrated in Table 12.1.

Finally, there is a new practice of hiring 'task workers' during harvest who are paid by the amount and quality of grapes they pick. For example, they are paid a base salary per kilo according to the yield per hectare, e.g. €0.146 per kilo for 10,000 kg/ha and more, but can also achieve a bonus for picking selected grapes, e.g. €0.015. The CIVC sets the standard limit for harvest amounts. It is currently at 99 hectolitres per hectare, which is equivalent to 6.6 tons per acre.

Wine production jobs, responsibilities and salaries

Probably one of the most respected and coveted jobs in Champagne wine

Table 12.1 Salaries for Champagne harvest workers, 2008

	Hourly salary (€)		
	0–35 hrs	*35–43 hrs*	*Over 43 hrs/Sundays*
Grape-picker	8.71	10.89	13.07
Cook's assistant	8.71	10.89	13.07
Basket provider	8.97	11.21	13.46
Manager of grape boxes	9.26	11.58	13.89
Vehicle drivers	10.33	12.91	15.50
Press worker	10.33	12.91	15.50
General cellar worker	10.33	12.91	15.50
Cook	10.33	12.91	15.50
Team manager of pickers	11.58	14.48	17.37
Team manager of press hands	11.58	14.48	17.37
Team manager of kitchen staff	11.58	14.48	17.37

Source: Data provided by David Menival, Reims Management School.

production is that of the cellar master (also referred to as the wine-maker and/or master blender). Most of the houses have two – a current cellar master with years of experience and one in training. For example, the current cellar master of the brand Dom Pérignon has 19 years of experience, and the assistant has five years. In addition to the two cellar masters, other members of the blending team may include family members, executives, and oenologists. Some houses have a rule that members of the blending team cannot travel on the same airplane together, because they cannot afford to lose the intellectual capital of the blending process and experience that resides within their heads.

Blending is considered to be an art form in Champagne, which requires years of training and experience, and an incredible palate memory. It is not uncommon to combine 150 to 300 different lots of wine for the non-vintage house *cuvée*. In addition, in Champagne, reserve wine from previous years is allowed to be added to the blend. It generally takes two to three months to assemble the final blend, and the goal is to achieve the specific house 'style'.

As mentioned previously, the position of riddler is unique to the spar-kling wine industry. This role requires specially trained employees with strong wrists and endless patience to spend six to seven hours per day tapping and twisting bottles to fit the *pupitres*. A good riddler can move 40,000–60,000 bottles per day. The advantage of a riddler over a mechanical gyropalette is said to be a more gentle movement and the artisanal marketing message that can be communicated to customers. This is why riddlers are usually only employed for the top house *cuvée*.

Other important cellar positions include the oenologists, lab assistants, supervisors and general cellar workers who monitor the wine production process and maintain the equipment. Most of the large wineries are now automated and include mechanized gyropalettes and robotic disgorging and

Table 12.2 Salaries for technical and administrative workers, 2008

		Scale	Hourly salary(€)	Monthly rate (151.67)	Extra hours (35–43 hrs)	Extra hours (over 43 hrs)
Technical workers						
Simple worker	Level A	1	8.71	1321	10.89	13.07
		2	8.86	1344	11.08	13.29
Specialized staff	Level B	1	8.97	1360	11.21	13.46
		2	9.26	1404	11.58	13.89
Qualified worker	Level C	1	10.33	1567	12.91	15.50
		2	11.03	1673	13.79	16.55
Highly qualified	Level D	1	11.58	1756	14.48	17.37
		2	12.28	1863	15.35	18.42
Administrative worker						
Simple clerk	Level A	2	8.86	1344	11.08	13.29
Specialized clerk	Level B	2	9.26	1404	11.58	13.89
Qualified clerk	Level C	1	10.33	1567	12.91	15.50
		2	11.03	1673	13.79	16.55
Highly qualified	Level D	1	11.58	1756	14.48	17.37
		2	12.28	1863	15.35	18.42

Source: Data provided by David Menival, Reims Management School.

bottling machines. Indeed in the last ten years, the houses have reduced their workforces by almost 30 per cent due to increased mechanization.

The story is the same in the large industrialized cooperatives where many of the grower–producers make their wine. Very few growers are large enough to purchase all of their own equipment. One of the largest cooperatives, Nicolas Feuillatte, produces 30 million bottles per year, with only 33 per cent for their own brand. The remaining production is owned by 80 grower–producers (RCs) and some large BOBs plus sales to houses. The facility has 240 employees and can disgorge, dose and cork over 9,000 bottles per hour.

In Champagne, cellar workers and administrative positions are divided into four levels based on skills and experience, as described in Table 12.2.

In addition, French law requires that the employer pay for meals if the employee works during regular meal times (breakfast: €1.66; lunch: €9.93; dinner €6.62). Finally, an interesting requirement is that holiday pay is based on the number of children the employee has – the more children, the more holiday pay. For example, an employee who has zero to two children only receives €415 in holiday pay, whereas one with three children is given €515.

Wine marketing and other professional positions

The houses of champagne have recruited some of the most innovative marketing, branding and sales professionals in the world. No other wine region has consistently produced such award winning, eye-catching and often extravagant promotions. Sophisticated adverts, billboards, Internet sites, contests, campaigns, movie placement and product linkage to key celebrities are common place – with new and more creative versions being launched each year. The houses vie with one another to hire top talent in this area, and will poach experts from other luxury marketing industries as well.

Related to this area is a focus on hiring the best export specialists. Most houses have many staff members or consulting firms devoted to researching all of the export issues such as taxes, trade tariffs, insurance, labelling requirements, and all of the other negotiations and paperwork required to ship and sell wine in multiple countries.

Protection of the brand 'champagne' continues even today, and so not only the houses, but the professional associations (CIVC, SGV, UMC) devote thousands of euros to hiring top legal experts to monitor and prosecute anyone who dares to infringe the use of their name. In addition, they spend much time lobbying government officials and organizations to continue to support and protect the champagne name and method.

Recruitment of key executives to manage the businesses – especially in the publicly traded houses – is critical. Strong CEOs and other key executive positions in finance, accounting, marketing, human resources, production, and information management are necessary to compete in such a complex global environment.

According to one CEO interviewed, 'champagne is the most difficult business in the world'. He explained the additional steps involved in the wine production process such as longer ageing, riddling and disgorgement, and mentioned the extra capital required for all of the equipment. He described the challenging climate of Champagne with cold winters and frequent frost; the complex grower relationships and conflict-ridden trade-union human resource issues. In addition he mentioned the need to stay up-to-date with marketing, advertising and innovation, and the challenge of providing short-term positive financial reporting to stockholders when champagne is a long-term investment with heavy inventory.

Leadership issues are equally challenging in the cooperatives and with small grower–producers, who often struggle with succession problems. 'I am an 11th generation grower', reported one small RM who sells 10,000 bottles per year. 'My son is the 12th and I am training him to be a blender and take over the business. I'm just lucky that he wants to, because he is my only son'.

Salaries and benefits for professional employees are very competitive – often above market rates in other countries. 'Champagne has the best human resource practices in France', reports one CEO. 'Our employees receive the highest salaries, the best health care, and other benefits'. At the same time, since so many of the large houses are global in nature, they also must manage international human resources issues including foreign salary structures, benefits, policies and tax rates for their employees who work abroad.

Analysing the work culture of Champagne

In examining the work history of the champagne industry and its current human resource practices and job positions, it becomes more apparent how this has helped to shape the culture. According to Schein (2005, p. 32), culture can be defined as 'a pattern of shared basic assumptions' and values that a group of people develop as they work through problems and situations together; it is taught to newcomers as 'the correct way you perceive, think, and feel in relation to those problems'. The culture of a group, organization, region, or country can be observed in the artefacts or symbols they use; the behaviour of the people; values, language, and unspoken rules.

Based on the long and tumultuous history of champagne, its current work processes and positions, and the strength of its regional brand today, it is obvious that there is a strong and deeply rooted work culture. In conversations with key players in the champagne workforce, major concepts and values are repeated often. These primary cultural components revolve around the three overlapping areas of: (1) balance; (2) customer focus; and (3) location/process, all of which are illustrated in Figure 12.2.

Balance – keeping a fine balance in Champagne

The workforce culture component of balance is perhaps the most pronounced. It is a term that is heard repeatedly in most conversations, and

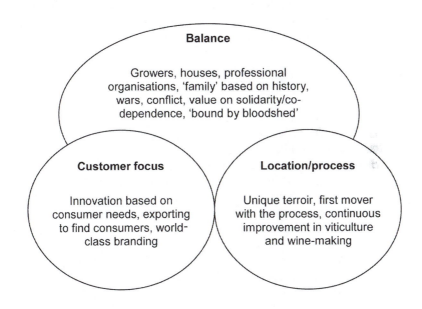

Figure 12.2 Culture components of the champagne work environment.

can be in reference to balance of the wines; balance of prices; balance of relationships between all parties; and balance of lifestyle. Following are several quotes from six different interviews with key members of the champagne workforce illustrating this concept:

- 'Balance is important here – between prices; between growers and houses'.
- 'In Champagne we try to keep a good balance of supply/demand. A fine balance is a slight shortage – all of the actors work together to create this'.
- 'Currently the growers are too small to worry the houses. It is a question of balance'.
- 'As long as growers do not sell the land, the balance will maintain'.
- 'If sales go down, we reduce production to keep the balance'.
- 'We see ourselves in the middle of a competition, but with a family focus . . . (we are balanced)'.

The balance between growers and houses is a key part of the work culture. In some ways, they see themselves as a large family forged together by years of history and bloody wars. As one house CEO reported, 'We should never forget that on this land where we drink the drink of happiness that great battles have been fought. The sense of history is very strong in Champagne'.

The sense of history and acting as one large family (though with frequent conflict between members) is quite apparent. Both the growers and houses recognize their co-dependence and there is strong solidarity. At the same time, they are still slightly wary of one another:

- 'My personal relationship with [the house] keeps me with them. It is important not to be too greedy' (Grower).
- 'There is a strong sense of loyalty and family in Champagne. We have solidarity in Champagne' (House).
- 'It was a shot gun wedding . . . [but we need to stay together]. If we lose that faith, we will kill the champagne business. We need each other, and not because the houses are good guys' (Grower).
- 'Ninety per cent of the growers are faithful and stay with their houses – because their grandfathers signed with them' (House).
- 'We understand that the houses helped to establish the brand of champagne . . . [we appreciate this] . . . The houses are the locomotive on the train to pave the way for the champagne market' (Grower).
- 'Like the Arabs have oil on tap; the growers have the tap here in Champagne . . . [we recognize that]' (House).
- 'History is beautiful. We are about family and history' (Grower).

This delicate balance is perpetuated by communication to new generations, and to some extent, by law and French pride. Within the grower ranks, the older generation trains the new generation to take over their vineyard. There is a great respect for the land. As one grower reports, 'There is a strong value to take care of the land in families'.

The growers recognize that their power lies in possession of 90 per cent of the grapes. However, if the new generation decides to sell the land there is not much to prevent them from doing so, except for the strong cultural tradition of maintaining the balance. There is also SAFER that allows the French state to intervene in the sale of land if the price seems inappropriate.

French pride also seems to be operating in maintaining the delicate balance of champagne, and keeping it under French ownership. For example, in 2006 when the extended Taittinger family had sold their house, it would have been resold to a large bidder from India had not the French bank, the Crédit Agricole, stepped in and agreed to finance the few members of the Taittinger family who wanted to keep the winery, and allowed them to repurchase it as a family concern (Frank, 2009).

At the same time, most of the large houses are global in nature and many have wineries in other countries. 'Some of the growers see this as a bit of betrayal', notes one observer. Yet the houses recognize the need to expand their market, and the wisdom of taking their wine-making expertise and strong branding presence to develop sparkling wine brands in other locations. And so the delicate balance between houses and growers continues with slight flare-ups on both sides whenever one party takes an action that may seem threatening to the other – all the while recognizing their co-dependence.

Customer focus – 'In Champagne we focus on making friends, not marketing'

The second major work culture area of customer focus is readily apparent in the history of Champagne as well as in its current workforce design and emphasis. Since the mid-1700s when Claude Moët travelled to Versailles to introduce the court and Madame de Pompadour to the wines of Champagne, getting close to the customer has been a key part of champagne's success and culture. And, since from its earliest days most champagne was consumed by royalty, it entered the luxury market from the beginning.

A focus on luxury marketing is very evident in the work culture of champagne. As one grower–producer stated, 'We make bubbles that make you dream'. This is an excellent description of luxury marketing which taps into the dreams and aspirations of consumers to such an extent that price is not as relevant, and they are willing to pay more to procure the luxury (dream). Furthermore, it is important to create an image of scarcity of the product, which the Champenois do so well with their supply/demand balance. Finally, with luxury marketing, 'selling' is considered to be rather vulgar, whereas relationships are key. As one house CEO put it, 'In Champagne we focus on making friends, not on marketing'. Other interviewed members discussed the luxury marketing of champagne:

- 'The psychological aspect of the product is important – the magic of champagne'.
- 'Champagne is the drink of kings. The bubbles are linked to being excited and lit up. By drinking it, you can join the festive occasions of the elite'.
- 'Champagne is an affordable luxury'.
- 'Luxury doesn't suffer crisis'.

Despite the enviable position of champagne as a luxury product, the Champenois recognize that this needs to be perpetuated – thus the very strong customer focus. Economic downturns throughout history have impacted sales, but in almost every case customer focus and innovation have pulled them through to new successes. When some customers in Britain asked for a drier style, they created it. When the Tsar was concerned that someone would place a bomb in the bottle, Louis Roederer invented the clear bottle which became 'Cristal'. In London nightclubs, when female consumers said they wanted a drink that didn't mess up their lipstick, some champagne houses responded by producing small bottles which came with a straw. Being responsive to consumer needs is a key part of their culture and success. The huge staff of luxury marketing, branding, and sales people within champagne houses today attest to this.

Location/process – sacred terroir and the birth of the bubble

The third work culture component of location and process has to do with the actual land and terroir, as well as the wine-making process. In terms of production, today champagne holds only 12 per cent of total global sparkling wine share. As there is currently almost no more land to plant, this share will most likely remain constant or decrease slightly as other countries increase their sparkling wine production, at least in the short term. However, the Champenois are not concerned by the limits on production, because this will only increase their desired image of scarcity, and make wine from Champagne even more special. Additionally, the concept of terroir – a distinctly French concept – is very clever in terms of strategy and competitive advantage. If there is only one place on earth that possesses a specific soil, climate, topography, geology, sunlight and water, then there is no way that a competitor can duplicate it – especially if it is protected by strong French AOC laws and organizations like the INAO. In Champagne, this is even more so because it is much smaller than other French wine-making regions, such as Bordeaux and the Loire – being closer in size to Burgundy. It is because of this that land prices are so high. Many of the growers who own the land have become quite wealthy with rising grape costs. As one interviewee suggested, 'they are peasants,[2] but with Mercedes'.

This strong competitive advantage emanating from the sacred terroir is reflected in the wine-making process. Champagne is credited with inventing the *méthode champenoise* (even though there are some accounts suggesting that British wine merchants did), and indeed have fought to ensure that they are the only producers in the world that can use that term on their bottle – most EU countries now conforming to the new designation of *méthode traditionale*. This first mover advantage and communication of the wine-making process in marketing messages – especially the art of blending – is mentioned repeatedly in conversations:

- 'We are the ones who invented the birth of the bubble'.
- 'It is our job to engender the mousse . . . and create magic'.
- 'The greatest asset of champagne is the blend'.
- '*Assemblage* is magical'.
- 'I do not make a Grand Cru because it will dilute all the other *cuvées* – plus I can sell the bottles with better forecasting, because of consistent style'.
- 'We use 500 samples in our blending. It takes us three months to assemble. We usually taste 15 in the morning and 15 in the afternoon. The blend sits for three weeks to marry'.
- 'I like to compare champagne to Russian Dolls – the small dolls are like new wine and can't speak that well; whereas the larger dolls are like the older wine and they can speak in a loud voice'.
- 'The longer the wine is aged, the more smooth and creamy it will become with integrated carbon dioxide resulting in very small bubbles'.

The rigour and art of the wine-making process is a key part of the work culture. Indeed the reverence for blending is quite high, because it also helps to create a distinctive house style which assists with branding. It is also heavily linked to the financial success of the industry, because as one expert stated, 'Brut NV is usually 90 per cent of sales in most houses'.

In addition, the Champenois do not rest on their laurels, but continue to make improvements. 'Innovation is continuous and more incremental in Champagne in the vineyard, the cellar, and in the bottles', reports one interviewee. Examples include reduction of pesticides in the vineyard by 40 per cent since 2001; the first region in France to begin carbon emission studies; adoption of a sustainable farming strategy; and experimentation with new and safer ways to remove the yeast from the bottle.

Finally, the grape-growing and viticultural process itself is enjoyable to many, and the pride and joy in the work is evident in the passionate dialogue and descriptions of workers. As one grower–producer reported: 'There is an intrinsic satisfaction in the work, because of the completeness. It's enough to have a good life . . . My pleasure is to make champagne'.

Conclusion – the future of the Champagne work culture

In conclusion, it can be seen how the strong work culture of champagne provides it with a unique competitive advantage. The reverence for balance in the wine, lifestyle, supply, pricing, and relationships between growers, houses, and professional organizations is strong and currently clearly understood by all parties. The relentless focus on customers as a continued means of financial success and differentiation is obvious. The pride in the land, unique terroir, and work processes in the vineyard and cellar are palpable. All of these currently work together to keep champagne strong.

The obvious question is – can this continue? Is the culture strong enough to withstand changing economic conditions and potential variations in values by new generations of growers and different leadership in the houses? Can they successfully pass on the work culture?

- *Land ownership.* As new generations of growers take control of the land, will they uphold the perceived sacred trust to care for it and not sell it to outsiders? Will the houses break with their tradition of not owning much land, and attempt to take control of the grape-growing part of the supply chain?
- *Publicly traded companies.* As new generations of leaders come forward in the houses, will there be more share offers created to gain fresh capital and the chance to grow larger? How will this impact the balance?
- *Mergers and acquisitions.* Will there be more consolidation of the houses so that only a few dominate the market – as seen in other parts of the world, (e.g. Constellation Wine and Fosters in Australia). Already in Champagne five houses own 60 per cent of the value of all the négociants. Further consolidation could upset the balance.
- *Growth of grower–producer and BOB market.* This segment has continued to grow for the past decade. Will there come a time when it is so large that it negatively impacts the houses? As one expert observed, 'There is no need for Goliath (the houses) to fear David (the growers) at this point, but it could change'.
- *Changing labour regulations.* France already has an extremely protectionist and generous labour law. Could changes in labour regulations make it hard to compete in the world market? Who will hand-harvest the grapes in the future?
- *Union relations.* Are there issues which can upset the balance with the unions? Could an increase in union power negatively impact productivity and profitability?
- *Succession issues.* More newcomers are entering the champagne workforce via publicly traded houses. How will this impact the delicate balance of grower–house relationships? How closely is leadership succession monitored to insure positive continuation of the culture of the blend?

- *Continued innovation.* Will champagne be able to continue its tradition of innovation and stay ahead of the competition in this area?
- *Changing technology.* Is champagne staying abreast of changes in technology and adopting those that make strategic and financial sense?

These and other challenges currently face champagne. However, based on its history and ability to find innovative solutions during times of both peace and war, the future appears positive for the region. Though there will be fluctuating economic cycles ahead, this great region has proven time and again that it can surmount most obstacles. Through it all – exploding bottles and riots alike – it has maintained a fine balance of working relationships in multiple arenas, and continues to produce bubbles that make consumers dream.

Note

1   Much of this discussion is taken from Johnson (2004) and Kladstrup and Kladstrup (2005).
2   The term 'peasant' in French does not have the derogatory overtones that exist in English, and many growers are proud to use the term to describe themselves.

Part V
Reflecting on champagne

13 Conclusion

Maintaining the delicate balance of champagne

Steve Charters and David Menival

As stated in the introduction, this book was not intended as a textbook on how to manage champagne, nor for any wine region seeking to emulate its success. Rather it has been designed as a perspective on how champagne operates at the beginning of the twenty-first century, seen through eyes both of academics who live and work in the region, and have a comprehensive knowledge of it, and of those from outside, whose focus is on wine business, and who can offer more of an arm's length view on what is happening there. Further, the book was designed to address both practical and theoretical issues and to be of use both to practitioners and students. Consequently it is relevant to summarize what the authors of the various chapters have concluded at both an applied and a conceptual level and to reflect on some of the issues which face the region in the future – factors which have a relevance well beyond champagne, to the wine, tourism, and food and agriculture industries more generally.

A number of key themes and issues emerge from this analysis. Some of these will not be surprising to those with an intimate knowledge of the wine and the region, and many of the challenges have already been spelt out. Others may be less evident, or – at least at the level of implementation – more difficult to engage with. We will start with an analysis of some of the key reasons why the wine has attained its present position – including its paradoxical nature, the idea of the territorial brand, and clusters and co-opetition. We then move on to how the business of champagne is changing and what the future may bring, noting some external constraints but examining in detail potential problems for the territorial brand, supply and financial issues and the changing structure of ownership and management.

The success of champagne

Resolving the contradictions of champagne

The first conclusion relates to the management of the myths which surround a product such as champagne.[1] The impact of history and geography on the development of champagne as a product, and the 'idea' of champagne, have been clearly set out and considered throughout the previous chapters. As Richard Mitchell and Nick Lewis make clear, the place (both as a wider socio-historical construct at regional level and in the micro as in the notion of terroir) are used to create a series of myths about what champagne means. There is also a common shared and accepted history. This integrates those common myths and stories which unite the key actors in defending the brand. However, it is important to be aware that this mythology changes – for it is often repeated in the region not just as accepted truth, but as unchanging truth as well. As Colleen Guy has suggested, 100 years ago champagne was a bourgeois consumption myth and a French national myth, but not a myth which provided internal cohesion in the region as it now does (Guy 2003).

This idea of the role of history, story and mythology leads to two further points. The first, more theoretical, is to note the importance of both internal and external myths, as was highlighted by Nick Lewis in his analysis of the role of the local newspaper, *La champagne viticole* about the use of terroir for internal as well as external consumption. The internal myths bind the region and explain its structure, resolve its tensions and provide it with a purpose. The external myths are used as part of the brand to explain to consumers why they must drink it. The second point is to be clear that as the mythology changes so it must be managed, and as the nature of champagne changes so will the mythology. To take just one example, how does the mythology of terroir or craft production continue as more consumers realize that the largest producers make 15, 20 even 30 million bottles per year?

One of the important paradoxes of champagne which has emerged from this study is that of complexity versus simplicity. Theo Georgopoulos, at a legal level, and Nick Lewis, when examining terroir, have shown how the operation and the story of champagne are not easily reducible to categorical statements. Yet as Tim Dodd has pointed out, part of the wine's appeal is the apparent simplicity of its message: three well-known grape varieties, a handful of linked consumption situations (conviviality, celebration, seduction and success) and one soil type. Additionally, the fact that there is a single AOC eases this presentation of the region, yet the management of this paradox is not easy and needs to be carefully handled by those involved in promoting the wine.

Finally, there is a sense of champagne 'exceptionalism' – reflecting in some ways the French notion of *l'exception française* (French uniqueness). Champagne is a wine, it is a terroir product – but it is also different. This is seen in production terms: champagne is the only quality European wine which can be made in a pink form by blending red and white wine (generally only red grapes can be used), or which can be made sweet by adding sugar, rather than solely by using super-ripe grapes. In marketing terms too, champagne is different. It is a consistent wine rather than one which displays vintage variation, it is very strongly branded, and it has – essentially – a single AOC. It is also a drink associated with dissipation and the *demi-monde,* which was 'invented' by a monk and became one of the symbolic elements of bourgeois life. Further, as has been underlined throughout this book, it is a world of both large and small companies, apparently working together for common goals and, as Martin Kunc suggests, sharing the value created by their efforts.

Engaging with consumers

First, as noted by Tim Dodd in Chapter 7, the Champenois have engaged very effectively with consumers. Rather than merely providing a wine and then expecting the consumer to drink it because it is of such evidently high quality, they have worked hard to understand their varying markets and to position their product not merely on the basis of its intrinsic quality but also on the basis of its symbolism. This engagement has included a willingness to seek out markets as actively as possible. Contributors to this book have noted the efforts of 'Champagne' Charles Heidsieck, and the focus of Madame Clicquot. Both of these have their equivalents in the modern age who travel the world promoting both champagne generally and the individual brands specifically.

Second, champagne is perceived by the consumer to offer substantial added value. At a merely utilitarian level one can question whether or not a bottle of wine which costs perhaps €9 to produce (for the basic non-vintage brut), and not substantially more for the more prestigious wines is worth the large mark-up paid by the consumer – yet it is the fact that it has been positioned so successfully at a symbolic and mythical level which allows this to happen.

One other significant aspect of how champagne functions and why it has been successful is the general perception that it is a luxury product. This book has not addressed discretely the issue of whether or not champagne is a luxury good (that would require a book in itself), and the idea is not universally accepted – indeed one can question whether or not a wine which sells locally for perhaps €11 and in French supermarkets for even less is indeed a luxury product. Nevertheless, whilst not a universal view, it is very widely accepted that champagne is a luxury product – and, it can be observed, this perspective is shared by most of the contributors to this book! Richard Mitchell pointed out that champagne is produced at the margins of viticultural tolerance and yet its mythology has it viewed as one of the world's greatest wines. This combines, as Tim Dodd suggested, with the celebrity status of some owner/managers/wine-makers (and, one could add, past actors) and it is the personification of champagne in this way which results in an emphasis on what Liz Thach notes is 'making friends' rather than 'marketing', which helps to distance champagne from the merely commercial – something which is essential for luxury products (Beverland, 2005). But, despite what was said by one interviewee and noted in Chapter 12, champagne does suffer from crises – even if there is a widespread view that luxury products generally do not.

Having said this, it may be that the engagement with consumers needs regular reinvention. As Richard Mitchell noted, the way the champagne producers present themselves to many visitors is seen as repetitive by some. Further, as Larry Lockshin suggested, it may be that the added value offered by champagne and primarily based at present on situations of celebration, extravagance and seduction needs to be broadened out, with a more general positioning as the definitive aperitif, or even as a wine to drink with food. The CIVC has addressed this issue in the past, but it is one which could warrant additional attention from the industry.

The territorial brand of champagne

One key notion which has been highlighted in this book is the role of the territorial brand of 'champagne', and of the CIVC as territorial brand manager. The idea of a territorial brand is only just emerging in academic literature, but is likely to become more significant in the future. A territorial brand is one which belongs to all the producers in a definable territory, and which necessarily exists because the product they make can only be created there and cannot be replicated anywhere else. Thus the territorial brand exists together and in cooperation with a number of individual proprietary brands of the same product (e.g. separate brands of gorgonzola cheese), or sub-brands producing an element of that product (farms producing milk or factories creating cheese).[2] This is a system which operates on a complex web of both cooperation and competition, involving a number of individual brands of the same product. The champagne houses buy grapes and wine from the growers or cooperatives to produce their wine, yet at the same time are in competition with the same growers and cooperatives for share of the consumer market. Furthermore, the houses compete with each other in markets around the world, yet need to cooperate in presenting a united front in their dealings with the growers. For many people in the wine industry, for whom the concept of brand is anathema, the idea that a regional identification, often formalized into an AOC, could be considered a brand is unacceptable and the contrast is often made between terroir wines and branded wines (e.g. Leeuwen & Seguin, 2006), so that, by impli-cation, the latter are somehow second class.[3] Indeed, we have heard a number of times the argument that champagne is not a brand, rather it is an AOC. But if one considers how champagne functions, and the fact that it gives value both to producers and consumers by identifying the product (Aaker, 1991; Kotler *et al.*, 1994), then it is a brand. Further, as has emerged in this book, the role of the CIVC is essentially the role of a brand manager, managing 'champagne' in conjunction with the houses' and growers' *syndi-cats*. It markets the product, carries out research and development, protects its intellectual property, mediates between the conflicting parts of the (regional) enterprise, and has responsibility for quality control just as any brand manager does.

Given that this is the case, then, one relevant question is how can the CIVC develop its role as a brand manager? Is it carrying out all the work that a typical brand manager would, and can it be further empowered to promote the brand? A further and equally interesting question is to ask if the model of a single, cohesive, territorial brand manager, as exists in Champagne, can be transposed to other wine regions. If Bordeaux had had a single organization promoting its wine over the last 20 years, as opposed to a myriad of syndicats for different sub-regions or product types, would it now be in such a crisis of overproduction with AOC wine on sale in French supermarkets for €2 a bottle? Whilst other reasons for the success of champagne over past decades will be considered below, the cohesion and simplicity of its single territorial brand is one very significant reason for its current worldwide position.

There must be a number of economic actors underneath the umbrella of the territorial brand, with no single proprietary brand being dominant; if that were to occur the dominant proprietary brand would probably usurp the position of the territorial brand and its manager. Additionally, all actors must remain willing to cooperate, and all must realize that their individual brand will only be profitable if the territorial brand is successful, so that some of their company's needs must therefore be subject to the latter's requirements. Sharing brand values in this way has a democratic dimension, and it is part of the role of the CIVC to develop this. Further, as well as values, value too must be fairly shared – something which Martin Kunc noted as one of the achievements of champagne – so that the two families both feel that they are benefiting from the success of their collective product and their individual efforts. In this way the territorial brand, and its carefully constructed shared mythology, have come to transcend the differences of the two families.

Clusters and co-opetition

Two other related ideas hang over this book – although they are nowhere expressly considered – the idea of clusters (Porter, 1998, 2003) and co-opetition (Nalebuff & Brandenburger, 1997). A geographic cluster offers its members economies of scale and of proximity, momentum, access to local research and development, and access to staff. Indeed, the wine industry (in this case in the Napa Valley) gave Porter (1998) one of his key examples of the effective operation of clusters where grape-growers, wine-makers, consultants and enterprises which provide goods and services work together (whether or not technically in competition) to develop a single, effective and renowned industry, co-ordinated in this case by the Napa Valley Grapegrowers, a voluntary body uniting the wine industry in the region. The same can be said to exist in Champagne, although in Champagne the CIVC has more formal, quasi-statutory powers. Clusters are not inevitably coterminous with a territorial brand, nor do they have to have that indissoluble link with the place from which they come, as is evident with Italian leather or German cars, where it is history rather than geography which has provided the *savoir faire* that gave them their initial reputation and allowed the cluster to develop. However, what also exists in the territorial brand – in a less legally structured way in the Napa Valley than in Champagne, but to a certain extent in both – is a means of co-ordination, marketing and strategically directing the whole cluster. Silicon Valley is a cluster, but with no common body which gives it a collective vision and direction; effective wine regions are different in having such an organization.

Porter (1998) argues that, for a cluster's evolution to be successful, there has to be both competition and cooperation. This interaction of the two helps to maintain individual strengths and an advantage based on shared information for the cluster (although, of course, it does not guarantee the success of any individual enterprise). This is termed co-opetition (Gnyawali *et al.*, 2008; Zineldin, 2004), and describes precisely the situation which exists in Champagne. Zineldin (2004, p. 782f.), proposes a number of preconditions for co-opetition to be successful, including effectively constructed 'organizational arrangements', 'cultural fit', 'interdependences', and 'institutionalization and integration'. As we have seen, through organizational structures, a shared history and mythology, a common vision and a sense of a single origin these all operate for champagne.

There is a view which argues that French (perhaps European) AOCs do not work as a cluster, because they are based on terroir (Ditter, 2005). Ditter concludes that 'terroirs', whilst they are 'local production systems' are not clusters because (1) they raise barriers to entry; (2) they do not therefore generate competition; and (3) 'terroirs are characterized by fragmentation' (p. 49), which reduces their ability to invest, find capital and develop the whole cluster. Thus they are both non-cooperative and non-competitive. Ditter's is an interesting and carefully argued analysis, but it seems to us to be flawed; rather, we feel, terroir (however defined) and clusters go hand in hand but are different; one is about production guarantees and brand identity, the other is organizational. The argument over barriers to entry could just as easily be applied to the Napa Valley, where producers with land outside the region are excluded from membership of the cluster. Further, competition is entirely possible both within a small terroir (Clos de Vougeot, with over 50 different producers situated within it) or a large one – such as Champagne. Finally, the whole use of the notion of terroir, as Nick Lewis has suggested, is subject to multiple interpretations, because it is in part a socially constructed idea, and therefore cannot be easily contrasted with a cluster. Ditter based much of his analysis on the Burgundy wine region, which has a very distinctive interpretation of terroir that is not shared even throughout France, let alone other countries.

The future of champagne

Champagne has been extremely successful by adapting to internal tensions and external challenges and opportunities. This success is not now static, however, and the region needs to continue with its strategic planning for the future. The danger is that the success of the past 60 years leaves the region more focused on the achievements of the past – the success of the CIVC in uniting the two families and protecting the name of champagne – than planning strategically for the future. At a personal level, it seems to us that over the past few years the region has concentrated very effectively on the immediate problems facing it (from 2002–2008 the increasing stresses on grape supply, and then from late 2008 onwards the economic crisis), which required an effective 180-degree turn in day-to-day activity. Even the plan to revise the AOC boundaries and increase the potential grape supply, which will only have an effect in about 15 years time, were the result of the culture and environment of the boom of the middle of the last decade. However, there seems to have been less focus on problems that are on the medium- and long-term horizon.

Most of this book has focused on the internal organization of champagne, and much of this section examining the future of champagne will reflect that. However, when considering where champagne is going two external constraints must be noted, at least in passing. The first is the threat, or otherwise, from sparkling wines produced in other parts of the world (including other regions of France), examined in more detail by Larry Lockshin in Chapter 8. As Larry suggested, there are two views on this issue: the first is that it is a substantial threat as champagne will be seen ultimately as just another sparkling wine and therefore could succumb to a sustained challenge from wines of Carneros or Tasmania or southern England, particularly if the challengers are shown to be of equivalent or better 'quality' to champagne. The converse argument is that consumers do not ultimately buy champagne because they can see it is the 'best' sparkling wine – but because it is champagne and is therefore the only wine appropriate for celebration and display. Indeed, by this reasoning, the growth of the global sparkling wine market may in fact benefit champagne – for the more that consumers drink 'fizz', the more they will need champagne for those special occasions. One final view on this perceived threat actually synthesizes both of these ideas. There will be no threat to champagne so long as it maintains its distinctive role, story and mythological symbolism. The threat from outside only becomes important if champagne undermines its position by incoherent marketing or a pricing approach which makes consumers believe that it is in fact no different from any other sparkling wine.

The other external factor is global warming, noted by both Martin Kunc and Larry Lockshin. The wine industry has recently begun to take the impact of global warming on wine production and styles seriously, and some Champenois have also begun detailed analyses of its impact on their region, led by Dominique Moncomble of the CIVC. This has resulted in the application of some new policies designed to modify the environmental impact and carbon footprint of champagne (Descotes & Moncomble, 2007). Nevertheless, the focus has been almost entirely viticultural and not managerial, and it can be questioned whether or not it is still taken seriously. For example, one of us was told a few years ago by a senior member of the industry that the managerial impact of global warming did not warrant any consideration at the present. Any such consideration deserves a much more detailed analysis than the current study is able to offer, but the impact of global warming on wine styles (and thus consumer perceptions of quality and authenticity), on the management of the AOC and the proposed changes to its boundaries, on the strategy of the large groups, and on the balance between the various actors in Champagne, deserves a comprehensive exploration. This thus forms part of the context for what follows, even if not specifically addressed.

Problems for the territorial brand

We have noted how effectively the CIVC manages the territorial brand of champagne. Crucially, however, there are some things that the CIVC cannot do at present that a typical brand manager would be able to achieve. We have already observed that it relies on shared brand values and the willingness of key actors to cooperate; if, however, decisions are taken which threaten the continued implementation of that shared vision there is no sanction. A decision which is perfectly logical and reasonable for the future of an individual company may weaken the image and reputation of champagne overall. This is regularly seen in the internal arguments within the region. One example of many, which has been considered in previous chapters, is the decision by some champagne producers (mainly houses, but also cooperatives and growers) to establish subsidiaries making, or being involved with the production of, sparkling wine in other parts of the world. There is a widespread view amongst many Champenois that this dilutes the reputation of the champagne brand, and perhaps threatens its future success. Whether or not that perception is correct (and the arguments are complex) it is currently impossible for the CIVC even to intervene in the debate, let alone issue any directives about it. Yet, at the same time, the CIVC can dictate to producers how long their bottles must age on lees in the cellar, and can carry out downstream quality evaluation.

These limits to the power of the CIVC have an impact on a debate that is likely to become increasingly important in the mid-term, over issues such as quality and authenticity. Classic economic theory would suggest that once the region's reputation has been established, one would expect the main brands to 'free ride' on that and reduce the level of absolute quality of the product whilst maintaining the price (Landon & Smith, 1998). It is to the credit of the region's large producers that this has not happened – indeed, if anything the view is that the quality of champagne has increased over the last decade or so rather than declined (Faith, 2008). Nevertheless, if a producer does chose to coast on the region's reputation in the future there is little that can be done about it.

A similar concern relates to the perceived authenticity of champagne. Authenticity is a key attribute sought by modern consumers (Gilmore & Pine, 2007) and for products rooted in place and tradition, as champagne is, it is especially important (Beverland, 2005), a fact stressed by Nick Lewis in his chapter. Whilst rarely addressed in detail the idea of authenticity has surfaced in most of the chapters in this book, notably in establishing the wine's superiority to other sparkling wines (Chapter 7) and the importance of terroir (Chapter 6) and tradition (Chapter 5) in sustaining it. Nevertheless, as suggested in Chapter 9, with the widespread distribution of large brands, authenticity is harder to sustain – and indeed may be threatened by the use of distribution channels which are 'modern' and 'industrial' (Muraz, 2010). Resolving this dilemma is a key issue for the people who are responsible for managing champagne as distinct from the individual brands of champagne.

The issues of quality and authenticity combine in two issues in particular, which may need to be resolved in the future to avoid the image of champagne being undermined. Both of these have been alluded to throughout this book. The first is the sale by individual growers of wines which are given their label, but which they have not made, and indeed have been made by a cooperative to a mass produced specification. It is almost unknown elsewhere in the world of wine that grape-growers sell wine with their label that they have not made (and thus for which the production process has not been controlled by the owner of the label) and which comes from grapes from vineyards other than their own (and therefore not from their authentic terroir). Whilst not a major issue in terms of the volume of champagne sold, this could at some point cause wider damage to the brand of champagne. The second quality issue relates to the use of *sur lattes* wines (see Chapter 4), champagnes which are made by one producer but marketed by another. The argument in favour of this procedure is that it smoothes irregular demand patterns for the wines of large producers, yet in effect it means that the consumer cannot be certain that the wine they buy with a well-known label on it was actually made by the company claiming it as their own. This is probably less significant as a quality issue – the purchasing company will attempt to obtain wines that broadly fit into their house style – but it does have an impact on the perceived authenticity of the brands, and by extension of champagne as a whole. Some of the houses, indeed, are aware of the danger of this practice, and will not buy *sur lattes* wines; some of the largest, however, do not deny using the practice.

A further paradox of the territorial brand in Champagne is its style of distribution. As noted in Chapter 9, in the discussion on the distribution of luxury brands, there is potentially a contradiction between wines which are presented based on brand image or on product attributes. The former, which also tend to be the highest-volume brands (although this is not invariably the case), risk the loss of authenticity and a self-defeating loss of scarcity. How does all this impact on the territorial brand generally, and the other brands marketed more on the basis of their product attributes, guarantee of authenticity, and intrinsic quality? There is the danger that the approach taken by one group of brands (with, say, a focus on glamour, presentation and celebrity) will undermine the overall success of the region, and the image of another type of brand. The territorial brand of champagne was founded on internal contradictions (the two families), which were resolved during the course of the twentieth century. It has, however, yet to negotiate how to resolve these external contradictions and differences which have resulted from the wine's very success and rapid growth over the last 30 years. This is a key challenge for the future of the territorial brand and its managers.

A final distribution-related issue involves the willingness of key outsiders to continue to work with the territorial brand. This also was highlighted in Chapter 9, particularly in the context of supermarket behaviour with champagne sales (especially influential in some countries), and the fact that their sole responsibility is to their shareholders and to maximizing the latter's revenue and capital growth, rather than to champagne. An interesting comparison is to consider the impact of supermarket demands on the reputation of the Australian wine industry. Fifteen years ago the reputation of Australian wines for quality and consistency was very high; however, a number of producers became locked into selling large volumes of wine where discounting and margin-shaving became more important than strong long-term branding. The result is now that Australian wine in the United Kingdom, at least, has a reputation for being safe but boring; it has lost the image of being interesting and different that it had a decade or more ago. However, once producers were organized to produce large volumes they found the relationships with the large retail chains difficult to discard, for this remained the only potential outlet for the amount of wine they were producing. This in turn locked them into a vicious circle of further discounting practices to secure their necessary distribution outlets. Whilst champagne producers blame high levels of discounting on the multiple grocers, the region needs to take care that such practices do not make it as dependent on these outlets as the large Australian producers became.

The guarantee and development of supply

For much of the last decade the overall level of grape supply and the provision of raw materials to individual houses have been perceived to be the most urgent problems in champagne. Rapidly growing demand put pressure on the supply of grapes, despite increases in yields. This, in turn, put pressure on contracts, with growers being offered incentives to enter new contracts with some of the houses. Concurrently there were suggestions from the houses that some growers were sitting on stock that could be released onto the market for either fiscal or superannuation reasons. It was projected by the Crédit Agricole in mid-2008 that demand would outstrip the total potential supply sometime between 2014 and 2016, even allowing for the onset of a global economic crisis. Whilst the bank may have underestimated the effect of the eventual crisis, there is no doubt that before the end of the current decade this crunch point is going to be reached.

The proposed revision of the AOC area has been referred to throughout this study, and its limits – particularly in terms of timing – have been noted. Critically, management issues around it also present possible future tensions for the region, and Al Seaman commented on the potential stresses on growers in Chapter 11. Although it was the SGV which initiated the review of the AOC area at the start of the last decade there is evidence that the view of the growers' leadership was not shared by its members, and that many growers are highly suspicious of any increase in the production area (Charters, 2009). Logically, if the growers' economic power is based on a limited supply then increasing that supply could reduce their power – depending on overall changes in demand. Many growers believe that the proposal is likely to see widespread purchases of potential vineyard sites by the houses, thus tilting the balance of power in the region towards the latter. Further, the logic of such a change would be to reduce the value of vineyard land, and thus the overall potential wealth of the landowners.

Equally important will be how that increase in the AOC area is managed. What measures can be taken to limit the speculative purchase of land? How will decisions on which land is included and which remains excluded be taken – a decision which could make some land owners multi-millionaires overnight whilst leaving their neighbours sitting on agricultural land still worth less than €10,000 per hectare. Finally, how will the new landowners who choose not to sell their land but to become growers themselves integrate into the world of champagne? As we have seen, this is a world with clearly established and dominant internal myths which provide its cohesion. What happens if the new actors do not share in that common history and story? How will that change the internal dynamics of the region?

Financial issues

Naturally, financial issues – particularly on the world stage – are currently uppermost in the mind of the champagne industry. It is clear from Chapter 4 that the market for champagne is cyclical, and the onset of crises can now be predicted with some accuracy (that of 2008 was foretold by a number of those involved with the region). Planning for future crises therefore needs refining; stock and price maintenance should not only be tools of response to economic downturns, but also of preparation. Further, the impact of the crisis, and the way it affects négociants then cooperatives and finally growers, could be more effectively managed for the benefit of all. Critically, is the overriding aim of the key actors to maintain collective cohesion? If we consider what may happen in the future for the négociants and cooperatives, it could be that ultimately they benefit from the poor situation of growers, allowing them to access more and cheaper grapes than during times of prosperity. Therefore, even though these large organizations face major problems during crises, some of them may on balance benefit over the longer term because of this enhanced access to raw material.

Critically, it is our view (and supported by a number of the contributors to this book) that if the long-term success of champagne is to be sustained, this has to be done without using substantial price reductions as a tool; these offer short-term relief but may be producing long-term structural problems. The pricing of champagne, suggested Larry Lockshin, 'is simple'; it needs to be maintained at a reasonably high level to continue to signal the quality and prestige of the wine. As we write, one well-known, large-volume brand is being offered by a British supermarket at a price of two bottles for £15 (€18) each, with another outlet proposing one of its major rivals for £13.14 (€15.30) – prices which are no higher than reasonably priced grower wines and little above the more expensive cavas from Spain. Larry continues that 'the best action for the region is to maintain the luxury image'; again we return to problems over the management of the territorial brand. Image generally is the responsibility of the CIVC, but as noted above there are limits to the CIVC's power, particularly with actions outside the region, and it cannot impose controls on pricing nor on how the wine is managed down-stream.

These are external financial concerns. There are also those which are internal to the region which have already been rehearsed, and do not require further detail – notably issues around the high price of grapes and the price of land.

The changing structure of champagne ownership

As is quite clear from earlier chapters, the structure of Champagne is changing, and its ownership and management is evolving. This is happening in both sides of the industry. First, as noted by Larry Lockshin, the structure of the houses is in transition: forty years ago all négociants were run by companies based in Champagne and all were owned by Champagne families. Increasingly production and sales are managed by companies which have owners from outside the region, and owners are often shareholders. This changes the focus of the enterprise, and that in turn has a dramatic impact on what the organization believes it is doing, and what its strategic goals are (Charters, 2006). This change has been essential for champagne: it has brought in a renewed vision for the product and capital to fund the expansion that has occurred since 1970. However, it also means that some organizations are owned by investors who have not been party to the development of the region's story and who, not being from the region, may have less commitment to the success of its territorial brand. Additionally, whereas family-owned companies can take a longer-term view on profitability and see much of their value as being tied up with enduring equity growth in the company, publicly owned organizations and their institutional shareholders often have a shorter-term view on the need for profitability and may see dividends as being more important than capital growth.

One consequence of this change of ownership relates to how the houses' image may be managed, especially during crises. The commitment of shareholders to a champagne house is primarily based on the creation of profit in the short term. Therefore, the financial situation becomes a key element in this profitability. The value of a share partially depends on the indebtedness of the company. Houses are potentially in a weak position because of the high level of stock they have to carry, resulting from the extended production time (the ideal is 3.1 years' worth of sales). They can manage this level during times of prosperity because of sustained and regular cash flow coming from shipments but they encounter real difficulties during each crisis, when stock-to-sales ratios may grow substantially. Faced with this dangerous situation, many houses prefer to sell their stock cheaply to recover their debt and thus limit the drop in their share price. As has already been suggested, this repeated decision steadily undermines the quality image of their label. However, for these houses, that may be preferable to the risk of frightening their shareholders because of unresolved financial difficulties. Indeed, the houses which decide to retain their stock rather than sell at low prices may lose apparent financial value and even become weak enough to be sold after the crisis has passed – yet for the longer term their wine's reputation is enhanced by maintaining a consistent pricing policy. The result is that a change of structure towards public ownership may lead houses to threaten their own reputation in the long term in order to bolster their short-term situation.

Linked to the change in ownership is another factor – that many of the managers of champagne brands (whether or not in the publicly owned companies) are no longer drawn exclusively from the region. Again this has been essential to the wine's growth, as new management practices and marketing techniques have been introduced; yet, again, these individuals may have less understanding of the place, less commitment to its long-term health and less awareness of the interaction between the social and economic aspects of the region. As Richard Mitchell has suggested, the centre of gravity has moved from a Reims–Epernay axis to a Reims–Epernay–Paris triangle, and some of the local actors are cautious about the new managers' ability to sustain the personal relationships on which the region depends.

Meanwhile, for the other family of Champagne, as Martin Kunc observed, agricultural work is perceived to have less cachet and appeal than before. Growers are increasingly unwilling to spend many hours in the vineyards in inclement conditions (something which has been mirrored during harvest by the increasing paucity of casual local workers picking grapes). For the time being cheap vineyard labour can be employed to make up for this, often sourced in from the eastern countries of the European Union, but this source of labour may not continue indefinitely. The limits on the use of machines in vineyards, particularly for harvest and some aspects of pruning, could exacerbate this. Meanwhile, as Liz Thach pointed out, succession issues are making the transmission of champagne businesses more problematic. It is already complicated by the impact of the Napoleonic code, requiring transmission to all the children of a deceased vigneron, but as many increasingly seek work away from a family business and outside the region the traditions and cohesive approach of the growers is likely to change.

Such structural changes are not specific to champagne; they are occurring worldwide (the Australian experience is again pertinent), and in many industries beyond wine. However, the particular configuration of champagne with its mesh of competition and cooperation means that resolution of these issues will have an impact well beyond an individual enterprise. Internal tensions can undermine the territorial brand manager, and the common vision of the region. All of this therefore has an impact on the social fabric of the region, and on the relationship of vignerons and *maisons*.

Conclusion

Champagne has been consistently successful. It will continue to be for the immediate future. The fact that problems have been highlighted does not mean that it is about to fail, nor that it will not continue to prosper even for the long term. The Champenois have shown themselves to be dynamic and adaptive in the past, and this has been a major aspect in the shaping of their wine's success. Even here, though, it is worth adding one caveat. The triumph of champagne occurred at a time when there were no external challengers; the fact that these now exist does make a well thought out and strategically managed response to a changing world essential.

Success is no longer automatic – it has to be maintained, and new challenges faced and dealt with. One comment made by Al Seaman is pertinent here – that it is difficult to change if an organization is being successful. This book has tried to account for champagne's success, and has also sought to examine the situation facing it, and particularly the challenges ahead. It would be unfortunate if the former – the success – undermined the ability to deal with the latter.

Notes

1   We use the term myth not in the sense of something untrue, but rather a story, whether true or not, which seeks to explain some hidden reality, or which is used to resolve a paradox in the cultural identity of a community (Freilich, 1975; Levi-Strauss, 1963).
2   As well as food and drink, tourism products are also classic examples of territorial brands.

3   Leeuwin and Seguin (2006, p. 3) have suggested that

> in today's wine production a distinction should be made between "terroir wines" and "branded wines". Terroir wines are produced in a specified location . . . . Branded wines are produced by blending wine or grapes from larger areas and from a variety of sources, which may vary from year to year.

References

Aaker, D. (1991). *Managing brand equity: Capitalizing on the value of a brand name.* New York: Free Press.

Alexander, M. (1996). *The myth at the heart of the brand.* Paper presented at the ESOMAR Congress. Accessed July 2011. www.semioticsolutions.com/pdf/Myth%20at%20heart%20of%20brand.pdf.

Anon. (2003). *Images, usages et comportements des consommateurs de Champagne en France.* Epernay: Comité Interprofessionnel du Vin de Champagne.

Anon. (2009). Some bottle ... mafia's fake champagne scam uncorked. *Mafia Today.* Accessed July 2011. http://mafiatoday.com/sicilian-mafia-ndrangheta/some-bottle-mafias-fake-champagne-scam-uncorked.

Anon. (2010a). *L'appellation.* Epernay: Comité interprofessionnel du vin de Champagne.

Anon. (2010b). *Le terroir.* Epernay: Comité interprofessionnel du vin de Champagne.

Anon. (2010c). *La Journee Viticole*, 12 May, p. 217.

Avellan, E. (2009). Grower Champagnes: Look closely – and get more fizz for your bucks. *Decanter*, 2 April. Accessed 5 September. www.decanter.com/people-and-places/wine-articles/484951/grower-champagnes-look-closely-and-get-more-fizz-for-your-bucks.

Bahans, J.-M. (2009). La réforme de l'étiquetage des vins. *Revue de droit rural* (December).

Bahans, J.-M., & Menjuncq, M. (2010). *Droit de la vigne et du vin – Aspects juridiques du marché vitivinicole.* Bordeaux: Feret & Litec.

Bainbridge, J. (2010). Sparking through the gloom. *Marketing*, 14 April, 34–35.

Banks, G., & Sharpe, S. (2006). Wine, regions and the geographic imperative: The Coonawarra example. *New Zealand Geographer, 62*, 173–184.

Banque de France. (1969). *Le vin de Champagne.* Paris: Fascicule de documentation de la Banque de France.

Barham, E. (2003). Translating terroir: The global challenge of French AOC labeling. *Journal of Rural Studies, 19*, 127–138.

Barker, J. P. H. (2004). *Different worlds: Law and the changing geographies of wine in France and New Zealand.* PhD thesis: Auckland, Law and Geography.

Barthes, R. (1972). *Mythologies* (A. Lavers, Trans.). New York: Hill and Wang.

Benjamin, B. A., & Podolny, J. M. (1999). Status, quality and social order in the California wine industry. *Administrative Science Quarterly, 44*(3), 563–589.

Beverland, M. (2003). *Building icon wine brands: Exploring the systemic nature of luxury wines.* Paper presented at the Third Annual Wine Marketing Colloquium, Adelaide.

Beverland, M. (2004). Uncovering 'theories-in-use': Building luxury wine brands. *European Journal of Marketing, 38*(3/4), 446–466.

Beverland, M. (2005). Crafting brand authenticity: The case of luxury wines. *Journal of Management Studies, 42*(5), 1003–1029.

Beverland, M. (2006). The 'real thing': Branding authenticity in the luxury wine trade. *Journal of Business Research, 59*, 251–258.

Bohmrich, R. (1996). Terroir: Competing perspectives on the roles of soil, climate and people. *Journal of Wine Research, 7*(1), 33–46.

Bohmrich, R. (2006). The next chapter in the terroir debate. *Wine Business Monthly*, 15 January. Accessed July 2011. www.winebusiness.com/wbm/?go=getArticle&dataId=42095.

Bourdieu, P. (1986). *Distinction: A social critique of the judgement of taste* (R. Nice, Trans.). London: Routledge.

Brennan, T. (1997). *Burgundy to Champagne: The wine trade in early modern France*. Baltimore, MD: The Johns Hopkins University Press.

Brouard, J., & Ditter, J.-G. (2008). *Regional business systems in the wine industry and the example of Burgundy.* Paper presented at the Fourth International Conference of the Academy of Wine Business Research, Siena.

Carlsen, J., & Charters, S. (2006). Introduction. In J. Carlsen & S. Charters (Eds.), *Global wine tourism: Research, marketing and management* (pp. 1–16). Wallingford: CAB International.

Charters, S. (2005). Drinking sparkling wine: An exploratory investigation. *International Journal of Wine Marketing, 17*(1), 54–68.

Charters, S. (2006). *Wine and society: The social and cultural context of a drink*. Oxford: Butterworth-Heinemann.

Charters, S. (2009). A delicate balance: The champagne business now and in the near future. *Tong, 4*, 3–8.

Charters, S., & Menival, D. (2009). *The marketing perspectives of small producers in the champagne industry.* Paper presented at Bacchus Goes Green: Fourth Interdisciplinary and International Wine Conference. Dijon, ESC Dijon.

Charters, S., & Menival, D. (2010). *The impact of the geographical reputation on the value created by small producers in Champagne.* Paper presented at the Fifth International Conference of the Academy of Wine Business Research. Auckland, AWBR.

CIVA. (2003). *Evolution de la commercialisation du cremant d'Alsace.* Accessed 6 September, 2010. www.champagne.fr.

CIVC. (2007a). *Channels of champagne distribution in France.* Comité Interprofessionnel du Vin de Champagne. Accessed 10 July, 2010. www.champagne.fr.

CIVC. (2007b). *The keys to the wines of champagne.* Epernay: Comité Interprofessionnel du Vin de Champagne.

CIVC. (2010). *Le comité champagne.* Comité Interprofessionnel du Vin de Champagne. Accessed 10 July, 2010. www.champagne.fr.

Clarke, J. B. (1999). Hermeneutic analysis: a qualitative decision trail. *International Journal of Nursing Studies, 36*(5), 363–369.

Clause, G. (1988). Les vignerons champenois du XVIIIe au XXe siècle: De la pauvrete contestataire de 1791 a la revolution de 1911. In *Etudes Champenoises: Vignerons et vins, de Champagne et d'ailleurs – XVIIIe–XXe siècle.* Reims: University of Reims Champagne-Ardenne.

Croidieu, G., & Monin, P. (2006). Competing 'terroir' and 'brand' logics, and violating genetic codes in the wine industry. The European Institute for Life-long Learning, Working Papers 2006/06. Accessed July 2011. www.em-lyon.com/ressources/ge/documents/publications/wp/2006-06.pdf .

de Sainte Marie, C., & Bérard, L. (2010). Taking local knowledge into account in the AOC system. In L. Bérard, M. Cegarra, M. S. Djama, P. Louafi, B. Marchenay, S. Roussel & F. Verdeaux (Eds.), *Biodiversity and local ecological knowledge in France* (pp. 181–189). INRA.

Descotes, A., & Moncomble, D. (2007). *Bilan carbone et plan climat de la Champagne: du diagnostic au passage à l'acte.* Paper presented at the Conference on Réchauffement climatique, quels impacts probables sur les vignobles? UNESCO Chair in Wine and Culture: University of Burgundy, 28–30 March.

Diart-Boucher, S. (2006). *La réglementation vitivinicole champenoise.* PhD thesis: University of Reims Champagne-Ardenne, Reims.

Ditter, J.-G. (2005). Reforming the French wine industry: Could clusters work? *Cahiers de CEREN, 13*, 39–54.

Draperi, J. F. (2001). Cooperation et regulation des marches: La production du champagne. In *Document de travail du Groupe de recherche Interdisciplinaire sur les organisations et le travail.* GRIOT.

Drucker, P. F. (1993). *The new realities.* New York: Harper & Rowe.

Eisenhardt, K. M., & Martin, J. A. (2000). Dynamic capabilities: what are they? *Strategic Management Journal, 21*, 1105–1121.

Euromonitor International. (2010). Global wine: Challenges and opportunities facing the wine industry. Accessed 10 August, 2010. www.gmid.euromonitor.com (May).

Faith, N. (1988). *The story of Champagne.* London: Hamish Hamilton.

Faith, N. (2008). Bubble bubble: Quality and change in Champagne. *World of Fine Wine, 21*, 94–100.

Findawine. (2009). Vinexpo: le eperformance barometer de la vente de vin en ligne. Accessed July 2011. www.findawine.com/blog/2009/07/02/vinexpo-le-eperformance-barometer-de-la-vente-de-vin-en-ligne.

Forbes, P. (1967). *Champagne: The wine, the land, and the people.* London: David & Charles.

FranceAgriMer. (2010). *Les achats de vins effervescents par les menages francais pour leur consommation a domicile, bilan annuel 2009.* Paris: FranceAgriMer Infos. No. 169, pp. 85–109.

Frank, M. (2009). Saving Taittinger. *Wine Spectator*, 30 June, 74–82.

Freilich, M. (1975). Myth, method, and madness. *Current Anthropology, 16*(2), 207–219.

Gade, D. W. (2004). Tradition, territory and terroir in French viniculture: Cassis, France and appellation contrôlée. *Annals of the Association of American Geographers, 94*(4), 848–876.

Gagnon, M. A., Jansen, K. J., & Michael, J. A. (2008). Employee alignment with strategic change: a study of strategy-supportive behavior among blue-collar employees. *Journal of Managerial Issues, 20*(4), 425–443.

Garcia, A. (1986). *Le vin de Champagne.* Vendome: PUF, Que sais-je.

Georgopoulos, T. (2011). La fiscalité du vin de Champagne: Quelles spéci-ficités? In T. Georgopoulos (Ed.), *La Champagne viticole: Quelles spéci-ficités juridiques?* Brussels: Bruylant Publishers.

Gergaud, O. (1998). Estimation d'une fonction de prix hedonistiques pour le vin de Champagne. *Economie et Prevision, 136*, 93–105.

Gerstner, E. (1985). Do higher prices signal higher quality? *Journal of Marketing Research, 22*(2), 209–215.

Gilmore, J. H., & Pine, B. J. (2002). Differentiating hospitality operations via experiences: Why selling services is not enough. *Cornell Hotel and Restaurant Administration Quarterly, 43*(3), 87.

Gilmore, J. H., & Pine, B. J. (2007). *Authenticity: What consumers really want.* Boston, MA: Harvard Business School Press.

Gnyawali, D. R., He, J., & Madhavan, R. (2008). Impact of co-opetition on firm competitive behaviour: An empirical examination. *Journal of Management, 32*(4), 507–553.

Guibert, N. (2006). Network governance in marketing channels: An appli-cation to the French Rhône Valley AOC wines industry. *British Food Journal, 108*(4), 256–272.

Guy, K. M. (1999). "Oiling the wheels of social life": Myths and marketing in Champagne during the Belle Epoque. *French Historical Studies, 22*(2), 211–239.

Guy, K. M. (2003). *When champagne became French: Wine and the making of a national identity.* Baltimore, MD: The Johns Hopkins University Press.

Hall, C. M., & Mitchell, R. (2008). *Wine marketing.* Oxford: Butterworth Heinemann.

Hancock, J., & Price, M. (1990). Real chalk balances the water supply. *Journal of Wine Research, 1*(1), 45–60.

Harreld, J. B., O'Reilly, C. A., & Tushman, M. (2007). Dynamic capabilities at IBM: Driving strategy into action. *California Management Review, 49*(4), 21–43.

Henderson, J. L., & Oakes, M. (1990). *The wisdom of the serpent: the myths of death, rebirth, and resurrection.* Princeton, NJ: Princeton University Press.

Holt, D. B. (2004). *How brands become icons: The principles of cultural branding.* Boston, MA: Harvard Business School Press.

Hopkins, J. (1998). Signs of the post-rural: Marketing myths of a symbolic countryside. *Geografiska Annaler: Series B, Human Geography, 80*(2), 65–81.

Jeandet, P., Vasserot, Y., Liger-Belair, G., & Marchal, R. (2010). Sparkling wine production. In V. Joshi (Ed.), *Handbook of enology – Principles and practices.* New Delhi: The Asia-Tech Publisher.

Jefford, A. (2008). Everything you always wanted to know about the Champagne area revisions but were afraid to ask. Accessed July 2011. www.andrewjefford.com/node/134.

Johnson, H. (2004). *The story of wine*. London: Mitchell Beazley.

Jones, G. V. (2007). Climate change: observations, projections, and general implications for viticulture and wine production. *Economics Department Working Papers*, No. 7, Whitman College, Oregon, USA.

Kawamura, Y. (2005). *Fashion-ology: An introduction to fashion studies*. Oxford: Berg.

Kelly, S. (2007). *Constructing and mediating spatial relationships in French winegrowing: The Burgundian example*. PhD thesis: Auckland, Law and Geography.

Kladstrup, D., & Kladstrup, P. (2005). *Champagne: How the world's most glamorous wine triumphed over war and hard times*. Sydney: Fourth Estate.

Koka, B. R., & Prescott, J. E. (2008). Designing alliance networks: the influence of network position, environmental change, and strategy on firm performance. *Strategic Management Journal, 29*, 639–661.

Kotler, P., Chandler, P. C., Brown, L., & Adam, S. (1994). *Marketing* (3rd ed.). Sydney: Prentice Hall.

Landon, S., & Smith, C. E. (1997). The use of quality and reputation indicators by consumers: The case of Bordeaux wine. *Journal of Consumer Policy, 20*, 289–323.

Landon, S., & Smith, C. E. (1998). Quality expectations, reputation and price. *Southern Economic Journal, 64*(3), 628–647.

Lash, S., & Lury, C. (2007). *Global cultural industry*. Cambridge, UK: Polity Press.

Le Heron, R., & Lewis, N. (2010). New value from asking 'Is geography what geographers do?' *Geoforum, 41*(2), 1–5.

Leeuwen, C. V., & Seguin, G. (2006). The concept of terroir in viticulture. *Journal of Wine Research, 17*(1), 1–10.

Lepak, D. P., Smith, K. G., & Taylor, S. M. (2007). Value creation and value capture: a multilevel perspective. *Academy of Management Review, 32*(1), 180–194.

Lerner, J. S., & Tetlock, P. E. (1999). Accounting for the effects of accountability. *Psychological Bulletin, 125*(2), 255–275.

Levi-Strauss, C. (1963). The structural study of myth. In C. Levi-Strauss (Ed.), *Structural anthropology* (pp. 206–231). New York: Basic Books.

Lewis, N. I. (2008). *Brand New Zealand. Where are we at and what more should we be doing?* Paper presented at Building Wine Brands: Proceedings of the Inaugural New Zealand Wine Business Symposium.

Liger-Belair, G. (2004). *Uncorked: The science of champagne*. Princeton, NJ: Princeton University Press.

Liger-Belair, G., Polidori, G., & Jeandet, P. (2008). Recent advances in the science of Champagne bubbles. *Chemical Society Reviews, 37*, 2490–2511.

Liger-Belair, G., Jeandet, P., & Polidori, G. (2009). Bubbles and flow patterns in Champagne. *American Scientist, 97*, 294–301.

Lockshin, L., Jarvis, W., d'Hauteville, F., & Perrouty, J.-P. (2006). Using simulations from discrete choice experiments to measure consumer sensitivity to brand, region, price and awards in wine choice. *Food Quality and Preference, 17*, 166–178.

Luo, Y. (2008). Structuring interorganizational cooperation: the role of economic integration in strategic alliances. *Strategic Management Journal, 29*, 617–637.

Lury, C. (2004). *Brands: The logos of the global economy*. London: Routledge.

Lury, C. (2005). 'Contemplating a self-portrait as a pharmacist': A trade mark style of doing art and science. *Theory, Culture & Society, 22*, 193–110.

MacIntosh, N. B., & Daft, R. L. (1982). *A departmental technology model of management control systems*. Paper presented at the American Accounting Association Conference.

Mankins, M. C., & Steele, R. (2005). Turning great strategy into great performance. *Harvard Business Review,* July–August, 65–72.

Mary, B. (2007). *The role of the banker in the Champagne industry and viewpoint on the future*. Reims: Crédit Agricole du Nord Est.

Maye, D., Holloway, L., & Kneafsey, M. (Eds.). (2007). *Alternative food geographies*. Amsterdam: Elsevier.

Mazzeo, T. J. (2008). *The Widow Clicquot: The story of a Champagne empire and the women who ruled it*. New York: Tantor Media Inc.

Mintzberg, H., Ahlstrand, B., & Lampel, J. (1998). *Strategy safari: A guided tour through the wilds of strategic management*. New York: The Free Press.

Mitchell, R. D. (2008). International business, intellectual property, and the misappropriation of place: food, wine and tourism. In T. Coles & C. M. Hall (Eds.), *International business and tourism: Global issues, contemporary interactions* (pp. 201–219). London: Routledge.

Moran, W. (1993a). Rural space as intellectual property. *Political Geography, 12*, 263–277.

Moran, W. (1993b). The wine appellation as territory in France and California. *Annals of the Association of American Geographers, 83*(4), 694–717.

Moran, W. (2006). *Crafting terroir: People in cool climates, soils and markets*. Paper presented at the Proceedings of the Sixth International Cool Climate Symposium for Viticulture and Oenology, Christchurch, New Zealand, 6–10 February.

Mueller, S., P. Osidiacz, L. Francis, & Lockshin, L. (2010). *The relative importance of extrinsic and intrinsic wine attributes: Combining discrete choice and informed sensory consumer testing*. Paper presented at the Fifth International Conference of the Academy of Wine Business Research. Auckland: AWBR.

Muraz, S. (2010). *Authenticity in the positioning of a champagne brand*. Masters Dissertation: Reims Management School, Reims.

Nalebuff, B. J., & Brandenburger, A. M. (1997). Co-opetition: Competitive and cooperative business strategies for the digital economy. *Strategy and Leadership, 25*(Nov/Dec), 28–35.

North, A. (2008). *The effect of background music on the taste of wine*. Heriot Watt University Working Papers. Accessed July 2011. www.wineanorak.com/musicandwine.pdf.

Oczkowski, E. (2001). Hedonic wine price functions and measurement error. *The Economic Record, 77*(239), 374–382.

Paxson, H. (2010). Locating value in artisan cheese: Reverse engineering terroir for new-world landscapes. *American Anthropologist, 112*, 444–457.

Pendergrast, M. (2000). *For god, country, and Coca-Cola.* New York: Basic Books.

Perrouty, J. P., d'Hauteville, F., & Lockshin, L. (2006). The influence of wine attributes on region of origin equity: An analysis of the moderating effect of consumer's perceived expertise. *Agribusiness, 22*(3), 323–341.

Peteraf, M. (1993). The cornerstones of competitive advantage: A resource-based view. *Strategic Management Journal, 145*, 179–191.

Phillips, R. (2000). *A short history of wine.* London: Allen Lane.

Plassmann, M., O'Doherty, J., Shiv, B., & Rangel, A. (2008). Marketing actions can modulate neural representations of experienced pleasant-ness. *Proceedings of the National Academy of the Sciences of the USA, 105*(3), 1050–1054.

Porter, M. (1998). Clusters and the new economics of competition. *Harvard Business Review, Nov/Dec*, 77–90.

Porter, M. (2003). The economic performance of regions. *Regional Studies, 37*(6/7), 549–578.

Quagrainie, K., McCluskey, J., & Loureiro, M. (2003). A latent structure approach to measuring reputation. *Southern Economic Journal, 69*(4), 966–977.

Rand, M. (2008). Terroir and appellations, sacred for Champagne? *Decanter*, 6 June. Accessed 5 September, 2010. www.decanter.com/people-and-places/wine-articles/485757/terroir-and-appellations-sacred-for-champagne.

Samuelson, P., & Nordhaus, W. (2005). *Economie.* Paris: Economica.

Sargent, F. O. (1952). Fragmentation of French land: Its nature, extent, and causes. *Land Economics, 28*(3), 218–229.

Schatzberg, M. G. (2008). *Seeing the invisible, hearing silence, thinking the unthinkable: The advantages of ethnographic immersion.* Paper presented at the Political Methodology: Committee on Concepts and Methods Working Paper Series.

Schein, E. H. (2005). *Organizational culture and leadership* (3rd ed.). San Francisco: Jossey-Bass.

Schlenker, B. R. (1985). *The self and social life.* New York: McGraw-Hill.

Schumpeter, J. (1939). *Business cycles: A theoretical historical and statistical analysis of the capitalist process.* New York: McGraw-Hill.

Shapiro, C. (1982). Consumer information, product quality, and seller repu-tation. *The Bell Journal of Economics, 13*, 20–35.

Sharp, B. (2010). *How brands grow.* Oxford: Oxford University Press.

Starbuck, W. H. (1993). Strategizing in the real world. *International Journal of Technology Management, Special Publication on Technological Foun-dations of Strategic Management, 8*(1/2), 77–85.

Stevenson, T. (1998). *Christie's world encyclopedia of champagne and spar-kling wine.* Bath: Absolute Press.

Tadelis, S. (1999). What's in a name? Reputation as a tradeable asset. *The American Economic Review, 689*(3), 548–563.

Teece, D. (2006). *Explicating dynamic capabilities: The nature and micro-foundations of (long-run) enterprise performance*. Working Paper, Haas School of Business, University of California Berkeley.

Tetlock, P. E. (1983). Accountability and perseverance of first impressions. *Social Psychology Quarterly, 46*, 285–292.

Tetlock, P. E. (1985). Accountability: A social check on the fundamental attribution error. *Social Psychology Quarterly, 48*(227–236).

Thornton, P., Jones, C., & Kury, K. (2005). Institutional logics and institutional change: Transformation in accounting, architecture, and publishing. In C. Jones & P. Thornton (Eds.), *Research in the sociology of organizations*. London: JAI.

Tuan, Y.-F. (1977). *Space and place: The perspective of experience*. Minneapolis: University of Minnesota Press.

Tuan, Y.-F. (1991). Language and the making of place: A narrative-descriptive approach. *Annals of the Association of American Geographers, 81*(4), 684–696.

Ulin, R. C. (1996). *Vintages and traditions: An ethnohistory of southwest French wine*. Washington, DC: The Smithsonian Institution.

UMC. (2010). Champagne grandes marques et maisons. Reims: Union des Maisons de Champagne. Accessed July 2011. www.maisons-champagne.com

Unwin, T. (1996). *Wine and the vine: An historical geography of viticulture and the wine trade*. London: Routledge.

Van Leeuwen, C. (2009). Soils and terroir expression in wines. In E. a. C. F. Landa (Ed.), *Soil and culture* (pp. 453–465). London: Springer.

Vaudour, E. (2002). The quality of grapes and wine in relation to geography: Notions of terroir at various scales. *Journal of Wine Research, 13*(2), 117–141.

Vigneron, F., & Johnson, L. W. (1999). A review and a conceptual framework of prestige-seeking consumer behavior. *Academy of Marketing Science Review [Online], 2002*(18 January), 1–23. Accessed July 2011. www.amsreview.org/articles/vigneron01-1999.pdf.

Visse-Causse, S. (2007). *L'appellation d'origine: Valorisation du terroir*. Paris: ADEF Publishers.

Vranken Pommery Champagne. (2008). Champagne as a luxury product. Reims: Unpublished Presentation/Powerpoint slides.

Weick, K. E., & Sutcliffe, K. M. (2001). *Managing the unexpected*. San Francisco: Jossey-Bass.

White, M., Whalen, P., & Jones, G. (2009). Land and wine. *Nature Geoscience, 2*, 82–84.

Williams, R. H. (1982). *Dream worlds: Mass consumption in late nineteenth-century France*. Berkeley: University of California Press.

Wolikow, S., & Jacquet, O. (2010). *Terroir is a historic construct, not a natural phenomenon*. Reprinted from Tong (no. 2), in *A victory of the unions*, Burgundy Report, Spring 2010.

Wortham-Galvin, B. D. (2008). Mythologies of placemaking. *Places, 20*(1), 32–39.

Zineldin, M. (2004). Co-opetition: The organisation of the future. *Marketing Intelligence and Planning, 22*(7), 780–789.

Index